PRAISE FOR *RICH PEOPLE THINGS*

"I am always searching for books that can educate my six grown-up children, not to mention certain recidivist friends, about how this country came to be seduced, pushed, and betrayed into its present state by the money power and its Wall Street–Washington nerve center. When I read Chris Lehmann's *Rich People Things,* I was so impressed by its wit, wisdom, and acuity on this matter, by the variety, aptness, and richness of its perceptions and examples, that I bought ten copies to give to family and friends. With my own money. Hard cash. Can I say more? Well, yes, I can. I wish I had written it."

—Michael C. Thomas, journalist and author of *Love and Money*

"Scathing, scintillating chapters on Malcolm Gladwell; on the *Times*, and on its 'chirpy' and delusional columnist David Brooks; on *Wired* magazine's breathless paeans to new media's broken promises; and on other ventures and adventurers who, often unwittingly, work hard to suppress or deflect their own and their audiences' understandings of what consumer and casino-finance capitalism are doing to us."

—*Talking Points Memo*

"Lehmann began his economic blog inspired by 'the omission of real economic conditions from the accounting of the republic's collective life.' Now in book form . . . Lehmann illustrates the ideas, institutions, and individuals he sees as tools for the rich to keep themselves rich—or make themselves richer. The list of offenders includes the US Constitution, the iPad, Reality TV, and the *New York Times* (in particular, columnist David Brooks). The author explores meritocracy, class warfare, the 'powerful intellectual opiate' called the free market, and other 'hoary American myths.' Chapters include a description of *Atlas Shrugged* as a 'doorstop-sized digest of ideological boilerplate disguised as fictional dialogue, plotting, and character development' and memoirs, or 'memoirs,' (James Frey makes the list) that allow affluent readers to 'cast one's fellow citizens as monolithically soulful, suffering, and exoticized others.' Lehmann concludes his wholly entertaining effort with a particularly astute explanation of how the myth of the middle class has left Americans with an inadequate vocabulary to discuss economic woes; instead, 'we are committed to the dogmatic belief that we are all affluent entrepreneurs waiting to happen.' Brutal."

—*Publishers Weekly*

"Perusing Mr. Lehmann's volume I found myself wondering, again and again, what exactly is the target psychographic of this veritable wardrobe montage of proletarian resentments? I visualized: employees of used bookstores and/or independent coffee shops, people who don't own televisions, people who do own televisions on which they occasionally watch *Portlandia* and other shows they are capable of enjoying with substantial reservations, people who commute to their titular jobs on bicycles they have owned for more than five years, bartenders with a higher than average propensity to reward 'regular' customers with complimentary beverages (thus cheating their bosses, which they excuse by some deluded ethical calculus by which the right to steal is a just reward for being sufficiently overeducated to command the loyalty of 'like-minded' freeloaders), titular business owners foolish enough to employ such mediocrities, people at once eminently capable of constructing formidable and eloquent arguments making the case for socialized health care on the basis of a litany of broad-based macroeconomic factors and yet chronically incapable of holding down jobs that provide health insurance, childish people who know nothing of money and yet ceaselessly attempt to provoke class warfare by plugging loaded terms like *rich* and *millionaire* into otherwise civilized conversations about aspirational luxury, tastemaking lifestyles, the urgent need for deficit reduction by way of entitlement reform, etc . . . . 'parasites,' in other words. Given that the authorship of a nonfiction book is widely understood to be an undertaking aimed primarily at marketing one's services as a paid motivational speaker, it's hard to imagine why Mr. Lehmann would squander 256 pages addressing such a fragmented and under-capitalized audience. Having read *Rich People Things* in its entirety, however, it occurred to me that the parasite class does, at least, have time to read books, and that Mr. Lehmann would be an abysmal motivational speaker."

—Moe Tkacik, unemployed leftist

RICH PEOPLE THINGS

Chris Lehmann

Haymarket Books
Chicago, Illinois

First published in 2010 by OR Books, New York

This expanded edition published in 2011 by Haymarket Books

Haymarket Books
P.O. Box 180165
Chicago, IL 60618
773-583-7884
www.haymarketbooks.org
info@haymarketbooks.org

ISBN: 978-1-60846-152-3

Cover design by Abby Weintraub.

Trade distribution:
In the US, Consortium Book Sales and Distribution, www.cbsd.com
In Canada, Publishers Group Canada, www.pgcbooks.ca/home.html

This book was published with the generous support of Lannan Foundation and
the Wallace Global Fund.

The body of this book is printed in the United States on recycled paper containing 100
percent postconsumer waste in accordance with the guidelines of the Green Press Initiative,
www.greenpressinitiative.org.

Library of Congress Cataloging-in-Publication data is available

10 9 8 7 6 5 4 3 2

CONTENTS

INTRODUCTION

American class privilege is very much like the idea of sex in a Catholic school—it's not supposed to exist in the first place, but once it presents itself in your mind's eye, you realize that it's everywhere. And as with the upholders of adolescent propriety for the Mother Church, the forces of repression in our political economy are well armed with orthodox articles of faith. Social critics and academicians have expended heroic amounts of ink to explain America's "exceptionalist" indifference to the distinctions of class—from the absence of a feudal tradition to the frontier thesis to the convulsions of upward social mobility across the generations. Scholars appealing to these forces have all preached, in one way or another, that the condition of wage earning in the New World is but a passing way station on the path to real wealth and entitlement. Why, after all, should anyone militate on behalf of the interests of an American working class when no one intends to remain within its ranks for very long? And, conversely, why should anyone insist there's anything amiss with a society that lavishly coddles those who are fabulously well-to-do when we all long to be borne aloft in their company?

These are, to be sure, compelling explanations of our country's curiously complacent outlook on the politics of wealth and privilege—but they also seem more than a little pat. Canada, after all, had a western frontier and no strong attachment to feudal tradition, and has nonetheless spawned a robust labor-led politics, a single-payer health-care system, and a rather hale welfare state securing basic income supports and social equality. Social mobility has of late been higher in the allegedly fusty Old World social orders of Britain, Denmark, and Sweden—places that can lay a far more legitimate claim to the conservative epithet "socialist" than the business-friendly centrism of the Obama Democratic policy elite—than in the deindustrializing, debt-ridden United States.

If we're to understand the stubborn resistance to the idea of social class—especially in the wake of the Great Recession of 2008, which all too plainly elevated the fortunes of the financial elite over the notional prosperity of America's declining middle orders—we'd do well to relax our fealty to the ironclad determinism of past explanations. In the spirit of the suggestible Catholic student, we should recur instead to the piecemeal psychology of the absent presence—to look more closely at the freestanding institutions that reinforce and strategically update the coordinates of the reigning social consensus on economic reward and punishment.

From this vantage, the lionization of wealth becomes less a fixed catechism in the American creed than a contingent set of post hoc rationalizations—attached here to the idea of undeviatingly gargantuan executive compensation for the financial elite, and there to the business press's delusional romance with the ever-mythical free market. This outlook has the advantage of making our state of chronic class denial much less forbidding than it would be as a destiny-shaping verdict handed down from our colonial past. But neither is that to say that its social power is diluted by virtue of its comparative rootlessness. Quite the contrary, in fact—the paper-thin and amnesiac way that we continue to reckon with questions of wealth and social privilege accounts in large part for its staying power. Writing in 1956 of the formative consensus that took shape on these issues during the Cold War, C. Wright Mills observed that it hinged on a PR vision of overclass achievement, whereby liberals and conservatives alike found the power elite "to be diversified to the point of powerlessness. So far as power is concerned, nobody really makes decisions; let us fall back upon official and formal images of representative government. So far as wealth or high income is concerned, that is without decisive consequence, although it does perhaps affect the tone of society at large. Besides, everybody in America is rich nowadays. This unserious liberalism is the nerve-center of the present-day conservative mood."[1]

That statement serves as a letter-perfect diagnosis of our socioeconomic plight more than half a century later—save that it's now a tad harder for consensus thinkers to insist that every American is rich. Nonetheless, it's been striking to observe just how little the present crisis has altered the basic terms of political engagement on all sides. When the US economy veered toward cataclysm in the 1890s and the 1930s, mass political movements registered a new national distemper. The People's Party of the late nineteenth century went so far as to advocate an alternate production-based system of currency and exchange, known as the Subtreasury, a reform that eventually got watered down into the Free Silverite attack on the gold standard when the party fused with the Democrats in 1896. And the thirties, of course, witnessed the enactment of many of the core reforms first advanced during the populist and Progressive eras—public ownership of utilities, federally funded income support and retirement plans, enormous national public works projects, and the like.

One might reasonably ask what it would take for the basic truths of class division to sink in on today's American scene, after the reckless expansion of our paper economy has consigned entire productive sectors of business enterprise into the dustbin of history; after the bailed-out financier class continues to rack up obscene performance bonuses on the government dime; after the securitization of debt has left millions of American homes foreclosed, and millions more underwater. Instead, we remain in thrall to an unserious liberalism that continues to entrust most major economic policy decisions to career investment bankers, and to a conservative movement rhetoric that equates "populism" with heartland-approved consumption habits and evangelical culture-wars posturing.

In this deeply incoherent state of affairs, it's little wonder that conservatives were able to oppose a stimulus plan that actually lowered taxes for the vast majority of Americans by characterizing it as a feckless big-government tax increase. Or that the anemic final version of health-care reform—larded with massive giveaways to the insurance and pharmaceutical lobbies—can be widely depicted as a "government takeover" of American medicine or, indeed, as full-blown "socialism." We appear to have descended to the point where political economy, formerly the central organizing force in our national politics, has become a floating signifier, intended to say more about the demographic profile of individual political actors than anything about the collective cast of our productive lives, and how the rewards for our labor can be distributed more fairly and equitably.

Among other things, this state of affairs leaves leaders and policy makers unable to offer coherent accounts of who is meant to benefit from efforts to revive and revamp our financial sector, our rights to form unions, or our system of health care delivery. If such incremental reforms come across in much of political discourse as perverse and sweeping expressions of an undifferentiated liberal lust for power, then prospects for meaningful change—truly nationalized health care, finance overhauls that reward productive industry ahead of speculation in the paper economy, dismantling of the savage inequalities that still govern housing markets, and education funding—seem like nothing more than utopian fantasy.

* * * *

When I began writing *Rich People Things*, I had nothing quite so sweeping—or so dispiriting—in mind. Indeed, the whole thing came about by accident. In early 2009, a couple of old laid-off editor friends e-mailed me about a Web site they were launching (called the Awl, for some reason) and invited me to contribute. At the time, I filed the idea pretty far back in my memory bank—especially since, as my friends explained in their pitch letter, they'd be unable to pay their writers. But a few weeks after the project launched, another friend directed me to a cover story that ran in my former workplace, New York magazine, itemizing the widespread sense of grievance and entitlement among the city's lords of finance in the wake of public outrage over the Troubled Asset Relief Program's no-strings giveaways to the financial sector.

Since I knew all too well the inside-the-bubble mindset behind this quisling dispatch from the money wars—the celebration of the money culture being the de facto mission statement for Adam Moss's New York magazine—I knew I couldn't stay quiet. And I also knew, the deferential politics of the publishing world being what they are, that whatever I wrote could only see the light of day at a place like the Awl. So I wrote my friends, duly submitted a piece, and just as it was about to go live, coeditor Alex Balk wrote to explain that his colleague, Choire Sicha, "designed a graphic for this with the rubric, 'Rich People Things.' Does that work for you?" To which I replied, 'um, sure?' " It was a fait accompli in any event, Alex replied, since Choire had "gallivanted off to lunch"—though they could easily just erase the rubric when he got back.

I don't know when Choire returned, but by that time, we'd all moved on to other things, and in the next week or so, I didn't give "Rich People Things" much thought, either as a column title or an ongoing writing project. Thanks to another friend, though, I came across another dispatch that showcased unthinking press fealty to economic privilege—this time, a Washington Post front page piece about how the Obama administration's spending priorities would unduly punish taxpayers earning more than $250,000 a year. This prospect, as the Post correspondents saw it, could well place small-business owners and upward-striving professionals—two plum political constituencies that broke for Obama in 2008—at odds with the allegedly ambitious social agenda of the fledgling Obama administration. As both

tax analysis and political kibitzing, the article reeked of horseshit—
especially since a number of the items on Obama's ambitious social
agenda, such as federally backed health insurance, would significantly
aid the bottom lines for small-business entrepreneurs.

Once my eye had grown sufficiently jaundiced, I started to see
material for the column everywhere—in lunatic manifestos from
Steve Forbes on corporate leadership and entire cover packages in
major newsweeklies addressing the future of work without containing so much as a single passing mention of labor unions. Even though
the United States was enduring its worst economic crisis since the
Great Depression, our major organs of opinion, most of the leadership in Congress and the regulatory world, and nearly all the major organs of the business press were carrying on serenely as though
American society remained more a study in moneyed abandon than
abandoned money.

I fancy myself a fairly practiced cynic, but it struck me that my
randomly acquired beat was profoundly out of sync with the state of
the real economy, so much so that the familiar run of business coverage and economic commentary started to strike my ear as exceedingly strange. It all seemed not so much a hard-nosed appraisal of the
way the world really works as a species of magical incantation, worthy
of the witches in the opening scene of *Macbeth*. From the point of
view of my own journalistic production, this was a great boon; finding suitable column fare was generally not much more arduous than
taking in a *Money* magazine feature on, say, the damage the downturn
had wrought on exclusive golf clubs, letting the outrage sink in, and
opening up a fresh Word document on the computer.

Slowly, though, it dawned on me that the odd pleasure of putting
the column together each week served as a footnote of sorts to the
more-or-less permanent character of these United States. The omission of real economic conditions from the accounting of the republic's
collective life was something that ran very deep—if also very diffusely—in our history. Unbidden, long-dormant snatches of my graduate

history education started to tug at me and worked their way into the margins of the column. It became starkly evident, for instance, that one couldn't snipe at *Newsweek*'s saucer-eyed speculations about whether the new generation of young workers would be unduly stingy about floating more of their incomes into the consumer economy in order to jump-start still-skittish demand without also noting that the last generation of deeply traumatized American savers—those who came of working age during the Great Depression—had the assurance of a robust public sector, a fairly militant labor movement, and the informal social contract binding together business, labor, and government in common aims of enterprise. All these factors helped ensure that the wages of Depression-era wageworkers at least kept pace with the inflationary pressures that came with economic growth, once it finally arrived. All today's young workers had, by contrast, were the rancid leavings of the Reagan-inspired war on New Deal social protections—together with the banker-friendly policy initiatives of a craven "New Democrat" leadership on the other side of the partisan aisle.

Rich People Things began life as an afterthought title for a column without any particular mission statement to push it forward; but I later realized that this pointedly dismissive phrase took in a good many more trends, movements, and institutions than I'd first assumed. What were the US Constitution, the perpetual campaign-and-election season, the civic religion of celebrity worship, urban development policies, and the cloistered state of high-literary debate, if not also Rich People Things in their own right? Why not, then, widen the aperture of my accidental column to take in more of the long view of the American scene? This is not to advance, mind you, any overarching materialist explanation of our past—strict economic determinism isn't an especially persuasive vision of history, and is anything but a lively one. Rather, the conceit of this book is something infinitely more modest—an effort to apply the roving one-hit methodology of an online column, typically composed with the phrase

"Can you believe this shit?" ringing in my ears, to somewhat sturdier features of our common life. In the impressionistic tract that follows, I've occasionally cannibalized my other published work, both in the Awl and elsewhere, as it pertains to the expanding Rich People Things waterfront, but mainly I've just sought to imagine how the writing persona I've developed in the post-meltdown aughts would be provoked, baffled, and generally trigger happy if the Doc's time machine plunked him back down in the US history colloquia that formed the backbone of his long-ago graduate instruction. It's been cathartic, if nothing else, and I trust that you, dear reader, might find a similar tonic effect in these wayward musings.

Rich People Thing No. 1

THE US CONSTITUTION

It's no exaggeration to say that the great confoundment of common sense that Americans bring to the class question is rooted in the very founding of the American republic. The ratification of the US Constitution has been accorded an exalted place in our civic mythology. Long before Glenn Beck began to heap his incoherent adoration on the Founding Fathers, early historians of the United States such as George Bancroft spoke of our Constitution in full seriousness as the fulfillment of God's will, "The movement of the divine power which gives unity to the universe, and order and connection to events."[1]

In reality, the debate over the Constitution was nowhere near so orderly; rather, it exposed the many divisions of social rank then assailing the fledgling United States. In the prosperous agricultural valleys of the fertile American colonies, planters formed huge landed estates—and put themselves forward immodestly as the model citizens and legislators of the new American nation after it had won its independence from the British Crown. One of the central propagandists for the ratification of the Constitution, John Jay, characterized the new leadership class baldly enough in a letter to George Washington: "The better kind of people, by whom I mean the people who are orderly and industrious, who are content with their situation and not uneasy in their circumstances."[2]

Inconveniently for these worldly theorists, however, the vast majority of eighteenth-century Americans *were* uneasy in their circumstances. Landholders not blessed with vast valley tracts scratched out subsistence livings in upland regions; sunk in debt and hostage to erratic growing seasons, they tended to support a smaller, more decentralized government and to oppose harsh creditor protections such as debtor prisons. Merchants and laboring men were likewise prey to boom-and-bust cycles of commerce, the dumping of cheap European exports in their domestic markets, and the constriction of currency as the post-Revolutionary republic began settling its massive war debts. This economic unrest exploded on the western frontier of Massachusetts in the rebellion led by farmer Daniel Shays, who militated to circulate paper currency to alleviate the crushing debt of the agrarian producing classes.

The uprising occurred in 1785–6, just prior to the calling of the Constitutional Convention. Even though it was put down in short order by state and federal forces, Shay's Rebellion was assuredly never far from the inventive minds of Jay, James Madison, Alexander Hamilton, and the other propertied advocates of the new structure of the national government. Jay indeed wrote at the time that the uprising betokened "some revolution—something I cannot foresee or conjecture. I am uneasy and apprehensive; more so than during the war."[3]

The whole question of indebtedness, currency, and the terms of credit runs like a hidden Guignol through much of American history, otherwise made to seem a calm procession of billowing abstract principles such as the extension of the franchise, the idea of popular sovereignty, and other pleasingly Whiggish notions. The effect of reviewing the founding chapters of our history through the lens of clashing economic interests is, indeed, not unlike the grotesque war canvasses produced by Francisco Goya, pointing up the fraudulent cast of rationalist dogma and nationalist conflict current during the Enlightenment. The lead apologists for the Constitution—who appropriated for themselves the sonorous title of Federalists and, far more important, branded their socially inferior opponents with the epithet

"Antifederalist"—took pains that the final document contained two critical protections for the moneyed creditor class: a prohibition on the issuance of paper currency and a ban on state-level interference with contract obligations. The codicils of property, which had been subject to shifting jurisdictions under the old Articles of Confederation, acquired in the new document the aura of sacred writ; as Madison wrote in Federalist 44, the "sober people of America" had long suffered under the yoke of "the pestilential effects of paper money on the necessary confidence between man and man." It amounted, indeed, to "an accumulation of guilt which can be expiated no otherwise than by a voluntary sacrifice on the altar of justice"—i.e., the surrender of money-issuing powers to the centralized nation, so as to "inspire a general prudence and industry and give a regular course to the business of society."[4]

From these confident assertions of monetary right flowed most of the Constitution's other robust acknowledgments of property's social priority—including the infamous three-fifths clause, which counted the legal slave property of southern planters as fractional persons so as to artificially inflate the planter class's representation in Congress. While it would be hard to sell the practice of enslavement as a species of contract, the same basic outlook held: Relations of property naturally superseded the terms of the rational Enlightenment social compact, so much so that the Constitution's foundational doctrine of popular sovereignty (which goes by the familiar shorthand of "one man, one vote") in this instance was to be contorted out of all humane and sensible shape so as to accommodate a central property-holding interest. Thomas Jefferson, who'd already been prevailed upon by cooler mercantile heads to strike his ringing denunciation of the British slave trade in the early drafts of the Declaration of Independence, was schooled on this general principle in a 1788 letter from the fiercely antimajoritarian Madison: "In our Governments, the real power lies in the majority of the Community, and the invasion of private rights is chiefly to be apprehended, not from acts of government contrary to the sense of its constituents, but from acts in which Government is the mere instrument of a major number of the constituents."[5]

The Antifederalists—whose leaders included such Revolutionary-era luminaries as Patrick Henry, Samuel Adams, and John Hancock (though these latter two prosperous merchants eventually came around to support ratification of the Constitution once the Antifederalist cause was plainly lost)—took a very different view of the social impact of the proposed system of government. In an address before the Maryland Legislature, Samuel Chase announced that the system was a scheme to elevate the rich and wellborn to legislative influence.[6] Further down the social hierarchies, the sentiments against the document grew much more animated. A Massachusetts Antifederalist named Amos Singletary contended that all power under the new Constitution would accrue to "lawyers, and men of learning, and monied men." Having already locked up "all the power and the money," they would use the instruments of government to "swallow up all us little folks."[7] South Carolina Antifederalist Aedanus Burke reported that when news of ratification spread through the poor backcountry, "in some places the people had a Coffin painted black, which borne in funeral procession was solemnly buried as an emblem of the dissolution and internment of publick Liberty." Indeed, he continued, these opponents of the Federalist plan "think that having disputed and having gained the Laurel under the banners of Liberty, now, that they are likely to be robbed of the honour, and the fruits of it, by a Revolution purposely contrived for it."[8] Pseudonymous Antifederalist writers cautioned that the Constitutional Convention was hatching a "monstrous aristocracy" that would "swallow up the democratic rights of the union and sacrifice the liberties of the people to the power and domination of a few."[9]

When progressive historian Charles Beard sought to put such claims to the test in his 1913 study, *An Economic Interpretation of the Constitution of the United States,* he found that holders of landed estates, financial securities, and regional commercial empires within the union indeed made up the overwhelming majority of ratifiers at the Philadelphia Convention. Such worthies, he wrote, "knew through their personal experiences in economic affairs the precise results which the new government they were setting up was designed to attain."[10] Among those results, Beard concluded, was the exclusion of the nation's "large propertyless mass," either directly or through state representatives, from the Convention's deliberations, and a finished legal product that "was essentially an economic document based upon the concept that the fundamental private rights of property are anterior to government and morally beyond the reach of popular majorities."[11]

Beard was roundly eviscerated by most sober mainstream political-science types of his day for reaching such brute materialist conclusions about the document that occupies pride of place in the American civic religion. But most of the quantitative research that later scholars have conducted into the economic profile of the framers has borne out the Beard thesis and drawn long-overdue attention to the political battles pitched well behind the foreground of the Main Street USA diorama that most consensus historians have made out the Philadelphia Convention to be.

There's a more fundamental sense, though, in which the inhabitants of Bailout America can confirm Beard's argument with their own eyes. Once again, the holders of massive, government-enabled debt have been functionally locked out of a series of procedurally iffy proceedings explicitly designed to benefit the nation's narrow creditor and speculative class. Once again, popular outcries over the upward redistribution of wealth, and the downward socialization of risk, have been dismissed as so much immature and dangerous rabble-rousing. And the long-term political health of the republic is regarded as all but synonymous with the interests of moneyed privilege, so much so that elemental reforms to curb the destructive securitization of debt in commodity trades have been stymied by industry-drafted loopholes dropped into last-minute committee revisions. The Constitution may not have been so reliable in observing the letter or spirit of its opening "We the People" clause, but viewed in the more dispassionate light of the real constituency it was drafted to serve, it truly is, as the well-born nineteenth-century poet-cum-diplomat James Russell Lowell put it, "a machine that would go of itself."

Rich People Thing No. 2

THE NEW YORK TIMES

Yes, I know: The American right has long derided the paper of record as a bastion of all things liberal, godless, and proto-communistic. But it's hard to give much credence to that view if you dally much with the actual brunt of coverage in the *New York Times*, which skews ridiculously toward the overindulged Manhattan elite. If you graze through the archives of, say, the Sunday business section, you'll see adoring profiles of executives since exposed as all-purpose brigands, from Goldman Sachs chieftain Lloyd Blankfein to former Citigroup chairman Sandy Weil, the man who crowed loudly that the 1999 legislation enacting the repeal of the Glass-Steagall Act restrictions on the giddy fusion of consumer and investment banking should have been called "Gramm-Leach-Bliley-Weil." Indeed, in a time of ruinous contraction in the news industry at large, and at the *Times* in particular, the Gray Lady has actually announced plans to increase its online business coverage, which speaks volumes about the company's image of its ideal reader.[1]

In a sense, though, every section of the *Times* is its business section. In the Sunday Styles section, for instance, readers regularly encounter features explaining how best to indulge a Wall Street bonus-backed shopping spree without provoking "populist" ire among the hoi polloi who might clog the sidewalks outside a Henri Bendel sale. Meanwhile, the unsightly high-end shopping magazine *T* at least cops more directly to pandering to a plutocratic demographic than does the regular *Times Magazine*, which usually dresses up its penchant for privilege-osculating in mock-sonorous columns on "The Way We Live Now." (The front matter so dubbed in the Sunday magazine would likely be briskly rechristened if the publication's editors bothered to read the Anthony Trollope novel of the same name, which places a fraudulent US railway investment scheme squarely in the center of its vision of Victorian-era moral decay.) Even the one reliable economically liberal voice in the paper—op-ed columnist Paul Krugman—is a still, small presence compared to the outsized free-market delusions routinely minted in his section under the bylines of Thomas Friedman, David Brooks, and Ross Douthat.

As the industry leader in the news business, the *New York Times* showcases in greatly distilled form the economic and journalistic crisis roiling our media markets. As readerships fragment, thronging to online and nichified news sources, general-interest papers now go to great lengths to narrowcast content for their prized cohort of readers in elite demographics—to flatter the sensibilities and taste preferences of the consumer markets who present the most robust prospect for would-be advertisers. However, this marketing mandate creates a near-intolerable state of tension with the professed journalistic mission of the newspaper—to serve as a national news source of first resort. In competing papers such as the *Washington Post*, chasing a shrinking readership down an ever-narrowing news hole has produced embarrassing scandal—as when *Post* publisher Catherine Weymouth publicized a plan in 2009 to pimp reporters out to advertisers at off-the-record policy salons in her home. In the more genteel sanctums of *Times* leadership, there's no talk of resorting to such coarse pay-to-play gambits—for the simple reason that the paper's class affinities are already on abundant display in its pages.

And as the *Times*ian dalliance with the money culture billows upward, so does its vision of the plight of working Americans grow evermore puzzled, voyeuristic, and patrician. It's true that the paper is one of the only remaining metropolitan dailies to still employ a labor correspondent, the truly accomplished and sharp-eyed Steven Greenhouse. But it's also quite distressingly plain that the general treatment of working Americans in Timesland is akin to the way that the *Weekly World News* handles the Bigfoot beat—a source of erratic goggle-eyed wonderment, but not in any way a constituency claiming a serious purchase on adult attention. Hence the Gray Lady's recent pattern of consigning coverage of the unfortunates who fall below the entry barrier of the respectable middle class to the most voyeuristic "color" hand available in the newsroom—the just-folks professional southerner Rick Bragg through much of the nineties, then the arch purveyor of crusty American oddities, Charlie LeDuff, who left the paper in 2006.

The paper's blurry collective gaze downward on the class hierarchy conspired most unfortunately to produce an epic multipart 2005 series clumsily crafted as Pulitzer fodder, and later released as a book, called "Class Matters."[2] Here *Times* scribes heroically sought to reassure the paper's privileged readers that social class did not in fact matter all that much, at least so far as those Americans marooned in the wage-stagnant lower orders were concerned. No, "social diversity had erased many of the markers" of former divisions of caste and class, we learned in the opening installment of the series; indeed, it appeared that in these United States "merit had replaced the old system of inherited privilege."[3]

Such gentle cooing could only be music to the ears of Ivy League–educated Manhattanites, but unfortunately it bore no relation to the way the actual economy works. In 2005, the United States was in the midst of a five-year phase of economic expansion when wages actually declined—the first such period in our history. Wealth was no more being apportioned on the basis of merit or social diversity than lollipops were growing on trees—yet the *Times* plunged serenely on, in misguided character studies that demonstrated little about actual working Americans beyond the way they confused and frightened *Times* correspondents. Writing on a food warehouse worker who

stubbornly defied the meritocratic mandate of obtaining a college di-
ploma, economics writer David Leonhardt described the poor sap as
though he were a lab gerbil who had inexplicably seized up into paral-
ysis midway through his morning wheel-routine. "Many low-income
teenagers know few people who have made it through college," Leonhardt marveled. "A majority of the non-graduates are young men, and
some come from towns where the factory work ethic, to get working as soon as possible, remains strong, even if the factories themselves are vanishing. Whatever the reason, college just does not feel
normal."[4]

Of course, college mainly tends not to feel normal if less privileged
Americans have to rack up mountains of debt to meet tuition expenses
that rise at rates that are often more than double the rate of inflation.
Even Leonhardt was forced to concede that a recent binge of social-
spending cuts from the Bush White House produced the singularly
perverse outcome in the university world that "high-income students,
on average, actually get slightly more financial aid than low-income
students."[5] But at the end of the day, the only explanation of stalled-
out meritocratic advancement sufficiently comforting to *Times* readers had to be cultural—that these curious wage-earning life forms
simply do not "feel normal" on the generously leafy grounds of their
local university campuses. Imagine if, say, Franklin D. Roosevelt had
permitted such patrician fretting over the feelings of working-class
kids to stay his hand from signing the GI Bill, which tore down forbidding class-based entry barriers at many elite universities.

I don't mean to dwell on Leonhardt's excesses here—in other
respects, he's a very capable, and sometimes quite astute, writer on
economic policy. But his arm's-length disquisition on working-class
mores typifies a glaring blind spot that's long assailed the nation's paper of record. Apart from occasional off-lead features about the impact of deindustrialization in the Rust Belt, the struggles of working
Americans are virtually invisible in the paper's coverage. Indeed, in
a little-noted breach of just about every notion of journalistic ethics,

the *Times* had a former Sony studio executive, Michael Cieply, cover the 2008 Hollywood writer's strike—a conflict of interest that's roughly akin to handing the media beat over to Sarah Palin.[6]

Meanwhile, in the aftermath of the devastating 2010 Haitian earthquake, *Times* correspondents Marc Lacey and Simon Romero filed a surreal dispatch that could readily be mistaken for a parody in the *Onion*. "Quake Ignores Class Divisions of a Poor Land," the headline marveled in a tone of patrician dumbfoundment.[7] The accompanying text is no less wall-eyed in its astonishment at an impersonal act of God so risibly heedless of the hard-and-fast social distinctions that make up the *Times*ian social world. "Earthquakes do not respect social customs," Lacey and Romero write, as though they are desperately trying to pinch themselves awake. "They do not coddle the rich. They know nothing about the invisible lines that in Haiti kept the poor masses packed together in crowded slums and the well-to-do high up in breezy places like Pétionville." Indeed, as our correspondents traipse those breezy streets, they depict a social world turned upside down, confounding the most elementary sense of a natural order: "The unsettling feeling of seeing one's home collapse, no matter the size, affected Haitians of all social strata. . . . Destruction. . .was on display up and down exclusive residential areas like Pacot, near the old center, and Pétionville, in the hills above the city. Mansions were flattened and monied families slept in the street in front of their destroyed residences, clinging to their possessions."

When the great Lisbon earthquake of 1755 devastated a European capital and claimed some 20,000 fatalities, the once-confident philosophes of the Enlightenment were shaken to their core and questioned the notion that such a devastating calamity could be the handiwork of a just, compassionate, and omnipotent God. Faced with a similar existential challenge, the *New York Times* was moved to reflect that here was the one instance where the carefully assembled trappings of privilege could not secure a safe and comfortable life.

Such oblivious patrician treatments of socioeconomic life are now routine fare in today's *Times*—an especially egregious state of affairs when one considers that the ruinous impact of the 2008 collapse on the ordinary American worker is, by any measure, one of the most significant stories of our age. Yet today, the *Times* economic beat is rendered as through the wrong end of a pair of binoculars, recording the heroic efforts of moneyed families trying to belatedly school their offspring in the travails of holding down an actual job, the regrettably downscaled real-estate ambitions of a Donald Trump or a Bruce Ratner, and the chastened business model of the hedge-fund world. It's a surpassingly glum statement on the class myopia of our paper of record that the most serious and in-depth treatment of the plight of working Americans in the actual productive economy comes from the broadsheet of the investor class itself, the *Wall Street Journal*.

But things are ever thus, it seems, in the elite provinces of midtown Manhattan journalism. Following the business coverage of the *Times*, one can't help recalling Robert Warshow's famous characterization of the *New Yorker*'s editors' abrupt, and generally unbecoming, lurch into "seriousness" in the wake of the atomic bomb's impact: "They never dreamed that the world's inelegance could become so dangerous."[8]

Rich People Thing No. 3

MERITOCRACY

Few words in American public discourse are so routinely mishandled and deliberately misunderstood as "meritocracy." We are beguiled by the brisk, efficient ring of the term, its reassuring undertone of futurism and office-park cleanliness. And of course the idea behind it, that every individual is rewarded on a strict, measurably fair basis for his or her best effort in the hierarchies of work and academic achievement, all but doubles as a national mission statement. Who, after all, could be against a system so self-evidently impartial, open-ended, and technocratic?

The person who originally coined the term, that's who. Michael Young was a British sociologist who studied family relationships and community bonds in industrial England. As he chronicled the relentless postwar expansion of the storied British civil-service ethos of measuring performance and assessing worth via intelligence testing, the seeds of a mischievous work of satire began taking root in his imagination. So in 1958, he published his satirical novel, *The Rise of the Meritocracy, 1870–2033*.

The book is packaged as a government white paper in a future time of political crisis—as a new coalition of redundant technicians who've joined forces with women conscripted into a domestic-service class are militating for the overthrow of the entire social order. The report's anonymous author—who coyly finds time in its footnotes to cite the long-ago scholarship of one "Michael Young"—revisits the postwar rationale for adopting the meritocratic scheme of social reward. As he presses placidly on, the reader gradually realizes that this is the anatomy of a chilling dystopia. The British Labour movement, which technocrats used as a convenient bludgeon to dismantle inherited privilege, is casually consigned to history's dustbin once the meritocrats have sucked it dry of all its intellectual talent and capable leaders. As our dispassionate narrator lays out the dilemma, Labour activists had merely failed to appraise the remorseless working out of the principles they endorsed. "They demand that equality be more than opportunity; they demand equality in power, education, and income; they demand that equality be made the ruling principle of the social order; they demand that the unequal be treated as though they are equal."[1]

This latter point, of course, becomes an intolerable contradiction in a society arranged around the idea of impartial reward of merit—inequality is the very calling card of the meritocracy. "Once all the geniuses are among the elite, and all the morons among the workers, what meaning can equality have?" our narrator coos complacently. "What ideal can be upheld except the principle of equal status for equal intelligence? What is the purpose of abolishing inequalities in nurture except to reveal and make more pronounced the inescapable inequalities of Nature?"[2]

Working from such organizing dictums, the meritocracy keeps social order intact via the planned redundancy of older workers in favor of their younger, copiously credentialed social betters and ever-greater emollients for the educated managerial class—lavishly compensated in a top-heavy salary system known as "merit money." Meanwhile, the brutish lower orders are kept in line via physical entertainments (known in official jargon as the "Mythos of Muscularity") and a revived domestic service, converting former manual workers into valets of the knowledge elite. The ultimate rationale for this caste-based upward distribution of resources was global competition in a new knowledge-based economy—the kind of reasoning that has a sickeningly familiar ring to readers of Thomas Friedman or *Wired* magazine. "To better withstand international competition, the country had to make better use of its human material," our writer observes. After all, while "the proportion of people with IQs over 130 could not be raised—the task was rather to prevent a fall—but the proportion of such people in work which called upon their full capacities was steadily raised. . . . The ranks of the scientists and technologists, the artists and the teachers, have been swelled, their education shaped to their high genetic destiny, their power for good increased. Progress is their triumph; the modern world their monument."[3]

However, the greatest joke of Young's satire is that the ideology of meritocracy has taken firm hold in the United States—not as Young intended, as a cautionary watchword for the social tyranny of the knowledge class, but rather as a virtual synonym for the hoary American myth of equal opportunity. (There is even, hilariously enough, an American publishing house that has reissued the book as part of its "Classics in Organization and Management Series," marking, so far as I know, the first completely unironic endorsement of dystopian fiction as fodder for management guidance.)

Young's fictional alter ego might well dub this willful misprision, had he set his sights toward the deeply confused social order across the Atlantic, the Mythos of Merit. Hence *New York* magazine writer Gabriel Sherman could summarize the rationale for sky-high executive compensation on Wall Street by pointing out that financial traders endorse as an article of faith "the virtue of efficient markets distributing capital to where it is most needed justifies extreme salaries—these are the wages of the meritocracy," i.e., an impartial and just reward for a socially useful service. Similarly *New York Times* scribes Janny Scott and David Leonhardt could offer this excursus on moneyed reward and social class in America: "Merit has replaced the old system of inherited privilege. . . . But merit, it turns out, is at least partly class-based. Parents with money, education, and connections cultivate in their children the habits the meritocracy rewards."

In both of these entirely representative examples, "meritocracy" is the tacit measure for justice in matters of income and wealth distribution. Sure, bond traders or wealthy families might manipulate the rules of access to meritocratic reward, but that reward itself is an unimpeachably sound principle of apportioning social worth.

One could only imagine that Young, who died in 2002, regularly greeted such naïve Yank misappropriations of his satirical construct with bitter guffaws. After all, shortly after Tony Blair's New Labour party came into power, bearing all the trademark Third Way celebrations of credentialed business privilege, Young editorialized that the newly installed prime minister should retire his promiscuous use of a term he plainly failed to understand. "If meritocrats believe, as more and more of them are encouraged to, that their advancement comes from their own merits," Young warned in the UK *Guardian*, "they can feel they deserve whatever they can get. . . . So assured have the elite become that there is almost no block on the rewards they arrogate to themselves. The old restraints of the business world have been lifted and, as the book also predicted, all manner of new ways for people to feather their own nests have been invented and exploited. Salaries and fees have shot up. Generous share option schemes have proliferated. Top bonuses and golden handshakes have multiplied."[4]

Young may as well have offered up a class anatomy of the United States in the Clinton era, a time when the ratio of CEO to average worker salaries exploded from 40:1 to 400:1, and the bottom tenth of wage earners lost ground from the tenuous livelihoods they were vouchsafed in the Reagan/Bush years. Yet shortly after Clinton's election, he was hailed by commentator Nicholas Lemann—author of a celebratory "meritocratic" history of college admissions testing called *The Big Test*—as "the first product of the American meritocracy to reach the White House," a figure with a bona fide "log cabin quality" to stave off traditional critiques of elite liberal aloofness.[5] And unto this day, liberal commentators like Lemann and conservative ones like David Brooks hymn the meritocracy as a hardy Yank solvent that leaches away the faintest whiff of an Old World upper crust on these shores. In one sense they're right—as products of elite private colleges, these pundits have been impressively insulated from the true import of this favored phrase via a basic lack of reading comprehension. Young's vision of a meritocratic educational hierarchy consciously designed to perpetuate gaping social inequality is, in other words, magisterially intact.

Rich People Thing No. 4

POPULISM

It may seem perverse, at best, to count the debased term "populism" among the notions contained in the overclass's sprawling warehouse of institutional vanity. The historical Populists, after all, were the sworn foes of moneyed privilege—debt-ridden farmers, industrial workers, and middle-class social reformers. Indeed, the Farmer's Alliance took such spirited issue with the depredations of the late nineteenth century's financial barons that its leaders advocated an alternate system of national currency and exchange, known as the Subtreasury Plan, which sought to reward labor and circulate goods and services on the basis of actual productive activity, as opposed to land-based speculation or the formation of market cartels.

But the actual economic history of populism has virtually no bearing on how the word is used today. It usually comes across in media dispatches as a catch-all term for spasmodic fits of popular anger—as when diffuse outrage greeted the news in 2009 that government bailouts were footing the bill for some $80 million in performance bonuses for executives at AIG, a firm whose recent performance had greased the skids of the US economy for a toboggan ride to hell. But the spasms always pass, and the fabled pitchfork-and-torchlight threat of populist mayhem never materializes.

Despite repeated stalwart efforts to revive the Populist brand—
behind harebrained third-party candidates such as Ross Perot, Ralph
Nader, and Pat Buchanan, via various culture-minded appropriations
of the idea, from the triumphalism of the cultural studies academy to
the recording careers of John Mellencamp and Bruce Springsteen—
no explicit movement or political formation attaches to the term. The
killjoy former editor of the *Partisan Review*, Philip Rahv, stubbornly
refused to believe in the New Left without first learning its mailing address; we might well say the same of the amorphous "Populist" mood
afoot in the land. Mainly, it's a lazy framing device, summoned by
pundits as an all-purpose scare tactic as a deadline looms or a cable
talking point beckons.

And that's also, not surprisingly, how populism has quietly bulked
into a Rich People Thing. Once you're able to separate it from any
coherent economic affiliation or program, populism becomes a
floating signifier—here an ill-defined reflex of downwardly mobile
resentment, there a broad-brush characterization of a voguish movie.
(Adjourn to your Google, and you will quickly see that just about
any vaguely demotic Hollywood production, from *The Hangover* to
Avatar, gets tagged as "populist," provided it hangs around at the box
office long enough—a singularly odd circumstance given the profoundly aristocratic, and punitively copyright-minded, cast of today's
entertainment industry.)

In this scheme of things, ordinary Americans who may or may
not possess legibly populist political leanings get consigned to what
might be called the reality TV version of Populism—or better yet, the
Populist Front. That is to say, today's populism convulses fleetingly
and anonymously through the body politic, leaving virtually no visible trace—and certainly no clear policy imprint of any kind. Meanwhile—and here is where things get really strange—populism on the
right is tricked out with a full complement of successful spokesmod-
els. There's Bill O'Reilly and his ostentatiously fake solicitude for the

easily battered cultural sensibilities of "the folks"; there's Glenn Beck and his emo tantrums on behalf of the Tea Party movement; there's Sarah Palin's politics of permanent grievance against the elite media, the scientific establishment, or anyone else (to paraphrase Bob Dylan) who knows more than she does. These are all among the leading augurs of the putatively populist outlook of our age, and they are all Fox News–branded millionaires.

Likewise, cast your gaze beyond the agoras of cable punditry, and you'll see that all manner of plutocrat routinely gets dubbed a populist, be it multibillionaire New York Mayor Michael Bloomberg, British airline-cum-banking mogul Richard Branson, or the Nebraska-based investment titan Warren Buffett. Hell, even George W. Bush—he of the Andover, Yale, Harvard Business School and second-generation presidential pedigree—somehow got pawned off as a notional national populist thanks to his occasional dalliances with the Spanish language and his tireless, and mendacious, packaging of tax cuts to the rich as downward transfers of wealth.

That's the paradox of an alleged free-floating populism, based on diffuse traits such personal bearing, attitude, and cultural taste: It is everywhere and nowhere, aligning only provisionally alongside the most fleeting impressions of a democratic public life. And since that image is itself largely a function of the market, it's no great surprise to see figures such as Beck and Buffett converted into stock populist heroes—they're either the self-appointed guardians of touchy cultural sensibilities (in Beck's teary case) or the avatars of savvy market intuition (as Buffett famously is for every aspiring day trader). Neither, of course, can afford to be viewed as somehow out of touch with heartland mores—hence Buffett makes a point of dragging visitors and interviewers from his modest ranch-house compound to Omaha steakhouses, and Beck inveighs on behalf of We the People against the depredations of a shadowy revanchist government elite. Yet all these populist pretenders betray an all-too-palpable contempt for the reliably silent majority they purport to symbolize. Like the ur-Populist figure of the television age—Andy Griffith's Lonesome Rhodes character in the Elia Kazan classic *A Face in the Crowd*—these figures only embody a populism of markets; beyond that core dogma, firm convictions about the proper direction of public life are strictly negotiable.

Nowhere has this dynamic been more evident than in the odd career of former CNN demagogue Lou Dobbs. Dobbs launched his cable career as an enthusiastic stock picker at the height of the late 90s tech boom—a persuasion that of course was hailed as deeply populist at the time, since the NASDAQ market was magically placing the instruments of capital ownership in the hands of the savvy day-trading masses. When that market fable collapsed along with the tech bubble, Dobbs was reborn as a truth-telling tribune of the beleaguered middle class, marooned in heartland communities with waning manufacturing bases and grim employment prospects—and surrounded, in Dobbs's account, by faithless immigrant workers, remorselessly driving their wages down. When the great economic collapse of 2008 rendered such bigoted brays objectively irrelevant—how could shifty immigrants be spiriting off jobs that weren't there in the first place?—Dobbs abruptly cashed in his pundit chips. Reportedly, he was pondering an independent run at a New Jersey Senate seat and duly set about reassuring that state's sizable Latino population that he had outgrown his whole on-air nativist shtick.

But in another odd respect, Dobbs unwittingly followed the sad career arc of many a disappointed nineteenth-century Populist. With the battle against the Money Power decisively lost in 1896, many populists retreated into racist demagoguery—most famously, former Georgia congressman and populist vice presidential nominee Tom Watson, who had bravely argued for a cross-racial alliance of working Southerners in the early years of his career. By the end of his life, Watson had degenerated into a one-size-fits-all Southern bigot, deriding African-Americans, the Catholic Church, and the immigrant hordes, and promoting the revived Ku Klux Klan with equal vigor. The only thing that would have accelerated the once-promising career of Watson yet faster into the mire of xenophobic racism would have been a cable TV contract. It's the surest means, after all, of convincing yourself that you're the People's mouthpiece as you transform legitimate economic grievances into hateful deliriums.

Rich People Thing No. 5

DAVID BROOKS

No matter how many times I espy *New York Times* columnist David Brooks patiently explaining the deeply antipopulist, economically astute, and mildly amusing features of the American character, I somehow always picture him in a straw boater and a striped jacket, affecting the jaunty mien of Harold Hill, the charming-huckster protagonist of Meredith Willson's *The Music Man*. That's because, like Hill, Brooks keeps up a steady, wisecracking patter meant to lull his eager auditors into a state of calm reassurance about the social order surrounding them. There's really just one salient difference: Hill was drumming up civic enthusiasm for the blandishments of school band class; and Brooks is pitching the stalwart myth of pseudomeritocratic worth, a system by which all just rewards spontaneously waft upward to the talented knowledge elite.

Brooks staked his claim as new millennial social seer with his breakout 2000 bestseller, *Bobos in Paradise*, which purported to gently mock the bohemian pretensions of the new American power elite. (These were, in Brooks's waggish telling, the "Bobos"—a lazy conflation of "bourgeois" and "bohemian" that Brooks claimed was a signature new formation on the American social landscape, even though bohemians have always been drawn from the ranks of the bourgeoisie, and rarely harbor any serious ambition to forsake their socioeconomic birthrights.)

But as with many works of pseudomeritocratic propaganda, Brooks's labored puckishness proved on closer inspection to be the sincerest form of flattery. For all its consumer excesses, the Bobo class was, in his account, brilliantly adaptive and surprisingly resourceful. Instead of lurching into the sort of cataclysmic hedonism that haunted the prophecies of more dour social critics such as Daniel Bell or Christopher Lasch, Brooks's affluent Bobos embarked on rigorous regimes of physical and spiritual self-improvement, practicing an enlightened "Modernism for the shareholders"[1] and possessing a "Midas touch in reverse," whereby everything they touch "turns to soul."[2]

Behind Brooks's gentle scoffing at the Bobo vogue for distressed furniture and overpriced cave-aged cheese at Whole Foods, in other words, was a tacit bid to extort a very old kind of social deference on behalf of this allegedly new social class—provided, of course, that its members summoned forth the right sort of nationalist fettle and noblesse oblige. In the book's closing pages, Brooks exhorted the feckless Bobo class to step up to the bar of history and claim its own proper role of stage-managing the world-defining American civilizing mission. Sounding very much like his own imperialist hero Theodore Roosevelt, Brooks fretted that "we may become a nation that enjoys the comforts of private and local life but that has lost any sense of national union and any sense of a unique historical mission. The fear is not that America will decline because it overstretches, but because it enervates as its leading citizens decide that the pleasures of an oversized kitchen are more satisfying than the conflicts and challenges of patriotic service."[3]

Lasch, a keen critic of Theodore Roosevelt's mugwump brand of imperial adventurism, astutely dubbed it "the moral and intellectual rehabilitation of the ruling class"—and that is very plainly what Brooks had in mind in his bid to marshal the home-happy Bobo elite into a gauzy ethos of national service. But of course, with the benefit of hindsight, we can appreciate how deeply misguided this reckless conflation of ruling-class rehabilitation and national mission can be.

Following the spirit of the Brooksian playbook to a tee, the United States became mired in a disastrous and illegal imperial mission in Iraq—a project that Brooks enthusiastically cheered from his perch at the *Weekly Standard* and the prestigious *New York Times* op-ed column he inherited from William Safire. And of course the whole rickety debt-based fantasia that permitted countless Bobo homeowners to leverage out their mortgages into upscale kitchen upgrades has collapsed into a smoldering ruin.

But the beauty of Brooks's brand of just-in-time valentines to the American knowledge elite is that you never have to say you're sorry— or really that you meant much of anything you said in the first place. Aligning one's pundit brand with the credentialed smart set means automatically, in these United States anyway, that one is on the right side of history. If anyone has mastered the flexible dictates of Modernism for the shareholders, it's Brooks himself.

Indeed, the hollowness of the "comic sociology" Brooks sought to perpetrate in *Bobos* was exposed the following year, when he composed a faux-anthropological cover story for the *Atlantic*, exploring the mysterious hinterland sensibilities of "Red America"—i.e., the virtuous right-leaning voting districts and states that went into the George W. Bush column during the hard-fought 2000 election—in Franklin County, Pennsylvania.

True to form, Brooks strung together plausible-sounding tossed-off observations about the shopping mores and cultural sensibilities of the place, all of which allegedly shored up the big-picture thesis of the piece: that Red and Blue America faced off against unfordable culture divides, which in the pie-eyed editorial vision of Michael Kelly's *Atlantic* translated into abiding class segregation as well. The only problem is that very few of the telling details Brooks crammed into the piece proved to be, you know, true. For instance, it was quite possible, contrary to Brooks's airy assertion to the contrary, to purchase a meal at a local restaurant for more than $20; high-end retail outlets were surprisingly common in a region Brooks claimed was pocked by Dollar Stores and thrift emporiums. Red States did not swarm with QVC home-shopping addicts, as Brooks casually claimed; the network's highest-volume sales demographic was, in fact, the posh ultraliberal 90210 zip code in Beverly Hills. Nor was Red America the hotbed of NASCAR adoration that Brooks assumed when he claimed that the average Blue State liberal couldn't name five professional stock car drivers; it turns out that three of the top five viewing markets for NASCAR are in so-called Blue States. And Blue America didn't abjure hands-on, motor-driven yard work for the convenient leasing of illegal immigrant labor, as Brooks contended; indeed, most major centers of illegal immigrant hires were in agricultural Red States.

When *Philadelphia* magazine writer Sasha Issenberg ran this litany of contradictory facts by Brooks for his sharply critical 2004 anatomy of both Brooks's research and mystifying popular acclaim, the young reporter got a sober lecture from Mr. Comic Sociology for his trouble. "This is dishonest research. You're not approaching the piece in the spirit of an honest reporter," Brooks chided his interlocutor. "Is this how you're going to start your career?"[4]

Brooks well understands, of course, that the way to confidently pilot one's career upward is to play shamelessly to the broad-as-a-barn cultural prejudices of an elite readership rather than challenging its sensibilities with empirical findings—one reason, among countless, that it is beneath parody for Brooks to have accused Isenberg of "dishonest research." But there's no doubt, in pure terms of career ambition, that Brooks had the best of this particular argument. Not long after the unhappy *Atlantic* episode, he was elevated to the plum perch as the lead conservative columnist for the *Times*—and from there, he was off and running with all sorts of similar grab-and-go generalizations about the deep-seated cultural determination of everything, from the rancorous mood of Major League Baseball playoffs to the course of global development policy and foreign aid.

But the shtick has worn threadbare as Brooks has turned his culture-bound pundit gaze on things of actual material import, as the course of events since 2008 has mercilessly forced him to do. On a dumbfounding appearance on George Stephanopoulos's *This Week* in late 2008, Brooks was holding forth on the prospect of government bailouts for US auto manufacturers, a policy that he of course opposed as a defilement of sainted free market principle. Bailing out automakers would unconscionably introduce "politics" into industrial policy (since, you know, unregulated market activity had done so much to secure our collective economic stability) and this would be a bootless prospect indeed, compared to the existing federal bailout of financial institutions to the tune of $100 billion and more. "That's a public utility," he airily proclaimed. When another panel member pressed him on this outlandish claim, he just shrugged. "It's a metaphor," he wheedled, in much the same condescending affect that came across in his churlish exchange with Issenberg.

Well, not so fucking much, actually. This particular government-supported metaphor drove millions of homes into foreclosure, destabilized global credit markets, and helped plunge manufacturing enterprises like the auto industry past the brink of economic viability. To call this the handiwork of a public utility is akin to awarding a peace prize to Benito Mussolini. But then again, this is someone who could publicly mourn the wayward course of the occupation of Iraq as the miscalculation of a country "blinded by our own idealism"— and then, a week on, seek to rally the flagging spirits of the Invading Faithful with the fanciful incantation that America would prove "adaptable enough to recover from its own innocence and muddle its way to success, as I suspect we are about to do." There's your Modernism for the shareholders, right there—a callow optimism of the will in the face of all the familiar ironies and calamities that have attended Western colonialism throughout its long and deeply unattractive history.

Not surprisingly, the Brooksian machinery of cultural determinism sours noticeably when it becomes engaged with questions of poverty and global development. In such awkward settings, it plods

remorselessly on, serenely oblivious of its jittery misfires and delusional outbursts, so that its proprietor has gradually shed his confident Harold Hill mien and comes evermore to resemble poor doomed
Norma Desmond in the late reels of *Sunset Boulevard*.

In the immediate aftermath of the devastating 2010 earthquake
in Haiti, for example, Brooks took to his column to mount one of
his favorite hobbyhorses: the notion that the ultimate arbiter of fortunes in squalid, poverty-wracked nations such as Haiti, a longtime
US protectorate that has witnessed violent political coup after violent
political coup ever since Western powers resolved to isolate it from
the global community in the wake of its successful slave rebellion is—
wait for it—the mystical force of culture. The startling body count in
the wake of the Haiti quake, Brooks wrote, arose from "a complex web
of progress-resistant cultural influences. There is the influence of the
voodoo religion, which spreads the message that life is capricious and
planning futile. There are high levels of social mistrust. Responsibility
is not often internalized. Child-rearing practices often involve neglect
in the early years and harsh retribution when kids hit 9 or 10. We're
supposed to politely respect each other's cultures. But some cultures
are more progress-resistant than others, and a horrible tragedy was
just exacerbated by one of them."

There are few things as distasteful as an opportunistic pundit
seizing upon the wrenching spectacle of mass death for the sake of
scoring points in a self-congratulatory sidebar to the culture wars.
Voodoo may be a fatalistic and not-entirely-rational belief system,
but it at least addresses its believers in the actual circumstances of
their lives and reserves a decent interval of genuine mourning for
the dead.

One can only fantasize about the retributions its deities would arrange for their counterparts in the David Brooks pantheon of household gods—his Patio Men, Organization Kids, and all the mythical,
meritocratic Bobos suffering from Status-Income Disorder. These superstitious pasteboard inventions are, much like the syncretic African

divinities who populate Voodoo forms of worship, bywords for capricious market forces that have ultimately proven no less impersonally deranging in the wholesomely progress-promoting cultures of Paradise Drive than they have in the slums of Port-au-Prince. But this exurban Götterdämmerung, pleasing as it may be to contemplate, shall never come to pass—there are just too many prestige editorial operations too heavily invested in the career of David Brooks for his chirpy pronouncements on the fitness of robust market ideology to meet with any serious challenge. Failing that, though, one might have at least hoped that Brooks could have packed up his smug market cosmology just this once and given the Haitian fallen what their own native faith at least guaranteed them—a humble and respectful silence.

Rich People Thing No. 6

THE FREE MARKET

Supplying a critical anatomy of the American romance with the free market is like trying to paint a white fence in a blizzard: Your target is everywhere and nowhere, firmly anchored in the landscape yet at the same time so diffusely scattered throughout the atmosphere that you hardly know where to begin.

The notion of a self-regulated market, magically governed by the invisible hand of self-interest, dates back, of course, to Adam Smith's famed eighteenth-century treatise, *On the Wealth of Nations*. Smith's Scottish Enlightenment vision of economic enterprise as a mystical haven of uncoerced social relations has always been catnip to the ownership class in the resource-rich and labor-stunted New World. Smith's thesis—a heady world-historical expansion of how he saw the division of labor unfold in a Scottish pin factory—seemed intuitively true in an early American Republic long on frontier expansionism and short on fixed class division and institutions of social welfare. If anywhere could be the natural home of a free market, why, this certainly must be the place.

Meanwhile, Smith's British compatriots took a far more dour view of his achievements. As economic historian Michael Perelman recounts, Francis Horner, the editor of the *Edinburgh Review* and chairman of the Bullion Committee in the British Parliament, declined an invitation to contribute an introduction to an 1803 reissue of Smith's book with this candid assessment: "I should be reluctant to expose S's errors before his work had operated its full effect. We owe much at present to the superstitious worship of S's name; and we must not impair that feeling, till the victory is more complete. . . . [U]ntil we can give a correct and precise theory of the origin of wealth, his popular and plausible and loose hypothesis is as good for the vulgar as any others."[1]

He might as well have added, "Turn the Yanks loose on it." But even on our shores, Smith has largely become enshrined as a post hoc prophet of market sovereignty for the modern right, which has made an industry of reviling the New Deal and the notion of government intervention in the economy. Perelman quotes a latter-day Smith scholar who observes, "There were more new editions of *The Wealth of Nations* published in the 1990s than in the 1890s, and more in the 1890s than in the 1790s."[2]

Those dates are not without significance in our economic history. The 1890s marked the full onset of the Industrial Revolution in America and set the stage for the corporatist model of business enterprise pioneered by Progressive economic and legal thinkers. Under this dispensation—notably the landmark 1888 Sherman Antitrust Act's corporate-friendly interpretation in the courts—the breakup of smaller family-held business empires produced the golden age of incorporation, as joint stock companies displaced the more parochial brands of nineteenth-century business ownership. Thus was born modern managerial capitalism, a system whereby, as historian Alfred D. Chandler puts it, a new professional class of managers "came to command those enterprises where financiers were originally influential. . . . [B]y the 1950s the managerial firm had become the standard form of modern business enterprise."[3]

This shift meant, among other things, that the conceit of a free market founded and protected by stalwart individual entrepreneurs—always a diaphanous account of the operations of industrial enterprise—had withered almost entirely under the sway of what Chandler calls the "administrative coordination" of the managerial regime: the movement of corporate enterprise outward into ever greater swathes of market share at the same time its systems of production and distribution recombined into vertically integrated cartels. And in the wake of the 2008 financial crisis, those tendencies have not abated; unlike the New Deal's battery of efforts to deconcentrate finance and industry, and thereby stimulate consumer demand and job growth in public-backed enterprise, today's economic regulators have doubled down on the cartelized finance sector with lavish too-big-to-fail bailouts. The result is virtually a photographic negative of free-market theory, with federal income support going straight into the coffers of finance capital. This boondoggle, when gamed by an exceptionally crafty charity case such as Goldman Sachs, produces yet another garish turn of the screw: Goldman made most of its fortune in 2009 by wheeling from the Treasury's welfare window to exploit the infinitesimally low interest rates the firm commands as a Potemkin consumer banking shop to vacuum up virtually free profits in the municipal and federal bond markets. Nary a pin has been made in the process.

And the odd thing is that in the face of such grievous gaming of the finance dole, public discourse has doubled down on free-market dogma. University of Chicago behavioral economist Steven Levitt has leveraged classical martketspeak into an all-purpose pop explanation of virtually everything in his "Freakonomics" franchise. Sales of Ayn Rand novels (tracts that make Smithian free-market orthodoxy seem like wild-eyed syndicalism by comparison) have spiked; and anemic legislative bids to expand health-care coverage and to gesture vaguely in the direction of re-regulating our debt-ravaged financial system routinely provoke hysterical cries of "Socialism!"

All of which prompts one to wonder if there isn't a deep overcompensating strain in the American worship of free-market pieties. The craving for Smith-style truism appears to kick in most desperately when economic reality comports least to elegant free-market theory—in much the same way that, say, the tribal incantations of the

1990s "men's movement" took deepest hold among stoop-shouldered Boomer office workers; or that preachers in hulking multimedia Sunbelt megachurches profess to bear the unsullied truth of the Holy Ghost and the primitive gospel.

In reality, the market has no organic existence at all. It has always been a contrivance of contract law, interlocking trusts, and trade protocols—and its putative freedom is primarily a function of who is best positioned to benefit from this or that set of advantageous relationships. The explosion of global "free trade" agreements that revved up in the Clinton era were free for many local manufacturing economies in the United States only in the bitterest sense, i.e., that one suddenly takes on a great deal of free time when one's job migrates south. Likewise, the free market in health care that conservative activists are now so hot to preserve from the federal government's meddlesome regulating hand is in fact an elaborate patchwork of gamed Medicare contracts, erratically enforced state regulatory codes that are still the only government curbs on the excesses of most major insurers, and the lobbying wish list of a pharmaceutical Leviathan that seeks to secure patent rights to its most lucrative products, like the next generation of microbionic cancer drugs, into perpetuity. But the myth of the free market remains a powerful intellectual opiate, and its pushers are legion, from Malcolm Gladwell to Steve Forbes to Sarah Palin.

Indeed, probably the most effective way to break the free market's spell would be to transform its most debilitating cultural products into a globalized twelve-step program. See, for instance, how New Economy laissez-faire ideologues like Virginia Postrel or Chris Anderson fare in the hypercapitalist but viciously authoritarian island paradise of Singapore. Or put Thomas Friedman to work in a Marianas textile factory for a couple of months and let him see how flat the market-mastered world looks to him then. Take the utopian theorists of "seasteading" libertarianism at their word, and let them fashion their stateless free-market utopia out of all reach of all international sea treaty enforcement. Put Steve Forbes to work as a union organizer in the shadows of the breathtaking architectural homage to investor-class excess known as the Abu Dhabi skyline—where the local construction industry is awash in sweated day labor. Indeed, I can see a whole *Survivor*-style reality television franchise in the offing: *Capitalist Detox Island*. True, it might be a hard sell to advertisers—unless, that is, you compel TARP recipients to purchase ad time. Now that's a manipulation of market forces I can get behind.

Rich People Thing No. 7

THE STOCK MARKET

Few forces in American life are as anxiously monitored and as ill understood as the index of investor trade volume that, for most professional and civilian dwellers of the republic of finance, defines the overall performance of the US economy. In reality, the traffic in stocks—itself a misleading shorthand, since a great deal of investment capital now goes into bonds, securities, hedge funds, and other instruments far more exotic than publicly traded common stock—only reflects the erratic mood swings of a narrow stratum of players in the financial industry. One wouldn't think this point needed any belaboring in the wake of the Great Recession launched in 2008, since that cataclysm exposed in operatically humiliating detail just how shoddy, perverse, and borderline fraudulent most routine Wall Street transactions were in comparison to the overall state of the productive economy.

Yet in stage-managing the federal response to that crisis, Bush Treasury Secretary Henry Paulson Jr. and New York Federal Reserve Director Timothy Geithner (later Paulson's successor under President Obama) responded with blinding alacrity to restore at least the picture of health to many of the market's chief malefactors—the obscenely overleveraged American Insurance Group, the cancerous securities machine known as Goldman Sachs (where both Paulson and his Clinton-era predecessor Robert Rubin were senior executives

before their notional careers as public servants), and bailed-out purveyors of toxic debt such as Morgan Stanley and Bear Stearns.

The rationale for the $700 billion spent on these and other co-
lossally bad market actors was that the funds were the surest and
quickest way to jump-start America's frozen credit markets. With the
elaborate and lovingly modeled instruments of debt securitization
that drove the Potemkin prosperity of the tax-cutting Bush years now
threatening to pitch the entire economy into the abyss, the once risk-
inebriated investor class had turned gun shy.

There is, of course, a measure of logic in this remedy; when credit
disappears from the private sector, federal regulators become lenders
of last resort, lubricating the flow of capital among the investor class.
But when past federal regimes have bailed out Wall Street, they have
exacted some concessions in return. Indeed, in the present global crisis, other more tightly regulated international markets became nationalized outright, as was the case in Britain. And when Iceland's
national economy was thrust into bankruptcy by the derivatives-
fueled deliriums of British, Dutch, and other overseas investors who'd
managed to topple a huge Internet-based banking concern named
Icesave, Iceland's citizens put the government's proposed bailout plan
to a referendum vote—which resulted in 93 percent of the voters re-
sponding in the negative.

By contrast, when the US federal government became share-
holders-of-last-resort in the major investment houses crippled
by the 2008 crisis, government regulators primly declined to exercise the voting rights that went with the public sector's own
shares in those houses. And government overseers only engaged
the pivotal question of executive compensation—which fuels both
the upward spiral of paper speculation to support the insanely
unmoored pay packages of the senior members of the financier
class, and the more fundamental and scandalous misallocation
of resources from the productive economy into the paper one—
with the faintest heart and narrowest reach of authority. Federal

"compensation czar" Kenneth Feinberg made a great show of establishing a $500,000-a-year ceiling on executive compensation at firms still collecting Troubled Asset Relief Program (TARP) funds, but abjured any deeper engagement with the inner structure of the investment models that kicked up our outlandish executive pay regime in the first place.

Indeed, as Feinberg explained to *New York Times* writer Stephen Brill, he interpreted his role not as an arbiter of a just wage for the titans of finance, but rather as a protective buffer to shield them from the public's ire. In his discussions with the leaders of TARP-backed firms, Feinberg told Brill, "What I tried to make them understand, was that if I didn't do something, the public would revolt, and Barney [Frank] would surely do something more drastic that would endanger the whole system." That, in turn, empowered Feinberg to assure his charges that he was not their disciplinarian so much as their cautious enabler: "I told them it wasn't Citi or Bank of America or the others against me, it was Citi and me or B. of A. and me, against them"—"them" being the public.[1]

Setting oneself up as a sort of policy valet, advising the class of boodlers under one's regulatory authority how to best sidestep accountability in the public sphere is, to put things mildly, a novel philosophy of public service. But of course, it barely rings a warning bell in our market-prostrate system of government—any more than anyone pauses to reflect why the Federal Reserve, which is tasked under federal statute with providing stability to the financial sector and the economy at large, only appoints bankers and financial-sector economists to its governing board, as opposed to, say, labor economists or consumer and small business advocates in the financial world. If the Fed exists to serve the public, why do only the advocates for the most lavishly overcompensated stretch of the private sector go about setting its agenda and crafting its policy?

As matters stood, Feinberg himself was a far more frequent target of public scorn than any of the bad financial actors in his charge ever had been. The financial world and its uncritical chroniclers in the business press typically treated Feinberg's policies—which only lasted the duration of a company's time on the TARP dime, and failed to rein in the true dosh that Wall Street executives savor via deferred stock compensation and other stock-based rewards—as a landmark lurch onto the road to socialism every bit as alarming as the founding of the Paris Commune. It speaks volumes about the state of debate over the stock market's operations and alleged public utility that far more Americans can recognize Feinberg's name than those of the AIG chieftains who presided over the company's epic and chaotic meltdown (Martin Sullivan, Robert Willumstad, and Maurice Greenberg, for the record).

Then again, the whole cavernous void in the American policy-making imagination in matters of financial and industrial policy speaks to how far the reflexive idolatry of the stock market has shaped, and distorted, our understanding of basic economic aims. Stock market performance directly affects the economic well being of less than 1 percent of the US population, yet is uncritically taken as an ironclad reading of the economy's overall health. "The markets" are anthropomorphized in daily press accounts as the final arbiters of policy success and failure—expressing "anxiety" over reports of belated new banking regulations from the Obama White House and joyously rallying when they pick up the whiff of another bundle of tax cuts or a reduction in interest rates from the Federal Reserve's Open Markets Committee. Bloomberg economics columnist Amity Shlaes, in her deeply dishonest account of the purported failure of the New Deal, *The Forgotten Man*, goes so far as to supply a running quote of thirties Dow performance at the head of each new chapter. The gimmick is meant to spook readers into affirming the brunt of her delusional argument that the real economy suffered and slowed down further under the impact of the Roosevelt White House's new policy of government intervention, whereas all that these fluctuations can persuasively show is what any student of the period already knows: Investors and financiers really, really disliked FDR and the New Deal.

This lazy endorsement of stock performance as a popular referendum on economic policy was also one of the central myths of the great 1990s stock bubble, when the rush on tech stocks converged with a faux-populist celebration of mutual funds as a great social leveler. This was the age of the IPO-vested "Microsoft millionaire," the folksy heartland stock pickers' social known as the Beardstown Ladies investment club, and James Glassman's hallucinatory tract of perma-Bull mind cure, *Dow 36,000*. This was also the time when the stupendously oafish notion of privatizing Social Security gripped many mainstream economic solons, a measure that, had the Bush White House managed to carry it over in its second-term domestic agenda, would by now have the vast majority of the nation's retirees toiling in workhouses—or in the new millennial equivalent of that late-life sentence, as thirty-four-hour-a-week, benefits-starved Wal-Mart greeters.

What few observers paused to mention in the midst of all this exuberant balderdash was that the market was already proving itself to be grievously out of sync with real economic conditions. As the labor market improved to a state of near full employment, for example, the stock market would invariably spike downward, since the prospect of a broader prosperity triggered inflation fears among skittish investors. Not that such increases were a serious prospect in the Clinton years, anyway—another Wall Street-related distortion of real economic performance was the stubborn failure of significant gains in worker productivity to produce commensurate increases in wages. One thing Wall Street has always hated is collective bargaining, which threatens an equitable distribution of the fruits of the nation's labor. This pathological distaste for economic fairness only steepened in the market-happy Bush years, when for the first time in modern US history the economy logged five consecutive years of growth without an accompanying increase in median wages.

One key reason the TARP bailouts went forward with so little real public deliberation or any effort to impose a modicum of federal discipline on the firms that had done so much to despoil the real economy is that the federal welfare fix has been in on Wall Street for more than a generation. Beginning with the Bush I–era bailout of the failed, Reagan-deregulated savings and loan industry, on through to the benchmark "too big to fail" rescue of the flailing Long Term Capital Management hedge fund, investors have rushed into risk-steeped, debt-ridden markets in the growing confidence that their antics will only produce symbolic rebukes from Washington, and then a new round of blank checks from the Treasury. Much the same dynamic held, one imagines, when the parents of many a modern-day bond trader had sighed indulgently at the news that their teenage boy had been expelled from one private school, and then pulled out their checkbook to arrange the young ruffian's transfer to another. Writing in 2000, well ahead of the present calamity, business writer Doug Henwood neatly summed up the new dispensation: "The welfare state may have been shredded for the poor, but not for big finance, which can screw up grandly and still count on an expensive rescue."[2]

Even though FDR was himself famously an aristocrat, routinely denounced in the moneyed East Coast orbit of the finance world as a traitor to his class, he firmly grasped the moral and political power of holding his political foes accountable for their actions. In an age that has seen the repeal of federal income support for the poor under the risible slogan-cum–legislative moniker "The Personal Responsibility Act of 1996," one wonders just what it might take for a political leader to show the reckless, petulant, and shiftless beneficiaries of today's Wall Street dole a bracing dose of personal discipline.

Rich People Thing No. 8

"CLASS WARFARE"

To paraphrase Chuck Palahniuk, the first rule of American class warfare is this: It is always waged upward, never downward. That's because it's an all-purpose rhetorical cudgel favored among conservatives any time public debate threatens to oscillate outside the approved range of questions such as "Tax Cuts: Super Awesome, or Merely Awesome?"

This reflex has become so firmly fixed in public discourse that it dictates much of our news coverage of revenue questions. To take just one entirely representative example, in 2009 the *Los Angeles Times* headlined a dispatch on the debate over redressing the federal deficit with the words, "Obama's Budget: Taxing for Fairness or Class Warfare?"[1]—even though the class hypothetically coming in for a marginal tax increase was earning an annual income of $250,000. If its members would be waging a war, they would be armed with fencing foils and lacrosse sticks; what's more, the tax increase being discussed would restore these earners to the tax rates they paid during the second Clinton administration—that time, you vividly recall, when the sansculottes ransacked the mansions of the titled aristocracy and the tumbrels filled with the severed heads of royalty.

Oddly enough, one doesn't hear anywhere near the same rhetorical firepower trained on the other main term in the *Times*' taxing dichotomy: "fairness." That beleaguered notion not only fails to galvanize headline writers and Heritage Foundation seminars but also is a nearly taboo term in reckoning American life outcomes. After a punishing generation's worth of rabid antigovernment rhetoric on the right, economic liberals rarely stir out of the defensive crouch of "Third Way" New Democrat policy-making—whereby sober technocrats administer tax cuts that are "targeted" as opposed to sweeping, traffic in "incentives" rather than redistribution, and promote "intellectual capital" rather than labor organizing. So when Americans talk about taxation being fair—let alone brokering wider access to other public goods such as housing, quality education, universal health care, and income support—it's hard to see what they could be getting at, in terms of an actual agenda. Industrial policy? Pell Grants? Enterprise zones? Query any lawmaker—Democratic or Republican, it matters little—on such discredited Great Society or New Deal notions, and you'll only get blank stares of incomprehension, and (if you're lucky) a sound bite echoing some variation of "The era of big government is over."

It's a bit disorienting, then, to hear no less a capitalist savant than multibillionaire investor Warren Buffett complain to no less a free-market propagandist than former Nixon White House speechwriter Ben Stein that, in the simple process of filing his annual tax return in compliance with the tax code—without benefit of a nimblefingered accountant or tax adviser—he winds up paying much less of his earnings, in proportional terms, than any of the workers he employs. "How can this be fair? How can this be right?" Buffett wonders. When Stein offers the standard conservative objection that introducing such ideas into discussions of stabilizing the federal budget amounts to class warfare, Buffett blurts out in reply, "There's class warfare, all right—but it's my class, the rich class, that's making war, and we're winning."[2]

But this, of course, is not how the American game of class warfare is played. A financial titan never volunteers that he's ever anything less than a put-upon and munificent creator of vast swathes of jobs-creating entrepreneurship; suggesting that the tax code has been rigged in favor of his entire overcompensated class is a bit like filling in "herpes sufferer" on the occupational section of one's Match.com application. No, the specter of open class revolt has to come from the unruly peasant orders—though, as is with the case with the nation's kindred romance with bogus populism, somehow the actually extant members of this threatening rabble never really materialize for public view. It would be tremendously helpful if some publication would follow the lead of the Fortune 500 list, or *Forbes* magazine's annual roster of emulation-worthy billionaires, and come forth with a glossy yearbook featuring all the likeliest fomenters of nationwide bottom-up class revolt—an attention-starved John Edwards, say, or maybe the cast of *Jersey Shore*.

But that's the other odd thing about the class war canard: It references a conflict without any conceivable mobilized army. That's because giving names and faces to the ill-defined lower-born proles lusting after the expropriators' dosh would negate the great sport of crying "class warfare!" in the theaters of moneyed privilege: the rare opportunity for plutocrats to put themselves forward in the role of history's victims. It's perhaps no coincidence that the "class warfare" slogan first gained wider currency during the 1992 election shortly after the collapse of the Soviet bloc—the precise moment, in other words, when the waning prospect of actual class warfare was banished from the historical stage. Who could blame the leading lights of our pecuniary elite for feeling a certain guilty nostalgia for their mortal enemies on the Commie side of the historical dialectic? Much like a churchgoing kid letting his imagination run wild at a forbidden burlesque performance, they probably let their gaze fall backward on the hulking gray legacies of the failed socialist order—the pinched worker salaries, the brutalist government housing, the humiliating courtship of the nomenklatura—and wonder to themselves, "What must it have been like?" And then, virtually in the next breath:

"What if the lumpen masses were coming for me? What if I were Winston Smith?"

It's not as preposterous an imaginary exercise as it may sound. Back in 1983, at the height of Reagan-era Cold War saber rattling, Norman Podhoretz published a *Harper's* essay plumbing that irresistible neocon fantasy, "What If Orwell Were Alive Today?" trying to claim *1984* as a tract monocausally obsessed with Soviet menace— and therefore a love letter to the American political scene. (George Orwell himself, for what it's worth, was far less admiring of his Yank cousins than Podhoretz might have liked, deriding "American materialism" as fully as he denounced "Russian authoritarianism" and reserving special contempt for the mandarin class of American elite journalists "with their glittering uniforms and stupendous salaries." He abjured an interview request from *Time* magazine after the novel's publication on grounds of the "shame-making publicity" the newsweekly provided for the Republican right wing.[3])

Viewed from this labored vantage, the class war fantasies of today's economic right lend considerable elegance and plausibility to the older versions of the same persecuted-millionaire tropes that used to provoke hearty guffaws from a more confident liberal intellectual scene. Here, for instance, was *New Yorker* press critic A. J. Liebling, in the middle of the last century, marveling at the way newspaper publishers would lease their own editorial pages as outlets for their own poor-mouth works of self-portraiture:

> Who, noting the press's reaction to a given situation, can fail to be cheered by how nearly it matches up with how the press reacted when a similar situation last occurred? Thus, with the word "labor" the newspaper's association (i.e., the publisher's, in this case the same thing) is "stubborn." To government, "wasteful"; to the poor, "pampered"—or malingering, or undeserving. The "taxpayer" is "overburdened"—but it occurs to me as I write this that he is always represented as a

small, shabby man in underclothes and a barrel (the kind of man who, if he had a wife, two children, and no imagination, might be caught for an income tax of about $8) and never as an unmistakably rich man like, say, the proprietor of a large newspaper. The man in the barrel is always warned that a frivolous project like medical care for his aged parents is likely to double his already crushing tax burden. The implication is that the newspaper is above worrying about his parents, and of course he is, because his old man left him the paper.[4]

Say this much for the ready resort to the jumpy siren call of class warfare among the members of our latter-day overclass: They don't employ clumsy props like barrels and underclothes. Instead, they're outfitted with high-priced apologists filling up all available primetime space on Fox News, plying jeremiads against the same confiscatory government health schemes in exactly the same register of anguished mogul pique. True, it costs a lot more to keep a Sean Hannity in wardrobe and haircuts than it does to commission an editorial cartoon on the investor class's economic woes. But when one's own vision of economic conflict is so resolutely cartoonish to begin with, why quibble over the delivery system? Anything's better than pondering the real meaning of class warfare.

Rich People Thing No. 9

THE DEMOCRATIC PARTY

We all know the Team A/Team B scripting of our national politics: Republicans excoriate government, cut taxes, wax skeptical about climate change and evolution, and fulminate about cultural decline. And Democrats—well, this is where things get odd. In mainstream depictions of party conflict, Democratic leaders will try opportunistically to portray themselves as defenders of ordinary working Americans, and the press for the most part lazily endorses that script, since apparent bright-line differences in economic policy make for familiar and reassuring racehorse election narratives.

Once, of course, this broad characterization made sense. The Democratic party of the New Deal vintage was closely aligned with organized labor, suspicious of the concentration of corporate influence, and hewed to the old populist critique of financial elites and the Money Power. But the contemporary Democratic party, still at a loss to confront the many policy and analytical failures concealed by the relentless antigovernment sloganeering of the Reaganite right, continues to ply a softer brand of "us too" politics in economic policy. Democratic leaders support incremental gains for many of the already privileged segments of the knowledge economy— family and medical leave, targeted tuition credits, visa clearances for foreign-born tech and software workers—while briskly tending to the long and detailed wish list of today's Money Power: financial deregulation, creditor bailouts, free trade accords, and welfare reform.

The main champion of the Democrats' dalliance with the wealthy has been the conservative Democratic Leadership Council, which was founded after Reagan's landslide reelection to focus the party's policy agenda on the mission of regaining the White House. Key to that game plan was erasing the perception that the party was antibusiness—even though, viewed more broadly, the defection of the white working-class voters who came to be labeled as "Reagan Democrats" was chiefly fed by cultural, rather than economic, resentments. In other words, coming out of a tax-slashing and deregulatory Reagan White House that presided over one of the most sweeping upward distributions of wealth in our modern history, the DLC prescription for economic policy was to. . .continue wooing the affluent upper class.

The DLC White House strategy hit inadvertent pay dirt with the 1992 Clinton campaign, when in the teeth of a major recession, the Democratic nominee—a former chairman of the DLC—assembled enough stalwart liberal campaign advisers to run as a compassionate populist critic of trickle-down economics. But Clinton the president governed stalwartly from the economic right, negotiating the North American Free Trade Agreement over the bitter protests of the party's working-class base, rolling back federal income supports, and signing unprecedented (and as it turns out, quite disastrous) legislation to deregulate the finance sector, in the Gramm-Leach-Bliley Act that dismantled the New Deal segregation of commercial and investment banking under the landmark 1934 Glass-Steagall Act, and the 2000 Commodity Futures Modernization Act. Both measures directly abetted the massive securitization of debt that triggered the 2008 economic meltdown.

This fundamental shift in the party's economic outlook wasn't lost on most of the American electorate. By the early nineties, a number of national polls were showing a majority of respondents identifying the Democrats as the party of the rich. By 2007, when the Democrats finally regained their congressional majorities after fifteen years of White House–driven DLC strategizing, this characterization—which came as a shock to the 90s pollsters and commentators who could still recall the party's New Deal heritage—was simple demographic fact. An analysis of IRS data in the country's congressional districts—single filers earning more than $100,000 a year, and two-income households bringing home more the $200,000 a year—found that Democrats represented the majority of those districts in the House, and controlled the Senate delegations in the eighteen states with the highest concentration of such high-earning households.[1] That survey was done by Michael Franc of the conservative Heritage Foundation and so Democratic leaders could and did dismiss it as ideologically skewed—except that a similar analysis of income distribution in congressional districts performed by *USA Today* researchers after the 2008 cycle yielded nearly identical results. Democrats now represented 57 percent—some 4.8 million—of the nation's $200,000-and-above households; by contrast, the 2005 GOP majority in Congress represented 55 percent of that income cohort.[2]

This economic realignment clarifies a good deal about the Democrats' singularly laggard handling of the aftermath of the 2008 Great Recession. At a time when bold egalitarian policymaking was essential to reviving a fair and functioning economy, the chief framers of the Democrats' economic playbook—Treasury Secretary Timothy Geithner and Council on Economic Advisers Chairman Lawrence Summers—abjured a more robust and employment-based stimulus plan and focused mainly on the financial bailout regime they inherited from the Bush White House's economic team. There are many authors, in Congress and K Street alike, of the enormous failure to produce meaningful health-care reform, but a White House policy team that stressed recondite budget tricks like "bending the cost curve" and ready accommodation of pharmaceutical and insurance company giveaways over the far more politically viable and self-evident case for a universal government-backed policy bears a sizable share of the blame for the fiasco.

And all the while that the Obama White House placidly gave away the policy store on health care, polls showed a steady majority of Americans supporting the so-called public option of a competitively priced, government administered national health plan—a politically popular solution that the narrowing probusiness caste of Democratic economic sachems showed no pressing desire to provide. Meanwhile, a purported measure to reform the derivatives deregulation masterminded by the last Democratic administration morphed into another predictable K Street giveaway session, with hedge fund and derivatives lobbyists drafting key portions of the bill for the Democratic-led House and Senate committees shepherding it on toward its eventual floor vote. Needless to say, the Employee Free Choice Act—the first major measure to expand union representation in the workplace since the Wagner Act of 1935—never made it out of committee, even though unions spent more than $300 million in the 2008 election cycle, mainly to bulk up the Democratic majority in both houses of Congress and have lawmakers finally ratify this crucial piece of legislation.

When one reviews the sheer scale of the Democrats' abject failure to promote anything more than the shallowest, most rhetorical sort of lip service on issues of economic fairness, all the loose talk in the media about the Obama White House's lurches toward "populist" approaches to issues like executive compensation and banking regulation seems like a grim joke. And all the confused partisans of the Tea Party right crying havoc over the incorrigible "socialism" of the Democrats in power seem to be speaking another language altogether—a fusion of Esperanto and gibberish that future medical professionals may simply diagnose as "Rand-olalia."

Yet such are the terms of engagement, it seems, when one major party effectively quits the field when it comes to drafting equitable— or to put it in bald political terms, viable majoritarian—economic policy. Media outlets and political opponents keep recurring to the fiction of a fully engaged battle on the fundamentals of economic policy, in much the same way amputees develop the conviction that they still possess a phantom limb. It never seems to occur to any of the major players—least of all to the members of the Democratic leadership itself—that the cul-de-sacs of Democratic lawmaking in the Obama age are all but structurally identical to the crushing failures of the first term of arch–New Democrat Bill Clinton. There's the politically popular, but procedurally bollixed, effort to fix America's gruesomely broken health-care system—an initiative never really permitted in either instance to go above the heads of the interested pharmaceutical and insurance constituencies in order to produce its long-promised benefits for the household budgets of working Americans. There's a string of overt betrayals of a labor agenda—NAFTA in 1993, EFCA in 2009, Gramm-Leach-Bliley in 1999, and the Dodd-Frank derivatives bill in 2010. There are even many members of the same echt insider New Democrat policy vanguard, in the persons of former White House Chief of Staff Rahm Emanuel (as well as Emanuel's successor in the job, former Clinton commerce secretary William Daley), economic adviser Lawrence Summers, and Secretary of State Hillary Clinton—who famously mismanaged the Clinton White House's health-care initiative and now prepares the ground for a new battery of free trade accords, via her aggressive diplomatic touting of the "Pathways to Prosperity" initiative first instituted by the Bush White House.

One can think of many descriptors for a party that plods so relentlessly down a path of upward-tending, corporate-driven economic aims—but "populist" and "socialist" are definitely not among them. While the Clinton years produced a tremendous boom in the tech economy—and in the financial sector underwriting its expansion— the unequal distribution of those gains actually spiked income inequality beyond the levels of the Reagan years. From 1993 to 2000, writes economist Robert Pollin, "both the average wages for nonsupervisory workers and the earnings of the lowest 10 percent of wage earners not only remained well below those of the Nixon/Ford and Carter administrations, but were actually lower than even those of the Reagan/Bush years. Moreover, wage inequality—as measured by the ratio of the ninetieth to the tenth wage percentile—increased sharply during Clinton's tenure in office." Meanwhile, in the same years, the poverty rate barely eked downward to 13.2 percent of the population compared to the Reagan rate of 14.1—a remarkably dismal holding pattern, given the scale of the expansion in the tech and paper economies. Indeed, the poverty gap—the gains in income required to lift a wage earner above the federal poverty line (always a woefully low reflection of the actual income required for subsistence in America)—actually increased from $1,538 in 1993 to $1,620 in 1999.[3] Clinton tax policy, shaped largely under the direction of Treasury Secretary Robert Rubin, a former Goldman Sachs director and chairman, significantly spurred this top-heavy drift, producing in the grotesquely misnamed Taxpayer Relief Act of 1997 an estimated $1,000 in savings for the nation's top 20 percent of income earners for every dollar saved by the bottom 80 percent.[4]

Of course, eight years of Bushonomics sent all these baleful trends into overdrive—stoking ever-greater sums of deficit spending with ever-more gratuitous tax cuts. But that catastrophic track record shouldn't obscure the larger truth about the moneyed complexion of the New Democratic Party. As Slate money columnist Daniel Gross summed up the Clinton White House's romance with the investment banking set in his admiring 2000 chronicle *Bull Run*, "It's more hip to be a Democrat if you're loaded than it was in the 1980s. And it's more hip to be loaded if you're a Democrat."[5] And say what you will about Barack Obama's economic priorities—the guy is nothing if not hip.

Rich People Thing No. 10

THE PROSPERITY GOSPEL

Pioneering students of the Protestant origins of Western capitalism depicted relations between dissenting religion and the spirit of enterprise as a complicated, quasi-furtive affair. Protestant believers virtually backed their way into worldly success, Max Weber explained, via their intense anxiety over their prospects for salvation. Because heaven only permitted 144,000 or so souls past the gate, and because God's soteriological designs were largely opaque to mortal humans, the surest way to keep robust Protestant spiritual anxiety from lapsing into debilitating dread was, well, to keep busy—to dedicate one's life to a worldly calling, burrow in to its demands, and keep strict routines of religious observance until one's number was called for judgment on high. Latter-day Americans can probably best equate the process to selection for the most competitive private universities—only without benefit of a legacy admission. Both procedures rely on near-hysterical levels of status anxiety; both require a great deal of unquestioning fealty to remote higher powers; and both, when followed devoutly to the letter, produce a kind of manically overachieving character type.

But the inward spiritual tensions producing what Weber famously called the "worldly asceticism" of Puritan-trained capitalists have largely lapsed in the contemporary religious scene. Why agonize over one's fitness for divine reward in the afterlife, after all, if the evidence of God's blessings is so abundant in consumer culture? Why erect such elaborate schemes of spiritual introspection when the path to heaven is so plain, straight, and short? God wants us to be rich, it turns out, and has obligingly recast most features of the millennia-old Christian faith to double as a sort of middle-management motivational seminar. Today's Protestant mainstream, in other words, has largely discarded *The Pilgrim's Progress* in favor of *Rich Dad, Poor Dad*.

Hence the enormous appeal of the Prosperity Gospel—the movement identified most prominently with the aptly named Creflo Dollar, a Georgia-based minister affiliated with the Word of Faith strain of Pentecostalism. His ministry's well appointed Web page offers a full complement of just-in-time abundance preaching, from podcasts that cultivate "Thinking for Success" to a spiritual "word on the go" text message delivered directly to registrants' cell phones. It also includes manuals of success-minded piety, such as "Overcoming the Fear of Lack," which exhorts readers to "experience overflow," because "God desires you to live free from lack" and, more than that, "to overcome the fear of running out, and develop faith in running over." (Dollar's wife Taffi also hawks similar tracts to a female demographic, featuring titles such as "Your Spiritual Makeover.")

Such casual excess is barely conspicuous any longer in today's spiritual marketplace, which throngs with kindred appeals from megachurch leaders like Joel Osteen, another preacher in the Word of Faith tradition, whose Houston-based Lakewood megachurch is the nation's largest congregation, claiming more than 47,000 worshipers. Osteen's message is nearly identical to Dollar's: "God doesn't want us to drag through life like miserable failures," he writes in his bestselling work of spiritual self-help, *Become a Better You*. On the contrary—God "wants you to succeed; He created you to live abundantly."[1] And so Osteen studs his advice book with testimony aimed at securing worldly success. "Develop a habit of smiling on purpose," he counsels.[2] Oh, and "you need to put your shoulders back, hold your head up high, and communicate strength, determination and confidence. . . . We know we're representing Almighty God. Let's learn to walk tall."[3]

Other devotees of the Prosperity Gospel contend that Jesus himself was well-to-do—citing scriptural references to a treasurer in the midst of the first apostles, his apparent ownership of a mule, and the New Testament account of Roman soldiers gambling for his clothes during his crucifixion. "I don't know anybody—even Pamela Anderson—that would have people gambling for his underwear," C. Thomas Anderson, pastor of a Prosperity Gospel megachurch in Mesa, Arizona, told CNN reporter John Blake. "That was some fine stuff he wore." Anderson added that the popular success of Jesus' ministry was further proof of his pecuniary distinction. "The poor will follow the rich, the rich will follow the rich, but the rich will never follow the poor."[4]

Empirical challenges abound to this line of spiritual argument—there's the inconvenient pronouncement in the synoptic gospels that a rich man is less likely to enter the Kingdom of Heaven than a camel is to pass through the eye of a needle. There's also the birth in the manger, Jesus' evidently homeless status, and the cruel process of crucifixion, a mode of punishment typically meted out to slaves and criminal outcasts. If Jesus was well born, how is it that he was flanked by petty thieves at the moment of his death?

But historical accuracy has never been the point of Prosperity preaching. Indeed, it stands firmly in the lineage of modern Protestantism's merger with the therapeutic mindset—an alliance dating to the early twentieth-century vogue of the Mind Cure and New Thought movements. Less scriptural-minded gospels of wealth such as the New Age grab-bag faith identified with the Oprah-endorsed bestseller *The Secret* likewise bespeak an evidence-averse will to equate subjective betterment of the self with overwhelming material gain.

Today's Protestant dalliance with the money culture is striking, however, for the simple reason that there is no competing reformist trend in mainline American Protestant worship. The Mind Cure faithful, after all, emerged at the same time that the Social Gospel took root in many Protestant denominations, preaching a faith that addressed the new social ills of urban industrial civilization, from labor unrest to urban decline. The Dale Carnegie–branded success gospel of the 1940s and 50s emerged alongside the austerely neo-orthodox faith of Reinhold Niebuhr—and the upsurge of activism within the black church of the South that later produced the civil rights revolution. Indeed, the Word of Faith ministries of Dollar and Osteen are rooted in the rural Pentecostal tradition that first spread among the poor, and overwhelmingly African-American, stretches of the American South and West during the early twentieth century.

Now, however, to be a good Protestant capitalist no longer entails any fretful self-inspection to assure you're meeting divine dictates of right conduct or right livelihood—and hence the reformist energies that propelled the abolitionist, temperance, suffragist, and Social Gospel movements throughout our religious history have largely gone AWOL. The calling card of Protestant piety is no longer activist, but accommodationist: tailoring the believing soul to the pattern of preordained individual success rather than reviving a believing community with the collective will to remedy injustice.

This social quietism converges with the other, far more overtly fatalist strain in popular Protestant belief: the literalist interpretation of biblical prophecy, as evinced in the blockbuster *Left Behind* series of post-rapture sci-fi novels. Where Creflo Dollar and Joel Osteen preach a Christian ethic that largely begins and ends with accruing wealth, *Left Behind* authors Tim LaHaye and Jerry B. Jenkins interpret current events so tightly in the grip of foretold prophecy that the individual members of their Antichrist-defying "Tribulation Force" face a distressing behavioral double-bind: Why mount a military campaign to hasten Armageddon when the drift of world events is so closely matching the inerrant message of prophecy—right down to an unlikely military assault on Israel from . . . Ethiopia? With everything so punctiliously choreographed from Revelation or the Book of Daniel, why not just lie back, as it were, and think of Zion?

There's no clear answer to this quandary in the plodding eleven-volume chronicle—for the same reason that Prosperity Gospelers can offer no clear rationale for charity and social reform other than the notion that such efforts will vaguely advance one's own chosen course of self-improvement and perhaps furnish a tax write-off or two along the way. The wealth-addled state of American Protestantism calls to mind a snatch of scripture in Revelation 3:17 that you're none too likely to hear preached from Joel Osteen's Lakewood pulpit or in the prophecy roll call of *Left Behind*: "Thou sayest, I am rich and increased with goods, and have need of nothing: and knowest not that thou art wretched, and miserable, and poor, and blind, and naked."

Rich People Thing No. 11

WIRED MAGAZINE

Oh, the digital revolution! What primordial social power doesn't it possess? We've heard about the myriad ways it remakes work into play; how it empowers vast news publics and online audiences to interject themselves into the shopworn one-to-many models of communication; how it's demolishing fusty old hierarchies of the workplace and the political order alike; how the rafts of user-generated content it's kicked up have upended old models of commerce, journalism, and social networking.

And the most reliable outlet for all this feverish hymning of the info-Valhalla has of course been *Wired* magazine. The San Francisco-based digital culture monthly, founded in 1993, was the brainchild of libertarian tech mogul Louis Rossetto, who cannily merged the faun-eyed Berkeley wonderment of Stewart Brand's *Whole Earth Catalogue* with the self-infatuation of Silicon Valley's new venture capitalist class—coming into its own, conveniently enough, via a medium devoted almost exclusively to self-celebration. In the magazine's founding manifesto, Rossetto announced that *Wired* presaged "a revolution without violence that embraces a new, nonpolitical way to improve the future based on economics beyond macro control, consensus beyond the ballot box, civics beyond government and communities beyond the confines of time and geography."[1] In other words, Wired's Heavenly Kingdom would be a minimalist state right out of the

F. A. Hayek playbook. For all its shiny graphical interfacess and end-of-history brio, the de facto mantra of the *Wired* cultural revolution was "Let a Thousand IPOs Bloom."

But as the Internet age wore on, the old hierarchies, governments, and business cycles stubbornly refused to crumble—and indeed, embarrassingly demolished many an online capitalist's utopian reveries. Undeterred, the magazine turned inward for its utopian proof texts, a bit like an overleveraged Amway distributor with an entire inventory's worth of stock on unsubscribed back order. The principal product of both the digital revolution and *Wired* itself, it seemed, was the trippy prophesying of the Rossetto set. So on rushed one *Wired*-affiliated manifesto after another: *The Long Boom*, published in 1997, argued that all known laws of gravity in the financial markets had been abolished, productivity would spiral up toward infinity, and no economic setback of any note would ever, ever happen again. *The Cluetrain Manifesto* came along a few years later, sporting a set of ninety-five theses about doing business in the model information society (short answer: with lots of free-trade pieties and almost no input from the regulatory state).

Wired's post-meltdown editor Chris Anderson has inherited the unenviable task of manning the manifesto bellows amid conditions of near-market ruin, but he's kept heroically at it, first with *The Long Tail*, which purports to chronicle—wait for it—how the explosion of seemingly infinite, user-customized "shelf space" in the Web's cultural distribution system has created a "wildly diverse new culture and a threat to the institutions of the existing one."[2] He then stoutly pursued this line of argument to its daft logical terminus in *Free*, which argues that the re-mediation of cultural production via creative hacking, copying, and the like is driving the price of a fast-expanding cohort of consumer goods to a point "approaching zero."[3] And this was a good thing, because, um, it's what markets want?

Anderson spelled out what he took to be the main thrust of the *Free* gospel for the *Wall Street Journal*: "It's a consumer's paradise: The

Web has become the biggest store in history, and everything is 100 percent off."[4]

This vision says nothing about the producers of content, who in Anderson's frictionless vision of labor economics cheerfully refine and tinker with software innovations, media delivery systems, and what have you without any pecuniary motive at all. Nor is it the case that most putatively free offerings in the grand online bazaar can or will remain without a price at some point along the very long train of transactions represented in your average browser click. Television, after all, originated as a delivery system of free content, but no one pondering the low-cost, ad-infested output of cable news or the reality-programming boom can seriously maintain that it's somehow overthrown the profit system. Indeed, most Americans now fork over monthly fees for the privilege of absorbing greater swathes of TV content already lavishly subsidized by ad revenues. There's no basis to believe that the Web, whatever its other geeky permutations, won't evolve precisely along the same lines in a social order as market addled as our own, however revolutionary free-content sites such as Hulu or FreeArcade.com might seem to a middle-school kid—or to a *Wired* editor.

Most criticism of the *Free* thesis held that Anderson stubbornly overlooked the awkward question of just how viable the free digital regime would prove without enormous subsidies of venture capital: Google purchased YouTube for $1.65 billion in 2006, clearly hoping the site's viral popularity would soon generate a profit—and if anything, the site has only grown more profit averse. But focusing on unproven business models misses the larger, elegant sleight of hand that Anderson has achieved: In proclaiming no end of pending, future-improving revolutions, while hewing to free-market libertarian dogma, Anderson and his fellow *Wired* prophets have actually landed back in a feudal model of enterprise, whereby managerial rentiers—people like Anderson himself—extract fees far upstream in the revenue cycle from where the actual creators of value work.

Any classical economist will quickly confirm that everything that appears free at the point of a given transaction actually carries plenty of concealed costs—a point that Anderson made inadvertently when the *Virginia Quarterly Review* discovered that he had clumsily plagiarized long stretches of his own book from entries on Wikipedia.[5] Follow-up inquiries showed that Anderson had a troubling pattern of presenting long snatches of other people's writing and reporting without any adequate paraphrasing or citation.[6] Anderson characterized the missing citations as "screw-ups" that arose chiefly out of the decision he had reached with his editors at Hyperion Books "not to run notes as planned, due to my inability to find a good citation format for Web sources"—an explanation that strains credulity at many levels, not least of which being that Wikipedia has a Creative Commons-BYSA license that expressly stipulates that quotations from the site be properly cited and its copyright safeguards protected.[7] Terms of Anderson's advance with Hyperion were not disclosed, but *Free* became a bestseller with a $26.99 list price—and Anderson, in addition to his generously compensated perch as a Silicon Valley mouthpiece, also rakes in generous lecture fees courtesy of a business managerial concern called the Lehigh Bureau.[8] In other words, far from demonstrating the ways that technology remorselessly drives down the exchange value of information in the marketplace, Anderson has been gaming that value upward in his own favor, taking the uncompensated and unacknowledged work of others and pawning it off as his own.

During more forthright eras of intellectual discourse, the polite term for this M.O. would be "hucksterism" or—not to put too fine a point on it—"theft." Most college kids caught in the same act would certainly get swiftly disciplined or expelled—and, one presumes, any contract writer in Anderson's employ would be just as quickly purged from the roster of *Wired* contributors had his copy been published with dozens of unattributed liftings from the work of others.

Nevertheless, Anderson's crassly opportunistic preachments on Internet commerce are held forth not merely as a business model, but as a dazzling brand of consumer empowerment. One can easily picture Cardinal Richelieu making much the same case to French peasants as they handed another harvest over to Louis XIV to help the Sun King execute some renegade Huguenots, or mount a fresh invasion of Strasbourg or the Walloon hinterland. "It's going to be a glorious revolution," the cardinal might proclaim. "You can bask in the King's reflected majesty entirely free of charge—and you'll be regarded as the best-appointed, most cutting-edge fieldworkers on the continent." And finally, scooping the family's last few sous into his cap, he'd announce, "That's for my speaker's fee."

Rich People Things No. 12

THE CREATIVE CLASS

In our tireless national quest to deny the existence of social class where it most naturally belongs—in the nexus of wealth concentration, housing segmentation, income inequality, and financial policy that dictates vocational fates and life outcomes—American social commentators have developed an overcompensating tic. They have divined exotic new brands of class stratification that have almost nothing to do with material living conditions, and endowed them with strange and wonderful new powers to reshape the urban social contract, drive tax and investment policies, and even reconfigure the coordinates of the Western self. In an arresting act of socioeconomic alchemy, these thinkers have conjured forth an elastic golem, using the cabalistic incantations of the new information economy, and dubbed it the Creative Class.

Of course, like any superhero saga, the story of the Creative Class has unfolded in fits and starts, with tests of adversity and identity crises preceding the final moment of existential vindication. Beginning with the first flush of globalization, Robert Reich espied a privileged new cohort that he called "symbolic analysts"—people whose principal work involved processing knowledge and value in the information and paper economies. Only Reich, who would soon become the most prominent—and hence redoubtably miserable—advocate of economic fairness in the Clinton White House, made the fundamental error that no self-respecting symbolic analyst would commit: He worried that these new lords of global enterprise would shun public life and social obligations. In Reich's account, the nascent knowledge elite would indifferently consign the urban wage workers suddenly thrown into international competition with cheap, nonunion labor markets in emerging economies to their sad plight while they disported themselves to gated suburbs with private security forces, immigrant landscapers, and for-profit trash collectors. Reich dubbed this trend the "secession of the successful," and back in the early 1990s, it seemed a tad alarmist. Sure, gated communities were creepy, but how could a rent-a-cop or two add up to a full-scale retreat from the American polis?

Of course, this was before our social commentators discovered the wonder-working powers of the new information elite. It turns out, you see, that the symbolic analysts hovering benignly above the receding industrial-age economy could conjure forth all sorts of revolutionary new shifts in the social order. *Washington Post* reporter Joel Garreau espied these bold new changes in exurban "edge cities" and praised the tireless entrepreneurial pluck of these new knowledge workers—ignoring the enormous subsidies of federal money that financed the centripetal march of suburban office parks. (Now that the once-booming edge-city outposts are in steep economic decline, the outward thrust of enterprise away from urban centers looks a lot less world-shaking, as regional developers are at a loss for what to do with the vacant office complexes and big-box retail husks that stud the borders of their fast-eroding new urbanist town centers.) Paul H. Ray and Sherry Anderson, writing a few years after Reich and Garreau, stalked the emergence of another bold socioeconomic formation, the "Cultural Creatives"—people who manage the key nodal points in the postindustrial economy, but share a deep inner affinity for environmentalism, exotic cultural experiences, and the most accommodating mainlines to spiritual truth on offer. "They demand authenticity," Ray and Anderson wrote admiringly of their new demographic cohort, who they claimed numbered fifty million, or one-fourth of the adult population of America "at home, in the stores, at work, and in politics," as though the quest for "authenticity" weren't already the biggest racket going in the planned obsolescence of American consumer culture.[1]

But the great synthesis still awaited. It fell to economist Richard Florida, then a professor at Carnegie Mellon University, to piece together the new class dispensation. In his breakthrough 2002 book, *The Rise of the Creative Class*, Florida seized upon the bohemian enclaves sprouting up in the deindustrializing urban center of Pittsburgh to divine nothing less than a new model of economic production—and along with it radically new patterns of work, leisure, social geography, and cultural expression. It was a new millennium, and it marked the dawning of the Creative Class—a force so undeniably world-transforming that, in Florida's usage, it must always Be Capitalized.

But what made this new economic vanguard tick? As Florida imagined things, the Creative Class was basically a roided-up version of Reich's symbolic analysts—brain workers who seemed to embody the reengineered spirit of new capitalism in their smallest lifestyle choices, from their hunger for "participatory" sports to the kinds of "street scenes" they idly habituate. Indeed, the members of the Creative Class all but ingested the very essence of post-material lifestyle innovation, much in the manner of Alice and her magic pill. "Marx had it partly right when he foresaw that workers would one day control the means of production," our social prophet confidently pronounced. "This is now beginning to happen, although not as Marx thought it would, with the proletariat rising to take over factories. Rather, more workers than ever control the means of production, because it is inside their heads; they are the means of production."[2]

But just because the Creative Class had solved the problem of alienated labor and production by virtue of its mere existence, that didn't mean that it possessed anything like real economic self-determination. Indeed, the rampant casualization of work in the information economy institutes what Florida takes to be a permanent shift in economic relations—away from any expectation that jobs can be held in one place for any extended period of time with any substantial benefits or pension plans. Of course, social critics of a fusty materialist persuasion might well point out that the class of workers whom Florida baptized into a great, all-purpose self-actualizing vanguard was starting to look a lot more like Marx's industrial reserve army—a corps of surplus service workers helping to make employment seem unduly scarce and wages artificially low. But such gnat-straining objections miss the bigger picture, as Florida patiently laid it out. "The new reality of chronic job changing has become internalized in the psyche of work," Florida explained. "People have come to accept that they're on their own—that the traditional sources of security and entitlement no longer exist, or even matter."[3] Why, just look back at the popular furor that greeted the waves of corporate downsizings in the 1980s and 1990s; today, when a company sends thousands of workers packing, consigning their quaint notions of employer loyalty, long-term health insurance and the like to the dustbin, and the reaction is "not much," as Florida sizes things up: "No picket signs, no demonstrations, not a peep from the politicians. . . . We simply accept it as the way it is and go about our busy lives. We acknowledge that there is no corporation or institution that will take care of us—that we are truly on our own."[4]

Margaret Thatcher made much the same point when she famously snapped, "There's no such thing as society." But that statement was greeted in the more class-bound British political scene with outrage and disbelief—and became, quite properly, identified with a predatory and reactionary system of market idolatry. In the brave new frontiers of Richard Florida's new political economy, the unencumbered, disenfranchised knowledge worker is a floating signifier. Here members of the Creative Class may pursue an exotic hobby, and there they may track down a funky urban subculture. (Florida even dotes at uncomfortable length on the scene of a number of high-tech CEOs and venture capitalists performing an informal rock jam session at the Austin, Texas, 360 Summit for the new millennium's info barons, as if this were by itself a profound statement on the fluid social identities of the Creative Set as opposed to another sad appendix to the death throes of a popular music form vaguely associated with a tradition of dissent and protest.) But here's the thing: These tireless seekers of what Florida calls the "experiential life" never much trouble themselves with the particulars of how economic power—let alone actual wealth and income—gets distributed.

This rather colossal blind spot crops up again and again in the most celebrated findings of Florida's book—surveys of forty-nine leading metropolitan areas that correlate the location of regional booms in high-tech enterprise to lifestyle measures such as "The Gay Index" (reflecting a high percentage of same-sex households reported in census findings) and "The Bohemian Index" (a less statistically exact correlation of tech firms to regions that boast significant indie-rock scenes). While these sorts of correlations can indeed be charted, they chiefly point up the rather banal trend of younger workers thronging disproportionately to tech employers in big cities and bringing more tolerant social outlooks—and indie-scene-sustaining disposable incomes—along with them. More curious, however, are the all-but-audibly-awkward moments in Florida's presentation when he's forced to concede that however much his beloved Creative Class may double as refined connoisseurs of cultural diversity and alternative lifestyles, they tend not to actually live and work among the less fortunate, and less white and Anglo, people who populate their favored "street scenes." "My own research shows a negative statistical correlation between concentrations of high-tech firms in a region and nonwhites as a percentage of the population," Florida concedes.[5]

On closer inspection, similar anomalies stud Florida's findings. Las Vegas, for instance, seems to be a big outlier in the Gay Index's correlation with New Economy growth. Because the local economy is closely allied with open sexual expression, gay equality is happily a nonissue in matters such as domestic partner benefits in Vegas. But the city is also home to a sprawling, and notoriously union-hostile, service economy. So while the city places fifth in the roster of gay tolerance, it is a woeful forty-second on the High Tech index. Perhaps cultural attitudes don't have the alchemical wonder-working powers that Florida imagines when the highly mobile, benefits-optional workforce tends to be poor.

Similarly, Florida is abashed to find that, for all the Creative Class's enthusiasm for global cultural diversity, the High Tech Index correlates poorly with metropolitan areas encompassing large immigrant populations. That's because immigrant workers, too, are overwhelmingly overrepresented in low-wage service jobs—and represent a still steeper challenge for union-organizing drives, since many of these people are also undocumented. It's true that there are stronger correlations in some regions with populations large enough to incubate workers in both the immigrant and creative sectors—e.g., Chicago, Los Angeles, and the Bay Area. But here again, the outliers tell a suggestive story: Providence, Rhode Island, places sixth on Florida's Immigration Index, but forty-forth on the High Tech one—suggesting, again, that lower living standards in communities with smaller absorptive capacities severely derail the Creative Class's natural evolution into a cultural utopia.

Indeed, the key cultural traits Florida assigns to the Creative Class could well have been cribbed from any employee orientation brochure in any Fortune 500 company: individuality, openness, diversity, and (of course) meritocracy. Far from possessing the power to revolutionize economic relations, and thereby banishing alienated labor from the historical stage, these qualities form the basis of the twenty-first century's corporate managerial mindset. This is not to deny the genuine virtues of diversity and openness, when they can meaningfully be used as remedies to practices of cultural, ethnic, or racial segregation. At the same time, anyone who thinks corporate America is overrun with these retrograde practices hasn't been paying very close attention to contemporary business culture—diversity consulting is a multibillion dollar industry, and "openness" as it pertains to sexual preference and gender identity likewise is closely monitored and officially celebrated (however awkwardly or ham-handedly) in one employee seminar after another. Nor is the reason for this mood of enlightenment especially difficult to fathom—in addition to reflecting genuine, hard-won legal victories in the battle for fair and equal recognition among oppressed populations, a more diverse and culturally tolerant world is also a far more market-friendly world. It's also, far from incidentally, a world in which wealth and income diversity never seem to achieve the same vaunted status as cultural and gender diversity.

In this regard, Florida's own impressionistic research is mightily suggestive. For as his dutiful reader plods on through his litany of the marvelously "experiential" makeup of the Creative Class, it becomes increasingly plain that the furious pace at which the Creative workforce adopts and reinvents provisional cultural affiliations requires boatloads of cash. "People in my interviews identify themselves to a tangle of connections to creative activities," Florida cheerfully reports. "One person may be simultaneously a writer, a researcher, consultant, cyclist, rock climber, electronic/world music/acid jazz lover, amateur gourmet cook, wine enthusiast or microbrewer."[6]

In addition to being the sort of person one dreads being trapped in conversation with at a party, this ideal-type Creative Class member would have to possess a prodigious amount of disposable income just to keep tending his extreme-hobby portfolio. Any one of these pursuits entails a significant commitment of resources and time up front—indeed, it's hard to interpret this array of sidelines as creative activities so much as consuming ones. One could make a case, I suppose, for "writer" being an exception here, but one can only assume if this Creative Soul is a writer in the afternoon and a rock climber at night (if we might again paraphrase Marx, and *The German Ideology*'s famed characterization of the life of the worker under Communism), then a good deal of pricey computer equipment is involved. Or else—dare I say it?—this edgy new millennial Fauntleroy might just be something of a dilettante.

The Creative Class, like so many other features of the pixel-and-paper New Economy, hasn't aged all that well. By 2010, Florida was publishing an old-wine-in-new-bottles sequel to his masterwork of social prophecy called *The Great Reset: How New Ways of Living and Working Drive Post-Crash Prosperity.* The prescriptions he lays out there are not so grand, sweeping, or world-transforming. For example, consider the book's calls for more flexible housing markets and improved systems of mass transit—the same sort of unobjectionable social-democratic aims that other chastened exponents of the nineties boom in high post-material theory have advanced. A funny thing, though: There's never any sense in any of this revisionist work that the zeitgeist-on-horseback heroes of these hectic forecasts of a brave new post-everything economy might have actually borne a good deal of the responsibility for the epic collapse of the old status quo. Then again, the best alibis usually are the most creative ones.

Rich People Thing No. 13

MALCOLM GLADWELL

It's critical, in any carefully ordered worldview, to have the unequal distribution of life outcomes be more than the fatalistic byproduct of capitalist enterprise. The touchy question of how an upward-ascending model individual secures and preserves the main chance must be nothing less than a defining trait of the natural order—a property, indeed, of the human mind itself.

This is where Malcolm Gladwell comes in. Gladwell is the best-selling author of fizzy zeitgeist titles of pop sociology such as *The Tipping Point, Blink, Outliers,* and *What the Dog Saw.* These books all, in various registers, serve as motivational slogans to the nation's ever-anxious managerial class, otherwise prone to deeply uncertain efforts to divine the market's true will and rampant second-guessing at the slightest setback. His breakout 1998 book, *The Tipping Point,* professed to deliver fresh counterintuitive insights into the logic of crowd behavior, but came bearing a galvanizing, not-so-tacit message for its business readership: "Your decisions and pop culture affinities could produce major marketing trends!"

In *Blink,* Gladwell refined this feel-good brief a bit further. The thrust of his popularized account of the mechanics of mental judgment told the same advice-happy lords of the marketing world that introspection and analysis are the oversold entertainments of the market's also-rans. "Trust your first impressions!" the big-haired business prophet preached. "If you dwell on a subject for more than thirty seconds or so, you're probably missing the point!"

The just-in-time paradigms of Gladwellian wisdom have marched on. The counterintuitive thrust of *Outliers* was that prime opportunities often lurk at the margins of the mainstream, and that conventional measures of achievement like academic performance are often worthless. Translation: "Use your snap judgments and market instincts to burrow out profitable dark-horse stratagems!" *What the Dog Saw*, meanwhile, offers a scattered, impressionistic array of portraits of entrepreneurial characters and movements to ply the oldest moral in the business self-help genre: "These geniuses and market fables provide valuable life lessons and role models: Heed them and succeed!"

There's just one problem with the Gladwell genre: It is, for the most part, empirically bankrupt. This is not merely my dyspeptic judgment, mind you. In a thoroughgoing breakdown of the typical Gladwell argument, neuropsychologist Steven Pinker noted that it commences with hyperbolic claims masquerading as truisms: that "we"—the legatees of conventional wisdom—believe that the elimination of risk makes us all safer, that jailing corporate executives serves as a deterrent to official corruption, and that genius is a property of individual self-will. Gladwell then knocks down the claims with some puckish insight gleaned from an investigator taking a skeptical, sideways view of the topic at hand and proceeds to alight, as Pinker put it, on "generalizations that are banal, obtuse, or flat wrong."[1] So when, for instance, Gladwell argues in *Outliers* that college football performance, teaching scores, and IQ tests are imperfect predictors of future success for footballers, pedagogues, and accomplished test-takers, he misjudges the point of such measures, which is not to forecast ultimate life outcomes, but to minimize risks for employers. Investors in fledgling professionals are playing the odds, just as their counterparts in financial markets are—and both groups have devised shortcuts that help them game the system. And thus, Pinker notes, "It is simply not true that a quarterback's rank in the [NFL] draft is un-correlated to his success in the pros, that cognitive skills don't pre-dict a teacher's effectiveness, that intelligence skills are poorly related to performance or (the major claim in *Outliers*) that above a mini-mum IQ of 120, higher intelligence does not bring greater intellec-tual achievements."[2]

Pinker doesn't extend his analysis farther back in Gladwell's oeu-vre, but much the same critique can be trained on *The Tipping Point*, which pivoted largely on the "Broken Windows" theory of commu-nity policing, a system that diverts greater resources to "quality of life" initiatives, such as basic neighborhood sanitation and upkeep, in the conviction that criminal behavior flourishes in the malign neglect of urban blight. On inspection, the Broken Windows thesis turns out to be something of a social-scientific bubble unto itself. Its main ur-ban showcase, New York when Rudy Giuliani was mayor and William Bratton served as chief of police, was actually experiencing across-the-board declines in crime before Bratton instituted a community-policing regime. Other cities adopting the system reported mixed or inconclusive results in crime reduction, at best. What's more, other social indicators associated with increased crime—such as teen preg-nancy, high-school drop-out rates, and child poverty—were on the downswing during the nineties heyday of Bratton and Giuliani.[3]

Similarly, many of the instantaneous social seers featured in *Blink* have not performed as advertised in the book's pages. Sociologist John Gottman's Seattle-based "Love Lab," which Gladwell features in the book's opening pages as a model of "thin-slicing" snap judgment, does not in fact predict the relative successes of marriages probed in Gottman's computer models. Rather, those models work backward, es-sentially instructing Gottman's software to devise formulas explaining why a given couple's alliance succeeded or failed over a six-year span. As writer Laurie Abraham has noted, this can be a useful analytic en-terprise in its own right, but it scarcely can be adopted as a classic case study of the power "we" all possess when we indulge our predictive first impressions, as Gladwell has argued. And because Gottman employed a small data sample—just fifty-seven couples—his findings don't lend themselves to falsification in broader control groups. "In statistics, you can't judge the predictive oomph of anything without knowing the population prevalence of the event or condition you're studying," Abraham writes. Allowing for false positives and negatives—the standard statistical test for verifying research results—in the sample used in Gottman's celebrated 1998 study would actually bring down his model's purported 80 percent "accuracy rate" (itself an unscientific designation). Gauged against the actual incidence of divorce in his sample of couples married three to six years, his successful prediction rate plummets to 43 percent, more or less equivalent to the success one would have in forecasting a marriage's future by flipping a coin.[4]

But what's more striking than the persistent pattern of error in Gladwell's work is the question of how this particular brand of sociological fable-making has won such an enormous following. Regardless of whether Gladwell is describing the way we actually behave and absorb new ideas and social trends, he is clearly offering a very appealing picture of how his readership wishes the world works. The chief hero in his work is the intuitive manager—a new millennial upgrade of the plucky upward-striving protagonists in the Gilded Age fiction of Horatio Alger. But where Alger stressed the character-building individualist virtues of thrift, hard work, and self-sacrifice—themselves already endangered traits in the new industrial order of the robber baron age—Gladwell is preaching an entirely consumption-driven model of the gospel of success. The idea in his market fables is not to light out for new economic territory with grit and invention; it is, rather, to establish a mystical bond with market forces and to surmise how the market most wants you to behave.

Hence a typical Gladwell profile subject like Rick Warren—the megachurch preacher whose *The Purpose-Driven Life* is now the bestselling nonfiction book in American history—is, in lieu of being a deeply conflicted figure packaging spiritual wisdom for a mass audience, simply "one of those people whose lives have an irresistible forward momentum" and his life story a case study in how a strong character obtains a sentimental education in market fealty.[5]

Significantly, Gladwell deliberately downplays the actual content of Warren's preaching in order to stress the man's prodigious marketing savvy. Doting on the "cell" structure of the Bible study groups of Warren's 20,000-member Saddleback Church in Orange County, California, and the online seminars Warren has produced schooling fellow pastors in church-growth strategies, Gladwell marvels at how Warren has purged the evangelical tradition of its dour talk of sin and translated the saving message of Christian faith into the sturdy creeds of the market. "In the argot of the New Economy, most evangelists follow a business-to-consumer model: b-to-c," Gladwell writes. "Warren follows a business-to-business model: b-to-b. He reaches the people who reach people. He's a builder of religious networks."[6] (Full disclosure: Gladwell quotes, and dismisses, my own review of *The Purpose-Driven Life* in making the case for the efficacy of Warren's post-theological message. Why fret about the mysteries of God's sovereign judgment or traditional theological riddles like evil and theodicy when, as Gladwell rather impatiently puts it, "Warren's great talent is as an organizer. He's not a theological innovator"?)

These networks, clearly, are the wonder-working miracles in Gladwell's version of the Book of Warren. "*The Purpose-Driven Life* is meant to be read in groups," Gladwell explains. "If the vision of faith sometimes seems skimpy, that's because the book is supposed to be supplemented by a layer of discussion and reflection and debate. It is a testament to Warren's intuitive understanding of how small groups work that this is precisely how *The Purpose-Driven Life* has been used. It spread along the network that he has spent his career putting together, not from person to person but from group to group."[7]

Like the vision of social change in *The Tipping Point*, the market forces fueling the Warren phenomenon are presented as an organic freestanding force of nature—and their success inevitably reflects a law of association that is only fully legible to the market-trained eye of a prophet like Gladwell. So even when Warren's book played a dramatic role in a Georgia hostage crisis—single mother Ashley Smith read aloud from the book to persuade her captor, a fugitive named Brian Nichols who had already killed four people, to release her and surrender to the police—Gladwell insists that the truly remarkable feature of the episode "is that it wasn't improbable at all.":

> [I]s it surprising that Ashley Smith would feel compelled to read aloud from the book to her captor, and that, in the discussion that followed, Nichols would come to some larger perspective on his situation? She and Nichols were in a small group, and reading aloud from *The Purpose-Driven Life* is what small groups do.[8]

But of course, to dwell on Warren's innovative, networked delivery system for evangelism is to discount the thing that matters most to him and his millions of followers: the vision of Christian faith that propels all this rapid churchly growth. In Warren's case, that vision is accepting of superficial social tolerance—he preaches in Hawaiian shirts, Saddleback provides day-care and Christian-themed AA services for congregants, and Warren typically delivers homilies to the strains of Christian rock. But this laid-back presentation accompanies a harsher message of scriptural literalism—as observers learned when Warren helped bankroll Proposition 8, California's anti–gay marriage ballot initiative, and refused to use his influence to denounce a barbaric law enacting capital punishment for the practice of gay sex in Uganda, one of the Third World nations Warren has adopted under his "purpose-driven country" initiative.[9]

A networked approach to Christian faith seems a lot less impressive, in other words, when that faith is steeped in unreflective and inhumane bigotry. Yet such discomfiting notions have no place in the beguiling smooth surfaces of the Gladwellian social world—for they hint at the still-more-disturbing idea that markets can produce invidious distinctions and unfair outcomes of their own, that fifty million middle managers could in fact be wrong, no matter how intuitive and swashbuckling their snap judgments might seem in the moment of their execution. The term "tipping point" was, after all, coined to describe just one such phenomenon of viral moral miscalculation—the juncture at which urban ethnic neighborhoods succumbed to white flight under the pressures of racial desegregation. For Gladwell to retrofit this idea to describe the benign ebb and flow of social fads seems a sadly instructive market fable all its own.

Rich People Thing No. 14

REALITY TELEVISION

The eternal, baffling conceit of all television is that it's showing you something real, when, more often than not, it's telling you how to think. This is especially the case now that producers have deranged the very notion of reality into a genre convention all its own. Viewers of the reality genre are expected to double down on the myth of televisual exposure, since reality TV purports to dig deeper into the human drama than mere entertainment fare does.

By staging competitions for scarce resources, as in the breakout network franchise *Survivor*, we're testing the core postulates about human behavior in the state of nature. By pitting aspiring singers against each other in *American Idol*—and putting them to a public vote—we're plumbing the wellsprings of the longing for success and recognition, while also (for good measure) shoring up the hoary talent-will-out shibboleths of the national gospel of success. By marching contestants through the Trump boardroom in *The Apprentice*, we're sizing up the proper quotients of ruthlessness, ego inflation, and sycophancy that form the forever-unstable compound of corporate achievement.

But it's never the case that reality TV is "real" in any meaningful sense. This isn't just because producers insist that at least one camera crew is on the scene to record the raw drama of interpersonal confrontation, replete with off-camera lighting and audio set-ups. No, more fundamentally, the sagas of the upward-striving reality format are unreal because they envision perhaps our culture's purest form of class contempt. Lavishly appointed depictions of overclass leisure, such as those in Bravo TV's *Real Housewives* franchise and the gruesome (and now, thankfully, canceled) MTV rite-of-pelf-laden-passage saga *My Super Sweet Sixteen*, provide a study in disaccumulative wealth and entitlement every bit as stark and provoking as the taxpayer-funded executive bonuses at AIG and Goldman Sachs. The surpassingly odd thing about these shows, though, is that they do profess to be natural reflections of our unquestioned social hierarchies; their pecuniary displays are evaluated on the spectrum of taste, not on any moral calculus.

In this respect, and countless others, today's reality-TV infatuation affords a dramatic contrast with the first great wave of documentary realism in film and photography of the 1930s. Then, an economic cataclysm spurred genuine curiosity among the country's makers of culture to try to record its impact on the lives of ordinary Americans. Dorothea Lange and Walker Evans harnessed the art of photography—heretofore largely devoted to stylized portraits and nature studies—to document the travails of Appalachian farmers and Okie migrant workers fleeing the Dust Bowl. And those works, in turn, informed extended written studies of the same subjects, such as James Agee's *Let Us Now Praise Famous Men* and John Steinbeck's *The Grapes of Wrath*. Literary critic Edmund Wilson felt the cataclysm of the Depression had transformed American culture and society so fundamentally that he made it his mission not only to master the literature of Western socialism, but also to report on the plight of the American worker in a series of dispatches for the *New Republic*, later collected in his anthology *The American Jitters*. Even Hollywood movies adopted quasidocumentary styles of storytelling in works such as *I Was a Fugitive from a Chain Gang*. The form became so common that by 1941, Preston Sturges was able to parody it in *Sullivan's Travels*, which made the case for escapist comedy as an equally legitimate artistic response to the Great Depression.

Now, no one expects a revival of such straightforward social realism in our own irony-addled age. Indeed, any member of our literary elite diving headlong into our economic crisis with the urgent abandon that seized Wilson in the thirties would trigger a series of pained guffaws. (The one honorable exception in this regard, former cultural studies maven Andrew Ross, is indeed the exception proving the rule. He has become a de facto labor sociologist, and his university cachet and MLA name recognition have plummeted accordingly.)

But it is bracing to consider, by contrast, how today's less-fortunate Americans fare in the pseudodocumentary genre of reality television. A slew of down-market reality series—from the VH1 reality-show castoff Guignol titled *I Love Money* to the TLC chronicle of the child beauty pageant scene *Toddlers and Tiaras*—remind us of the grotesque consequences that ensue when the wrong sort of ambitions take root in our working classes. Week after week, these lost souls are shown craving a kind of celebrity that is simply beyond their station. And then, in a display that's far worse, their personal weaknesses are forensically exhibited so as to showcase all the tawdriest symptoms of class exclusion—substance abuse, promiscuity, career failure, the transformation of one's children into trophy-objects—under the Klieg lights.

These spectacles treat their cast members as twenty-first-century equivalents of sideshow geeks—the carnival performers who would bite the heads off chickens for a nominal fee, and a pitiful amount of public attention. The pitiable ambitions and individual failings of these down-market souls are treated with such morbid interest because they are the clearest rationales for quarantining them from the ur-American pursuit of the main chance. As the conventions of the reality genre have it, they are asking for the treatment they get—and their casual ostracism by an indifferent mass audience is precisely what they have coming to them.

Even franchises that purport to deliver a class-based comeuppance to the arrogant rich, such as *Undercover Boss*, wind up deferring to the undeviating hierarchies of the success gospel. At the close of each episode of that show, the corporate CEO who has labored incognito in the lowest ranks of his company indulges a sentimental display of noblesse oblige, such as a promotion or a paid vacation—and in one case, a $5,000 down payment on a mortgage for an employee at a Roto-Rooter call center. The *New York Times'* television critic denounced this end-of-episode executive flourish as "embarrassingly feudal."[1]

But that's not the half of it. Back here in working-class reality, the executives who seem chastened by the hard-knocks curriculum of *Undercover Boss* continue to preside over deeply unequal workplaces, where an individual sentimental gesture from the executive suite rarely occurs—and would count for precious little even if it did. At the same time Roto-Rooter's CEO was learning the elementary lessons of service-economy kindness, his firm was settling a $2 million class action suit brought by California plumbers for unpaid overtime and working without meal breaks. Another firm featured on the show, 1-800 Flowers, is in the midst of a sex-discrimination suit brought by a former in-house female attorney, which alleges that senior management routinely referred to women as "babes," joked about her prowess in fetching them coffee, and kept up a steady stream of offensive, sexually themed comments directed at her.[2]

These beleaguered workers don't need to see their bosses undergo a heavy-handed, manipulated-for-the-cameras sentimental education every Sunday night. They need unions to safeguard their rights in their workplace and secure them fair wages and humane working conditions. They need legislation to protect their ability to organize in the workplace after a generation's worth of Reaganite strikebreaking and legal obstruction that has helped drive unionization in the American workforce to a historic low of 7 percent. They need federal and state regulators to stanch the epidemic of "wage theft" that now redistributes an estimated 15 percent of their incomes upward into the coffers of management.

But there's no titillation to be had in pondering such grim economic developments. So on the pseudodocumentary machinery grinds—with the occasional lurid intrusion from the actual real world to remind viewers that this isn't all quite the harmless fun and games we're all encouraged to think it is. In 2009, for example, VH1's gruesome bottom-feeding defilement of human intimacy, *Megan Wants a Millionaire*, was abruptly canceled when one of its contestants, an investment banker named Ryan Jenkins, was accused of murdering his real-life girlfriend, a swimsuit model named Jasmine Fiore, who was found crammed into a suitcase discarded in a trash bin in Buena Vista, California.[3] Jenkins later committed suicide while on the lam from authorities in Canada. (The network also pulled the plug on the third season of *I Love Money*, in which Jenkins competed and purportedly emerged victorious prior to his stint on *Megan*—though that horrific show was trundled back out for Season 4. Reality producers are only prepared to cultivate the illusion of decency up to a point, after all.)[4]

It's striking just how little a stir an incident like this makes in the inert and jaded universe of reality television. With Jenkins dead, we'll never know how much the full-surveillance degradation of his character contributed to his morally squalid end. But it should give all participants in the reality-entertainment world long and painful pause to consider that, in purporting to tease out the "true" nature of a living person weaned on fables of easy money and unearned overnight celebrity, they might have disfigured that nature into something resembling a monster.

No such introspection is on offer, though, among the fearless purveyors of this allegedly vital and enormously popular genre. In a remarkable self-congratulatory 2007 essay in the *Atlantic*, VH1 executive vice-president Michael Hirschorn made the straight-faced argument that reality television is "the liveliest genre on the set right

now. It engages hot-button cultural issues—class, sex, race— that respectable television . . . rarely touches. And it has addressed a visceral
need for a different kind of television at a time when the Web has
made more traditionally produced video seem as stagy as Molière."
Hirschorn went on to argue that the flat conventions of the genre
made for greater emotional exposure and produced in the process
a sort of pluperfect documentary style: "Where documentaries must
construct their narratives from found matter, reality TV can place real
people in artificial surroundings designed for maximum emotional
impact." He also assures us, as any give-the-people-what-they-want
mass-culture burgher must, that "the resistance to reality TV usually
comes down to snobbery." (My, that *is* a bitingly original approach to
the hot-button issue of class.)[5]

It seems reasonable to surmise that Ryan Jenkins did in fact experience some sort of "maximum emotional impact" during his tour
through the searing class-, sex-, and race-baiting rounds of reality
filming for Hirschorn's network. But such questions aren't fit to raise
for very long in the otherwise insatiably inquisitorial sanctums of reality programming. Hirschorn left VH-1 in 2008 to form his own TV
production company, ish productions; both *I Love Money* and *Megan
Wants a Millionaire* were produced 18 months after his departure.
Megan, of the eponymous millionaire-seeking franchise, first came to
reality renown, however, on VH-1's *Rock of Love*, which Hirrschorn
oversaw as an executive with the network. (One of Hirschorn's first
projects, at his new production venture it pains me to say, is a contract with Bravo to produce *The Approval Matrix*, a show based on
a feature I was forced to prototype during my tenure at *New York*
magazine. I can only pray that he forgoes using the introductory text
that I slapped on the first layout of the thing in 2004, and which has
unaccountably remained there ever since. And while I'm issuing disclaimers, I should also note that my wife briefly worked for Hirschorn
at his mercifully short-lived online media tip sheet, Inside.com. He
tried to dissuade her from quitting with the promise that they'd soon

launch an IPO and she could quit rich if she stuck out the soul-deadening gig a few more months—a claim that proved wildly off-base in the foundering tech economy of 1999, but did continue pointing up Hirschorn's feel for the hot-button class issue.) By the time he bailed out of his VH1 suite, Hirschorn was reportedly pulling down more than $1 million a year.

The reality genre, meanwhile, rumbles on, with franchises such as MTV's *Jersey Shore* contriving fisticuffs, debauched drunken scenes and regular sexual intrigue among participants recruited to represent a whole scorned demographic: Eastern seaboard Italian-Americans of the dead-end lower middle class. But the cruelest trick that *Jersey Shore* producers play in choreographing this particular class reality is in pretending to give the show's cast jobs over the franchise's filming run: They cool their heels in makework retail gigs, tending beach souvenir shops and gelato stores. In scripting such futures, reality programmers lets the viewership know the real social vision behind this plu-perfect documentary form: Seven-figures for the culture lords who stage manage these displays of class contempt, and symbolic service-sector obeisance for the players. Sure, the *Jersey Shore* cast members realize short-term gains for leasing out their dignity to the tabloid-reality nexus. But then again, the whole point of being a geek is getting paid.

Rich People Thing No. 15

DAMIEN HIRST

The most common complaint about the sterile Hollywood block-buster is that it reduces crowds to simply watching money on the screen—the pricey CGI effects and heavy-vehicle explosions merging indiscriminately with the bloated contracts of the proven box-office celebrity brands certain to survive all the harrowing, gleaming mayhem. So if that's what watching money is like, how does one characterize the experience of a Damien Hirst installation? Here, too, the chief aesthetic is driven by an obsession with surface control, tightly regulating the appearance of carnage underneath. Here, too, the accumulation of outlandish effects strains to provoke a kind of shock or outrage in the viewer, but ends up inspiring only a jaded sort of half-titillation. And here, too, all the prefab sentiment wrapped up in the clanking machinery is lavishly marketed as its own studiously branded, carefully modulated megaproduction.

There's one signal difference, though: Unlike most Hollywood productions, Hirst's work is usually sterile in the literal sense of the term. His signature work is a dead shark preserved in formaldehyde, bearing the portentous title of *The Impossibility of Death in the Mind of Someone Living*. Early in the 1990s, he came to the attention of collector Charles Saatchi, co-head of the UK-based faux-edgy ad firm Saatchi and Saatchi. The Saatchi/Hirst collaboration came to full fruition in the 1992 Young British Artists exhibition mounted at the Saatchi gallery. After a later YBA show netted the prestigious Turner grants, the YBAs were featured in a series of TV 4 specials, since the network was also a principal sponsor of the Turner award. Soon enough, the great Hirst shark and other Hirst productions in the same vein were hailed as the iconic representation of a lost generation of culture makers, and the "YBAs" became the more sweeping "Britart" movement before anyone had time to assimilate the meaning of the first catchphrase.

The art world's strategic alliance with the advertising industry involved much more than Charles Saatchi's individual enthusiasm for ponderously alienating art. As Chin-tao Wu argues in her important 2002 study, *Privatising Culture*, the emergence of firms like Saatchi into the front rank of arts patronage happened after the Thatcher government's complete recalibration of the arts-funding formula. On the one hand, Thatcher had slashed most public arts money from the UK's federal budget; on the other hand, the tax-cutting regime of the 1980s and early 1990s also relaxed capital-gains assizes to the point that arts investment became much more of an exercise in corporate branding and market share than the traditions of noblesse oblige or aristocratic whim that had heretofore propelled most rich folk into the oft-unstable arts markets. Consider the Swedish vodka maker Absolut, which has commissioned more than four hundred contemporary artists, from Andy Warhol on down, to re-create high-art variations of its tall rectangular bottle. This exercise inspired company literature to proclaim in all seriousness, "Art has become an important medium to express the basic values and magic of Absolut Vodka," as Wu reports.[1]

Absolut also got into the Young British Artists act, sponsoring regular student exhibitions and commissioning bottle depictions from Hirst colleagues like Chris Ofili, the Nigerian-born artist who would later gain great renown as the creator of the cow-dung-and-pornography portrait of the Virgin Mary in the Brooklyn Museum's Saatchi-sponsored "Sensations" exhibit. That show was arguably the last of the great arts-themed culture war dustups, which perhaps accounts for the spiritless going-through-the-motions feel of most of the featured works and all the controversy surrounding them.

Hirst was also prominently featured in the "Sensations" show—this time with a number of segmented cows preserved in formaldehyde, provoking the usual "You call this stuff art?" commentary from America's legion of conservative culture warriors, and the corresponding arch refusal to engage any serious public questions about either the message that Hirst conceived or the audiences he was seeking to address. Indeed, it's hard to avoid the supposition that the wearisomely familiar controversy around the "Sensations" show was perhaps its central aesthetic mission all along—it certainly helped consolidate Saatchi's standing as the unrivaled arbiter of all things edgy in the global art world.

Hirst, meanwhile, who'd already achieved a handsome living as a London restaurateur, has bulked into no less an imposing global arts brand than Saatchi or Absolut. His fortune was estimated in 2009 to be £235 million; one of his trademark shark productions was gaveled at a Sotheby's auction for a cool £9.6 million. (However, his most overtly avaricious, and reliably ponderous, work—a human skull garlanded in diamond encrustations and called *For the Love of God* has yet to fetch its official £50 million asking price.)

And in a fitting gloss on the new economics of the art world, Hirst was invited in 2010 to mount his first career retrospective by Prince Albert and Princess Caroline of Monaco—the very sort of high-art patrons that the old European masters had relied on, but that Hirst so clearly doesn't need. In a subordinate irony, the show was mounted in Monaco's Oceanographic Museum for the facility's centenary. Hirst produced a bigger-than-ever pickled shark for the occasion, a female Carcharodon, or Great White, preserved in 24,000 liters of formaldehyde. (The museum's floor had to be strengthened to accommodate the installation's thirty-ton weight, the UK *Telegraph* reported.)[2]

In another suggestive display of postmodern cultural synergy, one of Hirst's favorite bands, the psychedelic punk ensemble the Flaming Lips, was flown in from Oklahoma to perform at the show's opening, amid a riot of dry ice smoke and cascading gold confetti. For all the event's hectic juxtapositions of high culture and indie subculture, of old models of arts patronage and new ones, Hirst no longer bothers to come across as the enfant terrible he pretended to be when he first started plunking dead mammals in formaldehyde baths. Indeed, in conversation with the *Telegraph*'s patient correspondent, Tim Ecott, he sounds less like a transgressive art impresario than a standard-issue Tory propagandist in the Thatcher vein. "Money deserves respect," he announces. "It can be as important as love . . . and it opens doors. You need to respect money because there are so many people who don't have enough of it."[3]

Well, no, actually. Aesthetic values aside, the maldistribution of any social good is not a reason for it to command respect. Quite the contrary: That condition should invite public inquiry, and if need be, public scorn and protest about the prevailing social arrangements that enable and perpetuate such inequality. Historically, art has played no small role in highlighting such intolerable tensions, be it in Francisco Goya's celebrated cashiering for his all-too-realistic portrait of Charles VI's family, in Honoré Daumier's renderings of Paris's slum dwellers, or in Georg Grosz's pitiless depictions of the Weimar Republic's descent into privileged squalor and of the Nazi horror that ensued.

This is not to say that all art should be burdened with the narrow, oft-distorting expectation of serving as a topical broadside or a protest against injustice. It is, however, to say that when a restaurateur who's accrued a nine-figure arts fortune with the strategic backing of a status-anxious ad agency pronounces that money "can be as important as love," we have entered an aesthetic universe every bit as blinkered and morally obtuse as that of the Catholic Church, when it elected to suppress classical composers in the wake of the Napoleonic Wars out of the conviction that they presented an urgent Jacobin threat to the established order of things.

Of course, when Hirst's corporate-subsidized work is being mounted for an audience of royalty, the whole idea of engaging any world outside the inviting, shiny surfaces of the new global arts fraternity is pretty much a dead letter. Like most of what now passes for avant-garde expression in the arts world, the Hirst-branded spectacle, while fetching top dollar, is all but completely sundered from any meaningful idea of an arts public. And that, too, seems entirely fitting, since what chiefly distinguishes high art from its hulking mass-cult counterpart these days are emptier sanctums in which to watch the money.

Rich People Thing No. 16

AYN RAND

The surest recent sign of our country's deep derangement when it comes to sizing up fundamental shifts in economic life came in the early days of the Obama era. As the White House and Congress surveyed the smoldering ruin formerly known as the investment economy, and as economic advisers desperately sought out something—anything—that might prime the pump of frozen demand, free up the seized-up credit markets, or otherwise stave off the looming prospect of a new Great Depression, American readers rallied to the consoling, comically dogmatic fiction of Ayn Rand.

Rand's hulking thousand-page opus *Atlas Shrugged* became, in early 2009, an unlikely top title at Amazon.com.[1] A few months later, protestors at the demonstrations that launched the fledgling antigovernment Tea Party movement started brandishing that book's gnomic early refrain: "Who Is John Galt?"

Galt, for those who don't naturally gravitate to doorstop-sized digests of ideological boilerplate disguised as fictional dialogue, plotting, and character development, is the martyr-hero of *Atlas Shrugged*—a doctrinaire hyperindividualist philosopher king who nevertheless manages to organize a collective wildcat strike of the enfeoffed Industrial Age elite, and thereby bring American society to a crashing, disastrous halt.

Rand, an exile from the Russian Revolution of the early twentieth century, no doubt thought that the novel's plotline—buried beneath an ungodly amount of high-modernist hymning of the railroad and metal-alloy industries—was a canny transvaluation of values, to borrow the phrase coined by one of her philosophic heroes, Friedrich Nietzsche. Here was the true oppressed class of the twentieth century rising up in much the same fashion that Russia's dispossessed peasantry and intelligentsia had in the cataclysm of 1917—only this time, the economic rallying cry was not a communistic, or even a physiocratic, one. It was, rather, the hallowed creed of the reactionary Tory: *L'economie, c'est moi*. In its essence, Rand's thesis is a quasispiritual conviction that only the creative genius of the individual, unfettered not only by the gray dictates of the regulatory state, but also, in most cases, by the simple strictures of comity and civility, is the only enduring source of economic and, indeed, existential worth.

Nowhere in Rand's baby-simple sociological narratives is there the slightest room for any deviationist lurch toward the acknowledgment of any shared good, or even notional communities of interest, that her angry, atomistic ideal-type characters might have in common with each other, let alone with society at large. In no other works of fiction, ironically enough, does the parodic mantra ascribed to the Beat Generation's critiques of conformist culture—I blame society—apply with such complete, totalizing force.

One side effect of this airless dogma is the striking inability of any character in Rand's fiction to form anything resembling a lasting adult relationship. In both *Atlas Shrugged* and Rand's other reputation-making novel *The Fountainhead*, Rand's heroes are either profoundly estranged from close family members, or—the far simpler plotting device—rendered as orphans. Howard Roark, the angular, enormously irritating architect-hero in *The Fountainhead*, is the template for this character type. He appears not merely to be hewn from the granite earth that midwifes his beloved skyscrapers, but indeed to have sprung fully formed from the head of Athena, no doubt reciting the aphorisms of Albert Knock and Max Stirner at the moment of parturition.

"He despised causeless affection," Rand writes of one the central members of John Galt's new model army, "just as he despised unearned wealth."[2] That's the sort of uncritical equation of economic and emotional laissez-faire outlooks designed to send Frankfurt School Marxists into ecstasies of interpretation.

Rand's acute family-phobia is just one of countless reasons that the resurgent Rand vogue was an odd fit for a conservative movement that had brandished its fierce devotion to "family values." Another such irony is Rand's overt, no less dogmatic, atheism. One labored set piece in *The Fountainhead*, for example, involves Roark executing a commission for a guilt-ridden millionaire who is hectically trying to make amends with the Almighty in the winter of his grasping, pecuniary life. When Roark produces a modernist homage to the religion of humanity—replete with a scandalously pagan naked-lady sculpture in its central courtyard—he gets dragged into court for fraud, and the offending structure is converted (oh the cruel, collectivist irony!) into a facility for mentally impaired children. Meanwhile, the gloriously unclad female figure is packed off to the exits—only to serve as a crucial pivot in the novel's action when it catches the randy attention of a properly atheistic press mogul. (Such is the subtle genius of a Rand plot.)

I wonder how the John Galt wing of the Tea Party right regards this derisive view of the battle between religion and the arts—so close in structure and detail to the NEA battles of the 1990s, or the statue-covering mini-rampage of John Ashcroft's Justice Department in the early aughts, but with the rooting interests of the author's intended readership so plainly reversed.

Then again, the Rand brand of heroic individualism exhibits precious little patience with the niceties of philosophical consistency—for all of her protagonists' longsome tirades about the unassailable purity of their own integrity and uncompromising vision. And this quality also seems largely a function of their principled estrangement from the human community at large: The central paradox of Rand's novels is that her protagonists so revere the ideal of individual self-assertion that they usually fail to act in anything resembling a recognizably rational self-interest. To put things a bit baldly, their blind, exhibitionistic fealty to the high-professional, world-conquering songs of themselves seems genuinely to make them stupid. Hence Howard Roark doesn't merely shun career-making commission out of his own fastidiously high devotion to his aesthetic ideals; he rapes his love interest, the cool, nihilistic (and heretofore frigid) society architecture columnist Dominique Francon—and then, having of course tamed her into a state of total erotic submission, exults in her own collusion in his professional downfall.

She, too, can't bear to see Roark's genius sullied by commissions executed at the behest of the witless collectivist sheep who make up the client base of the modern architectural elite, so naturally, she works her prodigious professional and social connections to direct all major pending commissions to Roark's bitter professional rival—an absurdly convoluted view of, well, everything for a high-rationalist protagonist to take, especially when it would have made all sorts of sense for Francon to pledge herself to undermining Roark's career *because the asshole raped her.*

This same deeply incoherent set of motivations at the character level obtains with equally ludicrous force to the social canvas of Rand's work. Just as self-adulation exacts absurdly clotted forms of self-sacrifice in Randian affairs of the heart, so does the market utopianism of Rand's pet "objectivist" philosophy cast every social obligation as a disfiguring, destructive account of the true human interest. "Did it ever occur to you" Galt asks of one of his followers—another guileless heiress who's been connived into a submissive-cum-abusive relationship with our hero—"that there is no conflict of interests among men, neither in business nor in trade nor in their most personal desires—if they omit the irrational from their view of the possible and destruction from their view of their practical?" (And yes, Rand's characters really do talk like this—for pages and pages on end.) "No man is a threat to another," Galt's lecture picks up later, "if men understand that reality is an absolute not to be faked, that lies do not work, that the unearned cannot be bad, that the undeserved cannot be given, that the destruction of a value which is, will not bring value to that which isn't. The businessman who wishes to gain a market by throttling a superior competitor, the worker who wants a share of his employer's wealth, the artist who envies a rival's higher talent—they're all wishing facts out of existence, and destruction is the only means of their wish. . . . But men will not cease to desire the impossible and will not lose their longing to destroy—so long as self-destruction and self-sacrifice are preached to them as the practical means of achieving the happiness of the recipients."[3]

Stripped of the knockoff Nietzschean philosophical jargon, this clunky soliloquy does distill the essence of the Randian creed: The social world is, by definition, dark and invasive—a theater of sublimated inferior envy and unchecked "destruction" in the name of "faked" altruism serving the nightmarish mandates of a faceless army of "recipients." The market, naturally, is counterpoised as the forcing bed of the frictionless, unfaked "reality" that exalted souls like Galt apprehend so plainly. There is, in other words, no conflict of interest among men, if they simply recognize the mandate of deference to the superior high-modern Übermensch. It therefore follows that to exact market share from a "superior" business competitor or to compel an employer to part with his wealth in the name of workers is not only an unjust act of expropriation—it is a far more grievous defilement of objectivist reality. (The standing of certain visionary entrepreneurs and employers as superior is a given in this philosophical universe— something so self-evidently true and foundational that it's simply outside the terms of inquiry.)

It's true that Rand expressed this vision far more cogently in the first edition of her 1938 novel, *We the Living*. "What are your masses," she had a character ask there, "but mud to be ground underfoot, fuel to be burned for those who deserve it?" But it's also true that the vision of absolutist individualism in *Atlas Shrugged*, swathed in layers of obscurantist jargon, broke through to an admiring audience because it muffled its misanthropic scorn in the cult of economic genius. And that largely explains its unlikely standing as a popular American literary classic, both at the time of its 1957 publication and today. For the Randian worldview isn't so much a political scheme as a metaphysical one; it asserts the dominant interests of history as a category of being rather than an outcome of public conflict or organized deliberation.

As Rand envisions things, the individual will is simply prior to all such contingent, petty concerns. And so it stands to reason that society should be ordered to unleash the gifted minority who grace it with their genius. If an American Tea Party protestor resents the depredations of the taxing state, it must follow that he or she is possessed of the same primal stuff of genius that propels Rand's heroes into their tragic confrontations with the envious masses—and the expropriating federal bureaucrats who gleefully do their demotic bidding.

This callow Manichaeism flows from perhaps the most noteworthy appeal of Rand's writing—her early career apprenticeship as a Hollywood screenwriter. For all the absurdities of plot and characterization that riddle her work, Rand's potboiler fiction is also insanely readable. It is as agreeably broad, splashy, and romantically tortured as any major Hollywood production. The general effect of her novels on the reader is roughly akin to witnessing a Cecil B. DeMille adaptation of F. A. Hayek's libertarian manifesto *The Road to Serfdom*, under the influence of a mild hallucinogen.

Just as your average motion picture will divide its players into readily recognizable moral types—the amoral gangster or the shifty space alien versus the plucky ragtag band of cops or federal agents —so do Rand's paint-by-numbers morality plays divide humanity into two camps: the cringing, milksop phony altruists; and the heroic, forever-misunderstood absolutists. Every teenager who encounters

The Fountainhead fancies himself a Howard Roark, just as any kid seeing *Star Wars* wants to be Han Solo—and smite the collectivist state or the faceless minions of the Imperial Guard. Amazingly, though, Americans seem constitutionally unable to outgrow Rand's wish-fulfillment fantasies—as the lifelong devotion of Rand's best-known fan, former Federal chairman Alan Greenspan, makes all too painfully clear. Greenspan's career offers perhaps the most forceful imaginable real-world counternarrative to Rand's overclass wish-fulfillment fantasies. The young Rand confrere, after all, grew up to direct his own Randian adaptation in Washington, shunting aside pleas to regulate the derivatives market after the 1998 bailout of the Long Term Capital Management hedge fund, and hewing as firmly as any diehard Galt follower to the fiction that the market possessed the metaphysical ability to right all its excesses when left purely, and dogmatically, to its own devices. By 2009, one had cause to hope that, surveying the evidence of Greenspan's handiwork, the battered survivors of the former American middle class might realize they'd seen this movie before, and knew that it couldn't possibly end well. Instead, they promptly lined up in droves for the sequel.

Rich People Thing No. 17

THE MEMOIR

There's a long, honorable tradition of self-narration in Western letters, stretching back to St. Augustine. But sometime in the mid-1990s, the American publishing scene was overrun with a different sort of confessional genre—the Oprah-age memoir. And where Augustine and his motley band of successors up to the modern age, from Benvenuto Cellini to Jean-Jacques Rousseau, crafted the story of their selves as edifying glimpses of some universal principle working out its implacable logic on mortal human matter, the memoirs of our past two decades were almost uniformly sagas of individual uplift. In works ranging from Mary Karr's *The Liars' Club* to Augusten Burroughs's *Running with Scissors* to James Frey's *A Million Little Pieces*, we saw heroic narrator after heroic narrator conquering the impersonal machinations of a hostile social world.

In these stories, the finished memoir itself is a testimony to the hard work of spiritual conquest—an odd reverse-image of the Calvinist tradition of American confession, whereby the convicted sinner offers the narration of his corrupt and fallen exploits to diagram his richly deserved fate of eternal damnation. But in the secular, therapeutic redemption offered in our memoir age, the protagonists are blameless victims, initiated by rogue social forces into the rigged game of their own downfall via substance abuse, mental disturbance, or bad "magical thinking" (to borrow the title of another acclaimed recent memoir by belles-lettres essayist Joan Didion).

Most of all, the contemporary memoir is a tale of family dysfunction, where the neglect, abuse, or untimely death of parents (or parent-figures) short-circuits traditional filial attachments. Dave Eggers's Gen X saga of self, *A Heartbreaking Work of Staggering Genius*, is perhaps the best exemplar of the form. Within its first fifty pages, both of Eggers' parents die, leaving our narrator to light out for the West in the unencumbered literary tradition of Huck Finn. But even this self-empowered hero is still tasked with reconstituting a family life of sorts, serving as the parental guardian of his young brother Topher and inculcating him with the tribal canons of his media-saturated, wisecracking, recursively ironic generation.

The very particular family saga shared by today's memoir genre has prompted literary scholar Walter Benn Michaels to dub it the signature storytelling form for neoliberalism, the market-centered ideology of the new global economy. That's because, as Michaels notes, these pared-down chronicles of family life perfectly mirror Margaret Thatcher's famed right-wing aphorism, "There is no such thing as society."[1] And while Thatcher's free-market reign witnessed the privatization of all manner of social goods, from council flats to electric utilities, the memoir has facilitated a no-less radical privatization of the self, whereby readers vicariously see themselves as the authors of a postsocial destiny, conditioned neither by their own personal histories nor by the broader life outcomes meted out by the hierarchies of social class.

Indeed, this willed flight from the social world has played no small part in the great formal weakness of today's memoir genre—the embarrassing propensity of certain of its practitioners to wander off into to the inviting meadows of first-person fabrication. Even when these fabulists seek to address questions of economic privation and narrowing social opportunity—as in Margaret Seltzer's 2008 fake LA gang memoir *Love and Consequences*—the result bespeaks a telling failure of social imagination. Seltzer (who got the book published as the searing street testimonial of one Margaret Jones) recounts, for instance, nearly starving as a foster child under the care of a Dickensian Southern Californian foster mom, to the point of seeking nourishment by sucking the marrow from chicken bones.[2]

This set piece would have to involve a strange new chicken-ostrich hybrid breed to command even passing credulity from close readers—but that, in a sense, is precisely the point: Neither Seltzer—who, it turns out, matriculated at the same metropolitan LA boarding school that incubated Mary-Kate and Ashley Olsen—nor her dilatory editors were in close enough proximity to this kind of economic need to be able even to jury-rig a credible fictional account of what it would be like.

This broad lurch into lurid ghetto melodrama pocks nearly every page of *Love and Consequences*. The book opens with a Beirut-style vignette that has rampant gunfire riddling her room in the foster home that would sustain her into adulthood. It is her first night in the gangland wilds of South Central Los Angeles. Another overwrought set piece has Seltzer dropping a half-gallon of milk after she has just spent the family's last few dollars for groceries at a convenience store. After the glass shatters—another clumsy detail that a competent editor might recognize as a narrative red flag, since it's exceedingly unlikely that an inner-city convenience store would sell milk in anything other than a carton—she frets about her baby brother's prospects for nourishment as the white liquid mixes ominously with blood in the street; the byproduct of yet more ambient, and seemingly never-policed, warzone gunplay in the hood. In still another thinly imagined account of the struggle for ghetto survival, our protagonist rallies to pay a delinquent power bill under threat of a service shutdown by running home to cook up some crack in her bathroom, employing a recipe handed off to her by her foster brothers, who would have been nine and fourteen at the time.

This all bears repeating in some detail not merely to belabor the shoddiness of editing in the contemporary publishing world—though it is worth noting that entry-level book editing jobs are notoriously underpaid, and thereby select for family-subsidized children of privilege who would be far more credulous than most ordinary Americans in taking Seltzer's fables of inner-city privation at face value. Rather, Seltzer's invented testimony of ghetto adversity points up something far more disturbing: the unwholesome plundering of imaginary suffering for vicarious shock value, a kind of lived experience purchased on the cheap.

As such, *Love and Consequences* is not merely a neoliberal fantasy, but also, in emotional terms, a neocolonial one, serving as a sort of limit-case of the contemporary memoir's occluded social imagination. Seltzer's book also affords a revealing contrast with an earlier generation of inner-city autobiography, from Claude Brown's *Manchild in the Promised Land* to *The Autobiography of Malcolm X*. These memoirs are narratives of social awakening, in which the protagonists emerge from an early life of petty crime and family travail into the pivotal awareness that their life choices have been circumscribed by a racist social order that directly benefits from their economic and political isolation. These narrators move, in other words, from what's viewed as a degrading inward status of victimhood into a very public standing as political subjects.

The annealing wisdom won by our narrator in *Love and Consequences*, very much by contrast, is contained within her foster family—and her depiction of it is, not to put too fine a point on it, racist. Here, for example, is an all-too-typical soliloquy delivered by Seltzer's supposed foster mother, Evelyn—a large-armed, piety-moaning cleaning woman known to all her charges as "Big Mom"—prayerfully pondering her sons' descent into gang fraternization and the drug trade: "'I need help, Lord. I need help. This ain the world I knew. She shook her head slowly in disbelief, wiping at her eyes with a kerchief. I don't kno what ta do. Please, Lord, guide me'. Momma's shoulders collapsed under her burdens and she started to cry hard, head down on the table, one hand held up to God."[3] At which point, presumably, she broke out into a chorus of "Go Tell It on the Mountain."

The at-risk kids are rendered no more plausibly—their stereo-typed dialogue allegedly transcribed in sententious phonetic-style spellings that call to mind the "Klangs!" and "Baps!" of comic-book action panels. Here, for instance, is Seltzer's imaginary foster brother Taye, recently released from prison: "I done gave up on the whole family thing long ago. I mean I tried an tried again when I first got out. Y'all prolly hate me, but I jus hit this point where I got sikk of all Momma's hypocritical shyt, all the demands. I just figured that karin bout people was a bitch and I get all I need from the block and the homeboys."[4]

Before Seltzer's fraud was exposed, critics hailed the memoir as a rare and gritty chronicle of how life was really lived in the gang-ridden mean streets of South Central Los Angeles. Michiko Kakutani, writing in the *New York Times*, contended that the book's narrator does "an amazing job of conjuring up her old neighborhood . . . both the brutal realities of a place where children learn to sleep on the floor to avoid the random bullets that might come smashing through the windows and walls at night, and the succor offered by family and friends."[5] (In an especially nice touch, the patrician House and Home section of the *New York Times* published a photo-essay of Seltzer's quite lovely bungalow in Eugene, Oregon, treating it as a sort of half-way house permitting the traumatized South Central memoirist a well-earned rustic recovery—when it was in reality the boodle that a child of Brentwood extorted from a supremely cynical act of racial minstrelsy.)

But as the Seltzer case shows, the neocolonialist memoir isn't simply a falsified account of "brutal realities." More fundamentally, it's a bad-faith form of class voyeurism, meant to keep the misfortunes of others at a comforting, aestheticized arm's length rather than foregrounded in a self-consciously political narrative that directly engages the reader's conscience. It's a mark of privilege to cast one's fellow citizens as monolithically soulful, suffering, and exoticized others—just as it's something far uglier to pointedly want to know nothing else about them.

Rich People Thing No. 18

THE SUPREME COURT

Honestly, this shouldn't take much explaining, people. While the US Supreme Court has in recent years compiled a passable record on interpreting some of the core individual freedoms enshrined in the Bill of Rights, the nine appointed-for-life arbiters of constitutional law are a mite out of touch with the economic and political struggles of ordinary Americans.

One need look no further for proof of this claim than the atrocious 2010 decision handed down in *Citizens United v. Federal Election Commission*. In that case, a conservative advocacy group sought to publicize an anti–Hillary Clinton pay-on-demand movie within the thirty-day pre-election ban that prohibits corporations and unions from funding electioneering appeals under the McCain-Feingold campaign finance law. In the court battles leading up to the decision, Citizens United maintained that the market for on-demand films, being self-selected, couldn't distort political speech in the same manner that McCain-Feingold imputed to other election-themed appeals from groups bankrolled by "independent expenditures"—i.e., large chunks of cash from a corporate or union treasury.

The John Roberts Court had plainly been itching to overthrow the whole body of law curbing the undue influence of money on political debate back when it heard oral arguments on the case in September 2009. The chief justice, a former corporate counsel, contended that the federal government was, in all likelihood, being "extraordinarily paternalistic" in its presumption that individual shareholders wouldn't "keep tabs" on the diversion of corporate treasuries for political aims—though of course the general run of shareholders possess widely diversified 401(k)s and mutual funds, and would likely have to quit their day jobs to watchdog all the corporate political antics occurring under their notional ownership.[1] The question of how citizens who aren't shareholders can expect to wrest public accountability from the moneyed manipulation of the electoral process is a mystery unplumbed in the case's oral arguments and final ruling.

The text of that decision reads like an absurdist gloss on the principles of effective representative government—better suited to the work of arch surrealists like Alfred Jarry or André Breton than to the proudly rationalist drift of high judicial reasoning. "This Court now concludes," the majority opinion held, "that independent expenditures, including those made by corporations, do not give rise to corruption or the appearance of corruption. That speakers may have influence over or access to elected officials does not mean that those officials are corrupt. And the appearance of influence or access will not cause the electorate to lose faith in this democracy."

A strict literalist reading of that final assertion might be supportable, for the simple reason that the Roberts majority is not in fact describing a democracy of any sort, but rather an open-air plutocratic auction for public favor. How could the citizenry be said to lose faith in something that isn't there in the first place? As for the notion that access to generous complements of corporate cash creates neither corruption nor "the appearance of corruption," nor any quid-pro-quo scheme of legislation to power such appearances forward, that's an account of the daily business of DC graft so fanciful—and so readily dispelled by the two-word incantation "Jack Abramoff"—that one is tempted to mount upcoming High Court challenges to certify the existence of rainbow-colored unicorns.

But the sage dictates in *Citizens United* don't stop with conferring unearned virtue on a political system that even our sainted founders designed to be riddled throughout with base self-interest; the opinion proceeds to elevate the modern corporation into the status of a protected class, a gambit that requires absurdly acrobatic extensions of First Amendment doctrine. "By taking the right to speak from some," the Court speciously contended, any curb on campaign spending "deprives the disadvantaged person or class of the right to use speech to establish . . . respect for the speaker's voice" and—here's the real whopper—deprives "the public of the right . . . to determine for itself what speech and speakers are worthy of consideration."[2]

Got that? Not only is the rampant merchandising of the electoral process free of any imputation of corruption, but the consumption of corporate propaganda is also a first principle of democratic self-governance. And how better to acquire "respect" for a given speaker's voice than for said speaker to conceal his or her moneyed affiliations behind an anodyne civic nameplate like, let's say, "Citizens United"?

Sadly, all the self-administered gulling the Roberts Court has showcased in this decision marks the logical culmination in a long tradition of business-friendly jurisprudence from the Supreme Court. The granting of personhood—and hence most protections of citizenship—to corporations under US law dates back to Justice Morrison R. Waite's curt, precedent-free announcement in the 1886 *Santa Clara County v. Southern Pacific Railroad* decision that "the court does not wish to hear argument" on whether the Fourteenth Amendment secured rights of process and equal citizenship for corporate entities because, well, "we are of the opinion that it does."[3] (How this delusional aside became ironclad legal precedent is a tale unto itself, with author Thom Hartmann contending that the Court's reporter, J. C. Bancroft Davis—former president of the Newburgh and New York Railway Company—fished it out of oral arguments in the case and elevated it for inclusion in the syllabus account of the final published ruling.)[4]

In a series of subsequent rulings, the Court continued expanding the due process and equal protections of the Fourteenth Amendment for the legally nimble category of corporate persons—entities that could, for instance, readily shift their identities under new ownership structures, engineer strategic relocations across US borders, and lease and purchase legislatures without suffering any of the pesky legal consequences those actions might pose for mere living, breathing, mortal American citizens. At the same time, High Court justices drastically narrowed the application of those same clauses for the class of citizens Congress clearly intended them to apply to most forcefully: African-American freedmen and their descendants amid the brutal efforts of the southern white aristocracy to erect segregationist barriers to full political citizenship. Outlandish decisions such as *Plessy v. Ferguson* and *Berea College v. Kentucky* upheld the purported right of individuals and corporations to deny black citizens equal protection and due process, while a raft of railroad-funded litigation briskly minted the rights of corporate citizenship into a ready-made dodge against the differential levy of taxes across state lines. The early run of Fourteenth Amendment jurisprudence from the Court set the tone for its later interpretation; between 1890 and 1910 alone, the high court heard 288 Fourteenth Amendment cases addressing the putative rights of corporate persons, as opposed to just 19 devoted to the legal rights of African-Americans. As Justice Hugo Black noted in the 1930s, over the half century course of the amendment's test cases, "less than one-half of 1 percent [of High Court cases] invoked it in protection of the Negro race, and more than 50 percent asked that its benefits be extended to corporations."[5]

The Court continued to find new protections for corporations throughout the twentieth century: the Fourth Amendment (barring illegal search and seizure), the Fifth (against self-incrimination and double jeopardy), and the Seventh (absurdly enough, the right to trial by a jury of one's peers) have all been piled on top of the original *Santa Clara County* non-precedent.[6]

Still, those have been incremental upgrades compared to the briskly accommodating service the Roberts Court has provided to its corporate petitioners. In its short tenure, the Roberts Court's five-vote conservative majority has stricken down a 97-year-old central doctrine of antitrust enforcement and erected barriers to equal-pay litigation in the workplace so that Congress drafted new legislation to uphold legal remedies for workers victimized by gender discrimination. As Jeffrey Toobin has reported, that track record prompted Associate Justice Stephen Breyer, who votes in the court's moderate minority, to remark "It is not often in the law that so few have so quickly changed so much."[7] And that was *before* the egregious ruling in *Citizens United*.

This boardroom-first outlook on legal affairs is entirely in keeping with Roberts's career in private legal practice. "Shortly before Roberts became a judge," Toobin writes, "he successfully argued in the Supreme Court that a woman who suffered from carpal-tunnel syndrome could not win a recovery from her employer, Toyota, under the Americans with Disabilities Act. Likewise, Roberts won a Supreme Court ruling that the family of a woman who died in a fire could not use the federal wrongful-death statute to sue the city of Tarrant, Alabama. In a rare loss in his thirty-nine arguments before the Court, Roberts failed to persuade the Justices to uphold a sixty-four-million-dollar fine against the United Mine Workers, which was imposed by a Virginia court after a strike."[8]

Roberts's best-known case before the High Court was *Lujan v. National Wildlife Federation*, where he successfully argued that an environmental advocacy group had no legal standing to challenge a Reagan White House decision to place 180 million acres of federal wilderness land on sale to mining interests. The Wildlife Federation's complaint should be thrown out, Roberts argued, because it "was in no way distinct from the interest any citizen could claim, coming in the courthouse and saying, 'I'm interested in this subject.' "[9]

That dismissive reference to the policy hobby horses favored by "any citizen" makes for edifying reading—particularly coming as it does out of the mouth of a rock-ribbed antigovernment Reaganite, here making an inapposite, robust case for the unmolested sovereignty of the executive bureaucracy. But laid alongside the expansive protections afforded to the speech of our corporate polity in the court's campaign finance ruling, the logic of Roberts's *Lujan* argument at least looks consistent, if not sensible. It points out what the Court has long held, ever since it first began tussling with the awkward questions of social equality back in the nineteenth century: Some citizens are more equal before the law than others. After all, what is Citizens United but a slogan for a corporate front group?

Rich People Thing No. 19

HIGHER LEARNING

There's no firmer dogma in American social mythology than the idea that a university credential is an ironclad guarantee of upward mobility. And it is true that, according to a 2009 study by the Pew Research Center, adult children in the bottom quintile of household income increase their chances of reaching the top quintile from 5 to 19 percent by graduating college, while nearly half in the same bottom quintile who don't get a college degree just stay there.[1]

Yet the gaudier rise from the bottom to top occludes a bigger, and far less uplifting, picture. While poorer students may realize larger economic gains as a result of graduating college, not many of them get there in the first place. Students from the bottom two quintiles who placed in the middle third of math achievement scores enrolled at universities at a rate of 33 to 37 percent, compared to 47 to 59 percent for the same middling math kids in the top two quintiles. Meanwhile, university-level performance among student income groups follows strongly delineated lines of privilege; even high-performing students in the bottom half of the income scale fall behind—by 15 to 16 percentage points—the showings of their high-performing counterparts from the top quintile.

These figures only reinforce what anyone who's spent any time within a four-year university can see in virtually no time flat: Far from widening the path of economic opportunity, most of our prestige

institutions of higher learning function as engines of economic discrimination. The trends, as the Pew report notes, are easily sum-
marized: "Higher enrollment by students from families with higher
income; higher enrollment by students with higher test scores; and
at each given level of test scores, students from families with higher
incomes had higher percentages of enrollment than students from
lower-income families."[2]

Nor is the reason for this study in social stagnation any great mystery. For more than two decades, the cost of higher education has
been increasing at a clip well over the rate of inflation—most years,
more than double the inflation rate. As a result, postsecondary tuition
is the priciest social good on offer in the American scene, having ris-
en 439 percent, once adjusted for financial aid, from 1982 to 2008, according to a *Money* magazine analysis of federal inflation numbers.[3]
That's more than four times the consumer price index over the same
period, and nearly double the rate of increase in a medical system so
notoriously rigged with artificial cost hikes and third-party payola
that even Congress was moved to reform it.

There's been no similar public outcry over the tuition system,
which seems to glory in creating perverse incentives. Most high-end
and Ivy League schools spent the 1990s and early aughts pursuing a
senseless binge in luxury spending so as to draw a wider pool of high-
testing applicants—not because they had so many vacant spots to fill,
mind you, but because wooing bigger applicant pools permitted them
to reject more applicants and to continue burnishing their reputation
for exclusivity in the applicant market. In 2008, when lawmakers finally got wise to the scam and threatened to revoke the ridiculous tax
exemptions enjoyed by massively endowed institutions like Harvard,
Yale, and Princeton, most of these Ivied preserves of privilege hur-
riedly announced expanded aid programs for students from families
earning $120,000 a year or less.

By then, however, the tuition market had become so absurdly
distorted and top heavy that this miniature and belated land rush in

Ivy League aid wound up creating yet more pressure on major state universities. These schools had already begun evolving into "public Ivies" in the 1990s as more high-earning families got priced out of the skyrocketing Skull-and-Bones end of the market. As *Money's* Penelope Wang noted, "at the University of California, Berkeley . . . a family earning $90,000 would get little or no aid, so they'd have to pay the total cost of nearly $25,000. At Harvard, they'd now pay less than $9,000."[4]

Which would be great news, if most aid-qualifying students wielded Harvard-level test scores, alumni recommendations, high school GPAs, or other forms of lavishly appointed "social capital"—said in our civic lore to make individual achievement at the college level a sure thing. But with financial aid serving as the main arbiter of a post-secondary destiny, the lower orders face yet another battery of perverse barriers to entry. Federal Pell Grants, the most direct need-based outlays of tuition aid, declined in 2005, for the first time in six years. A Clinton-era set of cuts to the programs in favor of "targeted middle-class tax credits" for college students had already badly skewed the aid market away from students in the lower quintile. And these absolute declines occurred during the height of the great tuition binge—so that, as the National College Board notes, the proportion of tuition and room-and-board expenses that could be met by an average Pell Grant declined from 42 percent in the 2001–02 academic year to 33 percent in 2005–06—and that figure marks nearly a 50 percent drop from the 60 percent of expenses the average Pell Grant covered in 1985.

This aid squeeze, in turn, tends to ensure that the average lower-to middle-class college student, should she be fortunate enough to graduate, enters the workforce under a crushing burden of debt. In 2008, graduating students left school with an average of $20,000 in student loan debt—a gruesome prospect for the liberal arts grad, in particular, who earns an average yearly income of $33,000. And while Congress recently revamped the federal student loan program, most major loan providers have been swamped by recent scandals alleging artificial schemes to balloon student debt by sweetheart kickback deals with school loan officials, extending terms of "forbearance" to prolong the life of loans and the liabilities of borrowers. One of the most egregious offenders is the former government-service-enterprise lender Sallie Mae, which now appears to have the inside line on managing the bulk of loans under the "reformed" federal scheme.[5]

A cynic might well argue that, given the cartelized and crony-ized state of the rest of our economic life, being saddled with a mound of unscrupulously contracted debt might well be the best initiation into adult American life a young worker could expect—and that therefore our university leaders are indeed splendidly hitting their mark as the mentors of a new generation of workers. But that mordant thought overlooks a larger point—as, indeed, does the whole obsessive focus on education as a manufactory of economic opportunity. American public education was not intended to serve as a means of investment, or as a guarantor of enhanced life opportunities, in the first place.

Rather, the idea of Horace Mann's original "common school" movement was to educate Americans to be democratic citizens—not only to master the narrower civic curricula necessary to understand and execute the fundamental demands of citizenship and political judgment, but also to grasp and honor the value of education as a social practice in its own right. As Mann conceived it, public education was to be the principal means of refining the raw social sensibilities of the frontier—and that quality, paradoxically enough, would be a great social leveler by uniting common-school students behind the ideal life of the nation, as opposed to the tribal grievances of caste. "The spread of education, by enlarging the cultivated class or caste, will open a wider area over which the social feelings will expand," he wrote, "and, if this education should be universal and complete, it would do more than all things else to obliterate factitious distinctions in society."[6]

Clearly, our own education system, so skewed toward top-heavy privilege and so dogmatically bound by the functionalist demand that it bolster the economic standing of its students, has failed both of these missions. The content of most curricula, even at the college level, rarely bothers any longer with the conceit of using the rare margin of leisure culturally programmed into the adolescent experience to bring students in contact with philosophic, literary, or spiritual traditions that would permit "the social feelings to expand."

Indeed, overall enrollment in the humanities at American colleges have been declining steadily over the past four decades. As William M. Chace noted in the *American Scholar*, university graduates majoring in the humanities—history, English, foreign languages, literature, and philosophy—have declined nearly by half from 1970 to 2005, from 30 percent to just under 16 percent of awarded bachelor degrees. Business enrollment, meanwhile, increased by the same proportion, from 14 to 22 percent of degrees awarded over the same span.[7] To compete in these conditions of slumping demand, humanities departments now routinely acquire the protective coloration of their preprofessional disciplines, employing crass, functionalist pitches for a just-in-time, customized learning experience to would-be majors. Rather than professing to widen access to the rigors of learning, humanities departments now typically stress what their curricula can do for the harried, debt-ridden customer-student, conditioned in the culture at large to have all needs met in fastidiously narrow-casted fashion.

The Harvard English department, Chace notes, junked its standard undergraduate survey for English literature in 2008 in favor of what the department calls "affinity groups." So instead of encountering a shared and evolving "canon" (to employ the witless epithet of the nineties culture wars), Harvard students select from four high-concept clusters of voguish noun formations: "Arrivals" (i.e., influences exerted on English literature from cultures outside of it); "Poets" (an instructor-based selection of writers); "Diffusions" (the reverse of "Arrivals"—a selection of works reflecting English writing's thrust outward into the world); and "Shakespeares" (the plural form reflecting the bard's contemporaries—while also presumably intended to take down the notion of the great dead white male another conceptual-cum-ideological notch or two). The idea, explained the department's director of undergraduate studies, Daniel Donoghue, "was to start with a completely clean slate."[8] Apparently Donoghue and his novelty-addled colleagues never paused to reflect that "a completely clean slate" is pretty much the antithesis of teaching English literature—or indeed, of literature or teaching of any kind.

As elite humanities departments hustle for the attention of an ever-distractible overclass clientele, they're unwittingly following the canons of just-in-time pedagogy that have long been the rule in the more squalid and downscale end of the tuition market. The only difference is that these franchised outlets of the privatized higher-education future offer a product that's far less beneficial to students' self-esteem—or to their long-term economic standing.

Indeed, most of the recent enrollment growth in higher education has been in so-called proprietary institutions—multi-campus for-profit schools such as DeVry University and the University of Phoenix. These institutions deliberately exist in the shadowy frontier beyond the purview of the regulatory and accreditation authorities that oversee most conventional four-year schools so as to keep providing the most cheaply assembled product at the highest sustainable margin of profit.

It hardly need be added that they have obliterated any lingering Mann-style conceit of a university education serving any higher social good. The publicly traded schools embrace a curriculum tailored exclusively to the needs of corporate employers. In the words of its billionaire founder, John Sperling, the University of Phoenix is itself "a corporation, not a social entity. Coming here is not a rite of passage. We are not trying to develop [students'] value systems or go in for that 'expand their minds' bullshit."[9]

This unsentimental view has permitted Sperling's institution to become the largest university in the country, claiming an enrollment of more than 420,000 students with a faculty of more than 20,000 instructors. Yet by so aggressively mimicking the ethos of the corporation, the school has also adapted the cost-cutting model of mass-production to the marketing of academic credentials. More than 95 percent of the school's teachers are part-time, and none are tenured. It's perhaps needless to add that they aren't unionized either.

Students are encouraged to form their own self-administered "learning teams" to further drive down the expense associated with teachers' influence. Indeed, in 2006, under lobbying pressure of Phoenix's parent company, the Apollo Group, federal regulators dropped the going "50 percent rule," which had instituted an already laughably inadequate baseline requirement for aid so as to ensure that enrolled students received in-person instruction for half of their accredited time in school.

This was a major victory, since the University of Phoenix is also the biggest recipient of such aid in the perverse federal funding market for universities—another key to its corner-cutting business model. And for all the rhetorical stress that Sperling and other officials place on market results, the school graduates just 16 percent of its students, according to Department of Education statistics—well below the national average of 55 percent for public and private universities.

The idea is clearly to herd as many people into Phoenix programs as possible, charge inflated tuition rates, and leave them to ford through an indifferently conceived and executed curriculum largely on their own. A 2003 Department of Education investigation found that the university had broken the law by providing recruiters with cash incentives—kickbacks, in essence—to enroll unqualified students. The recruiters would mislead students about the scarcity of enrollment space in classes and campuses, lie to them about the amount of financial aid they would receive, and falsely claim that their Phoenix credits would be readily transferable to other four-year institutions. Nor has the public exposure of such abuses produced any significant change in Phoenix's recruiting methods. In 2009, the Apollo Group paid $67.5

million to settle a whistleblower suit that echoed most of the substantive claims highlighted in the Education Department's report, according to a report by ProPublica and NPR's *Marketplace*.[10]

These abuses are widespread throughout the burgeoning for-profit university sector. Two Government Accounting Office inspectors posed as unqualified would-be enrollees at one such school—the inspectors' report didn't specify which one, since the investigation was still ongoing at the time of its release. They both deliberately set out to fail the school's entrance exam. Administration officials read answers out loud to them, and when that technique didn't produce the desired effect (they were trying to fail, remember), the solicitous bureaucrats proceeded to cross out wrong answers and substitute the correct ones.

This manic emphasis on getting warm bodies through the door is simply a reflection of the for-profit university's quest for maximally profitable economies of scale. In 2008, the $3.2 billion in federal money the University of Phoenix received accounted for 86 percent of its total revenue.[11] What ultimately becomes of the poor slobs holding the notes on federal education loans is their own affair, once they've been processed at the front end, and the University of Phoenix takes its cut. According to federal figures, the loan default rate among graduates from proprietary schools is 11 percent—almost twice the overall 6 percent default rate among four-year graduates.

Those sobering loan figures, combined with the school's low graduation rates, indicate that the operation is less an institution of higher leaning than an Amway-style pyramid scheme. As long as recruiters are hustling new students through the front door and processing their federal aid forms, the low overhead associated with a casualized teaching corps and a footloose-to-virtual campus—the school typically sublets classroom space in office buildings, thereby sparing itself the heavy costs of maintaining libraries or physical plants—keeps the profit margins high. Indeed, even in a weak economy, the Apollo Group has exceeded its recent quarterly profit expectations, as the chronic shortage of decent-paying jobs has sent more students back into vocationally minded college programs.[12]

So the once-noble dream of a universal higher learning has been transformed, as have so many other social goods in America, into a brutally class-segmented market. The big money still goes into the elite Eastern Seaboard schools—and students at those institutions get customized, grade-inflated, kid glove treatment in lavishly appointed campuses and physical plants. Meanwhile, at the under-regulated frontier reaches of the college market, students are thrown largely back on their own resources—and systematically lied to by recruiters—mainly to furnish market subsidies in the form of federal aid to benefit a group of private investors. These shareholders evince no particular interest in educational quality, let alone the benefits that a liberal arts curriculum might bestow on a democratic citizenry. Indeed, it would be utterly irrational for them to cling to such notions, since doing so would only increase the company's production costs while dramatically narrowing its consumer base.

During a 2009 hearing of the House Education and Labor committee on abusive recruiting and loan practices at proprietary schools, California Democratic Representative George Miller said, "We're developing a process here that looks a lot like subprime student loans. Knowing that these people don't have the capacity to pay it back, knowing that they may not have the ability to benefit from this education, we go ahead and extend them the credit."[13] If anything, that puts things too diplomatically. There will always be more honor in being foreclosed upon than in getting mind-fucked.

Rich People Thing No. 20

THE TROUBLED ASSET
RELIEF PROGRAM

In 1933, when Franklin D. Roosevelt took office in the teeth of a ruinous global depression, one of his first acts was to declare a weeklong bank holiday to stave off the wave of bank closures then crippling the nation's financial system. Then after rushing an emergency banking act through Congress to stop the hemorrhaging of depositors' funds from a broken system, he set about restructuring the way the freshly recapitalized banking world would do business. Under the Glass-Steagall Act of 1933, commercial banks could no longer form holding companies that marketed investment products—a key factor in fomenting the collapse of the nation's paper economy in 1929. Nor could bank deposits be grossly undercapitalized. Under the regulatory eye of the Federal Deposit Insurance Corporation, banks were required to meet basic thresholds of currency on hand to qualify for federal insurance on their holdings. These requirements also fed the growth of community-based banks—particularly the savings and loans institutions that financed many of the mortgages Americans held throughout the twentieth century.

Now, of course, those structural reforms lay in smoldering ruin. The deregulation of the savings and loan industry in the 1980s helped stoke a wide sweep of economic calamity—from the farm crisis to the junk-bond crisis. The 1999 repeal of the Glass-Steagall strictures separating commercial and investment banking coincided with the gaudy expansion of grotesquely speculative and undercapitalized mortgages that fueled the outlandish growth of the securities market in the new millennium. Community banks resumed failing in wave after wave after the financial collapse of 2008. Now half of the nation's financial transactions involve a single megabank, Bank of America, which has absorbed flailing investment concerns such as the toxic Countrywide mortgage shop and the once-proud patrician house Merrill Lynch.

Just about every indication imaginable points to the need for drastic and far-reaching reform of the nation's banking system—be it the plan of de facto nationalization that the brain trusters used to ensure its healthy and reasonably equitable functioning, or the fundamental segregation of speculative gambling on stock futures from the productive investment needed to sustain the core middle-class institutions of homeownership and small-business proprietorship.

What we got instead was a seven-page piece of virtual draft legislation rushed through a Congress too panicked and jumpy to have any clear idea what it was doing. Once the Troubled Assets Relief Program (TARP) became law in 2008, the federal government had ceded virtually all effective leverage to make our financial infrastructure more fair and stable—let alone to prevent it from being swamped from any future meltdowns on the scale of the 2008 crisis that very nearly plunged our economy into all-but-permanent depression.

The whole idea of the banking system's assets being "troubled" was a masterwork of Washington euphemism, from the same people who christened the law gutting income support for families with dependent children the "Personal Responsibility Act of 1996." To suggest we were enduring a siege of "troubled" financial instruments was to view the meltdown as something like an adolescent phase—something to be outgrown with the proper combination of parental discipline and understanding, when the troubled teen moved out of the awkward age, discarded her bomber jacket, got her tattoos erased by a laser-removal service, and joined a campus sorority.

Certainly the particulars of the law were no more specific than those wishful parental reveries. Reportedly Treasury Secretary Henry Paulson Jr., Federal Reserve Chairman Ben Bernanke, and Timothy Geithner (later Paulson's successor, but then helming the Federal Reserve Bank of New York) bandied about big round fifteen-figure sums—$500 billion? No, make that $700 billion—to lend the plan the gravitas needed to assure Geithner's Wall Street clientele that the wheels were not in fact falling off the US investment economy.

Then, under the ridiculously wide authority Paulson in particular gained under the vague wording of the law, there were no efforts to negotiate reasonable terms of winding down the TARP bailouts from the banking giants now on the public dole—and even less of an effort to perform the basic forensic work of identifying counterparties in toxic debt transactions and derivatives trades who now needed to rethink their business models in the wake of the calamity they helped create.[1]

Hence was the groundwork laid for all the headline-grabbing outrage when the carefree bank executives collecting the public dosh would spring for lavish office accessories—like the $87,000 area rug and $1,400 wastebasket that Bank of America executive John Thain picked up for his office in what could have only been a what-the-hell Caligula-style decorating binge, and the $165 million in performance bonuses that AIG awarded the executives who had produced what most sane economic investigators would understand as the polar opposite of economic value.

In seeking to explain the singularly shoddy nature of the TARP agreement, much has been made of the pivotal role of Goldman Sachs—the high-rolling investment house that Henry Paulson Jr. captained prior to his Treasury appointment. Goldman is so choked with connections to the federal seat of power that it's come to be known as "Government Sachs." The house is more strongly identified with Democrats like Paulson and former New Jersey Governor Jon Corzine than with Wall Street's more exuberant defenders in the GOP. It was the largest private donor to Barack Obama in the 2007–08 election cycle, with Goldman-connected PAC donations and individual contributions accounting for more than $994,000, according to the Center for Responsive Politics.[2]

In a sense, though, the Goldman connection is incidental. If all that money were really dictating the particulars of lawmaking and economic policy enforcement, then Goldman executives would have been spared the serial embarrassment of congressional probes into the firm's market-making activities and a high-profile lawsuit—since settled—from the SEC. No, the larger point here is not that Paulson, Geithner, Bernanke, et al. were allied with a particular investment shop, but rather that they were in ideological thrall to the entire derivative-hawking model of financial speculation that fattened not merely Goldman's bottom line, but also that of Morgan Stanley, JP Morgan, and (before it was too late) Lehman Brothers and Bear Stearns and all the other name players in the collateralized debt market.

To use that phrase that must never be spoken in earnest in discussions of the American economy, the masterminds of TARP were pursuing a shared class interest. Yes, the counterparty that most directly benefited from the bailout program's lax scrutiny may have been Goldman—though the curious thing about the dark derivatives markets is that it's extremely difficult, even at this late date, to affix clear or certain rankings of any one house's exposure in a global market now estimated to be north of $600 trillion. But it may as well have been Morgan, or Deutsche Bank or Credit Suisse for that matter. The core logic of the deal would have remained unchanged, as the governing class consensus since the early nineties is that the investment economy is the American economy. Don't ask Timothy Geithner how keeping AIG afloat sustains job growth—it just *does*, all right? Small wonder, in short, that the TARP bailouts yielded this arch appraisal from the system's inspector general in January 2010: "It is hard to see how any of the fundamental problems in the system have been addressed to date."[3]

Nor is it hard to see why that should be the case. Since the great wave of Democratic-authored financial and trade deregulation in the late 1990s, the American economy has been lashed to the mast of the global neoliberal experiment, where the outward expansion of new markets steadily rolls back the state-refereed system of social welfare and public accountability that sustained growth through most of the developed world since Roosevelt's day. Under these arrangements, low-wage and nonunion service jobs proliferate and consumer debt skyrockets, the big money sloshes back and forth across national borders, and under business-friendly regional trade regimes, globalized firms seek the most beneficial—i.e., low-wage and under-regulated—conditions in which to produce maximum returns on investment. It's quite clear that the logic of the neoliberal expansion produces just the sort of crisis we endured in 2008, and that it is much more adept at spreading toxic debt and panic through the world financial system than the more locally based and tightly regulated national economies were in the last century. Just ask Iceland, or Greece, or Spain.

In this sense, the most sobering feature of the TARP regime isn't the bloated character of its initial bailout expenditures, grotesque as that chorus of snouts at the trough undeniably was. Rather, citizens should be far more worried about the stately yet emptily baroque character of the program's unwinding. All major TARP-backed institutions have booked a profit every day of their 2010 trading career—an achievement due, in nearly every case, to the Janus-faced character of their business model in the post-Glass-Steagall age. Houses like Goldman are able to get fresh infusions of federal capital interest free as part of the Fed's effort to prime the pump in the shell-shocked commercial banking sector. They're then able to purchase no-risk Treasury bonds at a 3 percent return simply by filling out a standardized form or two. So when federal officials like Geithner assure taxpayers that the bailouts have worked, that outstanding TARP liabilities are approaching zero and indeed realizing profits, just recall that the pea is going under the shell. Sure, credulous journalists and commentators will repeat those claims, but that doesn't make these core transactions any less subsidized or unproductive.

All this again affords an instructive contrast to FDR's handling of his administration's desperate banking crisis. Possessing a perspicacity and political vision that allowed him to understand that a banking system must serve a fundamental social good—supplying affordable credit for working Americans and stability to the communities they live in—Roosevelt tailored his banking reforms accordingly. Today's Democrats understand that their core constituency is the professional investment world. And just as certainly, they know that the neoliberal dictates of that world involve shoring up the key enabling fictions of the paper economy: that wealth isn't earned by workers in productive industry but rather manipulated into being by optimal shifts in market climates; that a healthy society's income is not clustered in the middling orders but rather moved toward the extremes at either end of the spectrum, in obedience to the wagers that create the speculator's claim to the main chance; that loyalty to national, let alone local, economies and financial controls is a dead letter in a feverishly globalizing financial order.

A propos of this contrast, consider the political case that FDR made for his financial reforms during a celebrated 1936 reelection speech at Madison Square Garden:

> We had to struggle with the old enemies of peace, business and financial monopoly, speculation, reckless banking, class antagonism, sectionalism, war profiteering. They had begun to consider the Government of the United States as a mere appendage to their own affairs. We know now that Government by organized money is just as dangerous as Government by organized mob. Never before in all our history have these forces been so united against one candidate as they stand today. They are unanimous in their hate for me—and I welcome their hatred. I should like to have it said of my first Administration

that in it the forces of selfishness and of lust for power met their match. I should like to have it said of my second Administration that in it these forces met their master.

There is not much of a question which forces are the masters of the post-TARP economic order. That's why when the Democratic Congress tried its hand at regulating the financial sector that brought the entire economy on the brink of collapse, no one on Wall Street was professing hatred for the new regime. Quite the contrary; as the *New York Times* reported, "Bankers and many analysts think that the bill approved by the Senate . . . will reduce Wall Street's profits, but leave its size and power largely intact."[4]

And why shouldn't they be pleased? According to data analyzed by the Center for Public Integrity, more than 850 financial institutions dispatched a flotilla of more than 3,000 lobbyists during 2009 and the first quarter of 2010, who billed a cool $1.3 billion to advance their congressional agenda, with the financial reform bill being Topic A, B, and C for most such institutions.[5] That effort has yielded vital loopholes for the industry in the bill, such as a huge exemption for so-called end-user derivative trades not to be traded on open public markets. By some counts, those trades make up as much as two-thirds of the multi-trillion-dollar global market in derivatives. TARP may be an unsightly perversion, from the taxpayers' standpoint, of the sturdy aphorism that you get what you pay for. But happily for the footloose financiers of the neoliberal order, members of Congress still produce ready value on demand.

Rich People Thing No. 21

THE LOBBYING WORLD

Some thirty thousand lobbyists clog the high-end restaurants and leafy suburban estates of the metropolitan world I live in. It's true that the ranks of registered lobbyists number just over 11,000—but lobbying, like the campaign fund-raising system, is a fungible thing; the majority of Washington's influence peddlers are tricked out nowadays with job titles like consultant, messaging strategist, or advocate—thereby sparing them the casual stigma of being identified with Jack Abramoff's profession, and more important, the pesky disclosures and conflict-of-interest disclaimers that come with full certification as a lobbyist.

These impresarios of federal messaging move in packs down K Street and up and down the high-speed trains of the Acela corridor, their gaily colored ties flapping in Washington's spring breeze like the royal standard of an advancing feudal army. They tool around town in purring European-made sports cars—usually top-down convertibles when the weather permits—and prowl the city's elite steakhouses and culture preserves diligently seeking status-minded entertainments. If you squint a bit you can imagine them in the image of their closest class forebears—the landed British gentry, out patrolling their country estates for fox and poachers.

In the stolidly anti-productive economy of the nation's capital, lobbying is referred to as an "industry," even though it produces little of value and much of objective harm. Certainly the sheer scale of the contemporary lobbying complex should command some sort of economic taxonomy. But it seems far more accurate to designate the business a joint-stock fraud than a productive economic sector. Like the great holding-company investment scams of the 1920s, lobbyists shift funds across purely notional boundaries of economic activity, promising to reward their gullible charges with the invaluable currency of insider access. And as they plunge onward with this or that policy agenda, they bid up transactional fees for each foray they make into DC's scrum of leisure events and trade promotions as they tirelessly seek to hold the attention of the country's 535 lawmakers. Those proceeds have helped make metro DC—and the outer-ring suburbs where the lobbying class takes its ease, in particular—a gilded Golconda. Northern Virginia's Loudon County—a horsey preserve of landed privilege stretching back to the nineteenth century that now is studded with baronial lobbyists' spreads—is the richest county in America, measured by per-capita income.

Unlike private-sector Ponzi schemes, the lobbying combine is largely recession-proof. When government shrinks, a battery of lobbyists fans out to ensure that it does so in a manner that benefits its clientele; when government expands, a still greater complement of influence-brokers goes forth to direct the growth into proper business-pleasing channels.

So while the activist conservative citizenry gets het up over health-care reform as socialism, or when a Fox News hector brands financial reform as a death knell to the spirit of free enterprise, the lobbying class can only look down from its skyboxes and chortle. From where they sit, the fix had long been in on these measures. The two-year battle over health-care reform had more than 1,750 businesses employing more than 4,500 lobbyists—eight per lawmaker, according to the Center for Public Integrity.[1] The legislative fight over financial reform, which ran nearly as long, kept some 3,000 members of influence-brokering class gainfully haunting the Capitol and the pricey entertainment venues nearby. That works out to five lobbyists per lawmaker, the Center notes.[2]

In popular lore, lobbying is regarded as a byword for the corruptions of public office—and that perception is eminently justified. No less than 168 of those lobbyists on the health-care measure were former members of Congress or onetime congressional staffers, according to a joint study by the *Chicago Tribune* and the Medill School of Journalism at Northwestern University. That number swells to 278 when you include non-health-care firms, like those allied with the US Chamber of Commerce, who were lobbying on the bill.[3] Among their number were fourteen former aides to Democratic Majority Leader Steny Hoyer and thirteen onetime staffers of Senate Finance Chairman Max Baucus—a pivotal player in the final version of the Senate bill—the report noted.

Clearly, the point of the big fees these Hill veterans now command in their new private-sector vocations is to market their personal access to key legislative gatekeepers. That nexus of influence is what lubricates the fabled "revolving door" between government and business, and spurs the anemic efforts to hold former lawmakers, at least provisionally, out of range of the tractor beam of private-sector pelf via public registration requirements and "cooling off" periods between public service and the commercial leasing of a congressional CV. These feeble restrictions are easily evaded, with former Hill chieftains simply waiting out their hiatuses in the euphemized messaging trade, keeping their valuable personal alliances with businesses very warm indeed.

Tempting as it is for us to break off the subject by simply summing up the truly fetid state of the lobbying-government status quo, official corruption is really just the window dressing for the real product on offer on K Street. Just as the selling of indulgences was the symptom of far deeper institutional and theological ills in the Reformation-era Catholic Church, so is the peddling of influence in Washington largely the side effect of the private-sector lobbyists' true mission statement: the manufacturing of social inequality.

It's no coincidence that the great boom in lobbying has coincided with the consolidation of the Reaganite conservative revolution in the 1980s, as Thomas Frank has argued in his 2008 book *The Wrecking Crew*. On the face of things, this shouldn't stand to reason. The conservative revolution was all about shrinking the size of the federal government, after all, and instituting crucial market-inspired reforms into the supposedly inefficient and bloated federal bureaucracy, such as cost-benefit analyses of proposed federal rules on private industry. The Reagan White House even instituted a separate federal agency, the Office of Information and Regulatory Affairs, granting affected industries the opportunity to reverse proposed new federal rules that presented too big a potential setback for their bottom lines. The ideologically charged brand of conservative misrule that has so deeply disfigured federal governance is not, Frank argues, the stuff of happenstance or personality-driven scandal. It is, rather, "the consequence of triumph by a particular philosophy of government, by a movement that understands the liberal state as a perversion and considers the market the ideal nexus of human society. This movement is friendly to industry not just by force of campaign contributions but by conviction; it believes in entrepreneurship not merely in commerce but in politics; and the inevitable results of its ascendance are, first, the capture of the state by business and, second, what follows from that: incompetence, graft, and all the other wretched flotsam that we've come to expect from Washington."[4]

Yet, even while these measures took hold, the lobbying sector continued to burgeon—and indeed, grew at a dramatically increased clip. What was going on?

As Frank and others have argued, the purported small government reforms of the Reagan and Gingrich revolutions didn't so much shrink the size of government as radically privatize the calibration of government's impact. Each time a new deregulatory initiative cleared

Congress—from the pillaging of the S&Ls in the 1980s to the banking and investment giveaways of the 1990s to the dividends and estate tax cuts of the aughts—a new armada of lobbyists would sprout up, seemingly overnight, in order to advise clients in how to game the privatized economic rulebook to their maximal advantage.

Indeed, our generation's most notorious "superlobbyist"—the gloriously unscrupulous Jack Abramoff, now imprisoned on fraud charges—almost seems to have been perfected in a laboratory to distill and fortify these trends. Abramoff mastered a supremely cynical Reagan-era experiment in deregulation—the expansion of sovereign legal status to the Indian nations previously marshaled onto largely non-arable, poverty-ridden federal reservations—so that the newly empowered tribes could create freestanding casino gambling empires outside the reach of federal US oversight. Abramoff and his colleagues got rich by billing client tribes outlandishly inflated fees in exchange for pledges to obtain federal certification to establish new casinos on their lands, often playing rival tribes against each other as they bid up their own exorbitant billing statements by prolonging the rival claims—playing both ends off the middle, in other words, in violation of just about every conflict-of-interest stricture. In an especially nice bow to the original Reagan coalition's callous exploitation of the conservative evangelical agenda, Abramoff contrived an inspired shakedown effort using his colleague Ralph Reed, late of the Christian Coalition, to launch "values-voter" branded anti-gambling ballot initiatives in the backyard of rival area tribes so as to gain an inside track on federal certification for their own casino plans.[5]

The casino racket was just the biggest and gaudiest Abramoff dalliance with the consolidation of deregulated boodle outside the formal reach of American regulators. Another big-ticket Abramoff client, the Northern Marianas Islands, similarly exploited its status as a US territory that falls outside the ambit of stateside minimum-wage and labor laws to set itself up as a kind of theme park for wage-slashing textile concerns—as well as to host a wildly profitable island land-rush in

the sex-worker trade. It was not for nothing that former GOP Majority Leader Tom DeLay, a longtime Marianas booster and Abramoff
crony, dubbed the place "a perfect Petri dish of capitalism."[6]

While most press coverage of the Abramoff affair focused on
the corruption angle, the real scandal here was the way in which
Abramoff's lobbying franchise was but the limit-case extension of the
way most major lobbying operations in Washington do business. Even
though the "public option" of a government-administered insurance
plan for poorer Americans priced out of the private insurance market
proved consistently popular in public-opinion polling throughout the
health-care debate, no Democratic congressional leader pushing for
health-care reform ever made a serious effort to keep the proposal in
the final version of the bill. That's largely because insurance and pharmaceutical lobbyists had already expended heroic time, effort, and
cash outlays to ensure that the Democratic caucus in both chambers
of Congress couldn't be swayed in favor of the plan. (A public option
was not in the sprawling health-care lobby's own interest, as there's no
effective way to selectively game a universally available public benefit
to an individual client's advantage. That's why you see private-sector
lobbyists closing ranks to repeal Social Security, but never to protect
it.) It's no exaggeration to say that industry-lobbying concerns were
treating Congress in exactly the same way that Abramoff and Reed
treated the Indian tribes they shook down—as convenient leverage
points to secure a predetermined outcome in a Potemkin version
of meaningful political debate and expression. Indeed, the activities
of the private health-industry lobby—together with its unassailable
Hill-seasoned pedigree—supplied the most succinct answer to the
greatest mystery of the draining health-care battle in Congress: How
could a piece of legislation grow so plainly and implacably worse the
longer that the people's elected representatives spent time preparing
its passage?

Of course, the genius of the conservative regime that created this
stupendously toxic lobbying climate is that most Americans who follow

the doings of Congress in our context-challenged national media see something like the backward march of meaningful health-care reform and write it off as yet more evidence of the inherent inefficiency—nay, the actively evil nature—of government. Never is there any sustained engagement with the question of how and why the institutions of our government became hollowed out, to their innermost core, by the pre-rogatives of a class of congressional interlocutors that's positioned itself as the arbiter of just how far a bill may be permitted to venture in the general direction of the public good. Fingering government as the cul-prit in the private and systematic delimiting of the government's sphere of legitimate activity is certainly a neat trick—a bit like a mugger suc-cessfully mounting a court defense that his victim had his treatment coming to him by carrying money around in public.

Hence we now see the ultimate reaping of this particular cyni-cal whirlwind: The reformist half-measures of an accommodationist New Democratic presidency—kept scrupulously within the industry-friendly channels of acceptable policymaking—are stoking a genuine popular uprising against the handiwork of industry lobbyists as the telltale signs of state socialism run amok. And providing crucial or-ganizational and logistical support for the Tea Party uprising is Dick Armey, the former House Majority Leader, who, after a few years billing half a million a year at the lobbying giant DLA Piper, now directs the political messaging shop FreedomWorks. Armey is also co-author, with his FreedomWorks colleague Matt Kibbe, of the fire-breathing *Give Us Liberty; A Tea Party Manifesto*, which sports an image of a colonial "Don't Tread on Me" flag on its cover. If you listen closely, you can hear the skyboxes echoing with horselaughs.

Rich People Thing No. 22

LIBERTARIANISM

The day after Kentucky GOP voters awarded insurgent Tea Party candidate Rand Paul the nomination to the US Senate, Paul—a so-called small "l" libertarian—hit the interview circuit. In sessions with NPR and MSNBC, he explained that while he was an opponent of institutional discrimination on the basis of race, he nonetheless opposed provisions in the 1964 Civil Rights Act that ban private businesses from practicing discrimination. "If you decide that restaurants are publicly owned and not privately owned," Paul asked Rachel Maddow, "then do you say that you should have the right to bring your gun into a restaurant even though the owner of the restaurant says, 'Well, no, we don't want to have guns in here'?" The issue boiled down to a philosophical question, he said: "Does the owner of the restaurant own his restaurant? Or does the government own his restaurant?"[1]

Within a day of the exchange, the candidate had walked back from his position, saying that, in fact, he now supported all the provisions of the landmark legislation. And there's no question that his retreat was dictated entirely by electoral politics. If headlines continued announcing that a Southern conservative had come out against the fundamental right of all citizens to equal public accommodations—and presumably to employment as well, another title within the law that dictates practices for private business owners, unmentioned in Paul's pronouncements—then the Kentucky GOP's fling with the Tea Party would result in electing the state's first freshman Democratic senator since 1974.

Voters, in other words, recognized Paul's libertarian philosophy as something deeply out of synch with a core, if extremely hard-won, American principle—a commitment to equal protection under the law. At the same time, the reason the Paul dust-up proved so compelling was that Paul was speaking very much within the new American mainstream, extolling the core libertarian creed that any obstruction of the market is a philosophical crime, abridging foundational principles of liberty.

Paul comes by his convictions via his father, Texas GOP Representative Ron Paul, who ran as a large "L" Libertarian candidate for president in 1988 before settling into his role as a small-government protest candidate within the GOP. And back of that lineage is the line of purist economic thought of "the Austrian school," pioneered by F. A. Hayek and Ludwig von Mises—a brand of classical free-market theory so dogmatic as to be a hallucinatory description of the world inhabited by living, breathing participants in consensual reality, and heartily endorsed by Paul the elder and younger alike.

Indeed, Rand's ill-advised bit of dorm-room debating on the Maddow show was nothing compared to the high-flown postulates of the Austrian set. Von Mises argued that capitalist economic growth was not—indeed, could not—be prey to volatile downturns and crises. All such disturbances had to be traceable, in one way or another, to some unholy molestation of uncoerced free-market relations by the ever-spiteful, dismally inefficient government. The social theory of the modern state hews, after all, to the theory of conflict among interest groups: capital versus labor, the country versus the city, the middle class versus the upper and lower orders, and the like.

Contravening this view, von Mises held that all social relations under the system of private ownership of property gravitated naturally toward an organic convergence of interests. "Any increase in total capital raises the income of capitalists and landowners absolutely and that of workers both absolutely and relatively," he posited. "As regards their income, any shifts in the various interests of the different groups and strata of society—the entrepreneurs, capitalists, landowners, and workers—occur together and move in the same direction as they pass through different phases in their fluctuations; what varies is only the ratio of their shares of the social product. The interests of the land-owners oppose those of the members of the other groups only in the one case of a genuine monopoly of a certain mineral. The interests of the entrepreneurs can never diverge from those of the consumers. The entrepreneur prospers the better, the better he is able to antici-pate the desires of the consumers."[2]

It is all, you see, gloriously self-regulating—as markets must ever and always be. Under this fundamentally sunny view of how mar-kets work—always tending upward, growing almost magically more frictionless and fairer as they proceed—the problems of defining and sustaining the public good (the problems of politics, in other words) get reduced into a simple formula: "The task of the state," von Mises declares, "consists solely and exclusively in guaranteeing the protec-tion of life, health, liberty, and private property against violent at-tacks. Everything that goes beyond this is an evil. A government that, instead of fulfilling its task, sought to go so far as actually to infringe on personal security of life and health, freedom, and property would, of course, be altogether bad."[3]

One can readily see the internal logic lurking in Rand Paul's gaffe: The Civil Rights Act curbed the freedom of business owners to extend their goods and services to whom they would choose. The law was therefore an infringement of freedom and property, and therefore illegitimate at best, and evil in intent at worst. Paul's pro-nouncements were not a slip of the tongue, but rather a reflection of this market-minded Manichaeism. When reporters started dig-ging into his past, they found his words were in line with his other doctrinaire libertarian positions, opposing the Fair Housing Act and the Americans with Disabilities Act, which likewise employed state power to illegitimately impinge on the freely contracted workings of the market.

This worldview leaves out a universe or two of historical and social causation. In the civil rights case, there is, just for starters, the legacy of the systematic enforcement of Jim Crow *by* business owners working hand in hand with the machinery of the state to deny civil, economic, and political equity to a people who were themselves treated as property under the neocolonial system of capitalist labor known as American slavery. Indeed, once that institution was legally abolished, Jim Crow arose out of exactly the same set of formal economic and political alliances to institutionalize discrimination in every commercial and political sector of American society. Blockbusting and restrictive covenants, redlining and debt peonage, served as the core bulwarks of segregation just as surely as literacy tests and poll taxes had—and, indeed, permitted it to continue as a de facto condition of our social life long after de jure principles of unequal citizenship had been abolished.

Libertarians can't make these elementary connections between the consolidation of social and economic power because, under basic terms of libertarian thought, they are not categorically possible. Racism cannot be systematically woven into the foundations of the market order any more than that order itself can be inherently unstable: The model simply doesn't permit it.

Hence, in his replies to the questions about the private-business provisions of the Civil Rights Act, Rand Paul—who asserts quite believably that he holds no racist opinions and abhors discrimination—clung rather pitifully to the notion that Congress should only legislate against discrimination in public venues and workplaces, as though Jim Crow had been conceived entirely in some cloistered market-free social laboratory, a sort of Klan-administered version of the Tennessee Valley Authority.

The truly curious thing, though, is how such an analytically deficient political philosophy could command enough assent in twenty-first-century America to propel the Tea Party social movement that launched Paul's meteoric political rise. After all, even Adam Smith, the great Anglo father of laissez-faire, subscribed to principles of public welfare and state regulation of the economy's inevitable social ills that are strict anathema to adherents of the Austrian school. And the modern American middle class is to a remarkable degree a creation of all manner of government subvention, from government land grants and jobs to the interstate highway system that midwifed the modern suburb, as a whole range of scholars from Lisabeth Cohen to Bethany Moreton have persuasively argued.[4] This is especially the case in Rand Paul's native South, which has prospered on the federal dime ever since FDR entered into his fateful, diabolical pact with Southern Democrats to backburner any push for civil rights legislation in exchange for broad intraparty support for the New Deal.

It's difficult to ponder the social privileges widely taken for granted, and just as routinely derided, in libertarian circles and not find yourself wondering if there's a deeper current of bourgeois self-hatred in the true market faith as libertarians articulate it. When Rand Paul's dad ran his protest presidential campaign for the 2008 GOP nomination, many of his younger supporters instinctively took up the rhetoric and imagery favored by the sixties-era breed of middle-class protestors in the New Left. That Paul campaign was dubbed a "Revolution," and its signage presented the backward "love" in the orthography of the word in the stylized big block type made famous by Robert Indiana. The same core ethos of privatized personal "liberation" that drove the New Left out of the distressing, compromise-ridden bummerhood of agitating for political change and into the personal quest for self-exploration echoed in the new millennium's tax-hating, government-slandering ideal of unconditioned freedom and "liberty." When I attended the landmark "9/12" Tea Party rally in Washington that Glenn Beck summoned into being out of his cable time slot, one supporter was joyously brandishing a sign declaring, "This is My Woodstock." It was framed as a half-ironic message, but came across in the same tonal register whereby many half-ironic gestures actually betray a deeper affinity for the subject being mocked.

Many critics on the left regard the contemporary libertarian as a kind of nihilist—favoring the callow social bullying of Ayn Rand or the rational-choice maunderings of University or Chicago law professor Richard Epstein, dean of the fanciful "law and economics" school of legal scholarship. But that misses the mark, I think. The recent libertarian renaissance is, much like the senescent New Left, a cult of self-expression—indeed, of self-expansion. At the movement's outer limit are the same sort of unhinged utopian reveries that made the New Left so deeply unpleasant for so very long. There are the advocates of space colonization—all to be carried under a regime of private investment and not via that rickety government boondoggle NASA, which merely launched the space program. There are the "sea-steaders"—the lawyers and social prophets who have plotted out the dream of a government-free society aboard some giant watercraft moored in the neutral waters untouched by the Treaty of the Seas. (In my more ungenerous moments, I wonder to myself why they don't spare themselves all the intricate advance planning and theoretical exertion and migrate to a preexisting, land-based society already operating without the loathsome intrusions of a functioning government—like, say, Somalia.) And there are the Extropians—the trippiest libertarians of all—who preach life extension, age reversal, and cryogenic preservation in a transubstantiation of the more-is-better creed of the market onto the life cycle itself. The founding father of the Extropian faith is an Australian philosophy professor who's adopted the name Max More in homage to his principled rejection of all human limits. I have seen this man dance at a wedding, and I was properly terrified at the sight.

The affinities go well beyond formal movements into matters of temperament as well. Like the Flower Children, libertarians subscribe to a fundamentally melioristic view of human nature and a noble-savage-style view of presocialized human existence. And like the bleary-eyed theorists of counterculture revolt, the new libertarians betray a tellingly dogmatic attachment to all things Dionysian—hence, in conducting a content analysis of leading conservative magazines, libertarian scholars Daniel Klein and Jason Briggeman report in notable distress that these publications "have preponderately failed to take pro-liberty positions on sex, gambling, and drugs."[5]

This is all to say nothing of the dramatic embrace of libertarianism by the lords of the new high-tech information economy in Silicon Valley, where the spirit of the counterculture so manifestly crawled away to curdle and ossify. Of all the social forces now going, the tech sector best exemplifies the modern libertarian spirit—expressive, market-obsessed (yet also, curiously, management-heavy), and, above all, beholden to the culture of money. The running joke among many left-inclined libertarians is that a libertarian is an anarchist who got rich, and that could well double as the civic motto for Mountain View, California—or be embossed on the business card of virtually any tech mogul, from Larry Ellison to Eric Schmitt. The cyber-libertarian dogma commends itself to believers, much as the Misean brand of political theory has, chiefly on grounds of its baby-simple catechism: Information wants to be free; the wireless transfer of information is the most potent shaper of the market civilization of the future; and the tainted legacies of industrial-age production—labor unions, tariffs and trade barriers, national borders, and industrial policy—must be cleared away as so much dead historical underbrush. Do all this, and the state eventually just withers away under the superior, invincible pressure of a truly free global market in data.

You would think that this outlook might have been chastened somewhat by the great tech crash of 2000—to say nothing of the far more gruesome, tech-and-data-enabled global economic calamities that have followed in its wake. But evidence that fails to fit the pure libertarian formula is, without exception, the product of some devious statist trick or another. This is another discomfiting respect in which the purist strain of libertarianism resembles the woollier

brand of left dogma. Just as Marxist purists used to dismiss the hor-
rors of Soviet rule as an epiphenomenal glitch in the working out of
the materialist dialectic—the inconvenience of "historically existing
socialism"—so do today's market purists wave away all the abundant
evidence of ruinous market externalities, from climate change to
workplace deaths, en route to the utopia of wholly uncoerced capitalist exchange.

To return to edifying case of the younger Paul, his most distressing pronouncements don't concern the Civil Rights Act's provisions—
which, as a practical matter, are not in danger of imminent repeal.
That distinction belongs to his continual dismissal of any federal role
in the regulation of business. This dogmatic view hasn't drawn the
degree of scrutiny that his civil rights critique has—for the simple
reason that it inheres so squarely in America's post-Reagan political
consensus on economic policy. Just as our fortieth president used to
gaily snipe that "government isn't the solution to our problem, it is
the problem," so do the Paulian libertarians howl over any faint sug-
gestion that government can perform any useful social function, be
it in the public-school classroom or on the assembly line. The day after his MSNBC debacle, Paul told an ABC interviewer that President
Obama's efforts to hold BP fully accountable for the catastrophic 2010
Gulf spill offended his ear "because there's something un-American
in his criticism of business." Such excesses are "part of this sort of
blame-game society in the sense that it's always got to be someone's
fault," Paul went on to explain, "instead of the fact that sometimes accidents happen . . . we had a mining accident that was very tragic and
I've met a lot of these miners and their families. They're very brave
people to do a dangerous job. But then we come in and it's always
someone's fault. Maybe sometimes accidents happen."[6]

Paul's "un-American" swipe at Obama rode through half-a-day's
news coverage, since it was, after all, of a piece with the fringe right's
belief that the president was not in fact an American at all. But the
notion that criticizing business was somehow un-American got no

scrutiny, for the simple reason that, at this late stage in our political economy's decay, most Americans take it for granted as a long-established truth. God knows how Paul's followers would greet the news that the founding father of twentieth-century Republicanism, Theodore Roosevelt, made a habit of inveighing against "malefactors of great wealth"—and dramatically beefing up enforcement of anti-trust laws. Or that Richard Nixon instituted the Earned Income Tax Credit, and Bob Dole helped institute the federal food-stamp program. Under the Paulian worldview, these are all hideous signs of runaway socialism. And since no major media outlet picked up on Paul's equation of economic criticism with treason, a host of other troubling questions went completely unaddressed. Are, say, food safety regulations an illegitimate exercise of state power? Is it a faithless, unthinkable critique of delicate business sensibilities to restore Glass-Steagall Act barriers separating out commercial and investment banking—or indeed, to regulate financial speculation in the derivatives or mortgage markets at all?

Meanwhile, Paul's truly appalling ignorance of mining safety received no significant attention whatsoever—even though he was speaking less than a month after the horrific Massey Energy mining cave-in in West Virginia that claimed the lives of twenty-nine miners after the mine's parent company was cited for hundreds of safety violations that were not enforced in any meaningful way by an industry-captive federal regulatory regime. (Paul appeared to be specifically referencing a smaller tragedy in Kentucky's Dotiki Mine, but in either case, the same egregious lack of federal oversight applies.)

What's more, while an extremely strained and inadequate case could be made that oil spills are an inevitable byproduct of offshore drilling (even though all sorts of evidence in the Gulf spill case points to shocking abrogations of routine safety precautions in BP's mad quest to maximize production and profit from furiously pumping undersea wells), no such sophistry can apply in the case of mineral mining. Mining occurs in an entirely artificial and man-made environment; it is the basest kind of nonsense to assert that cave-ins and gas releases in these settings are some kind of natural occurrence.[7]

Yet Paul ceaselessly repeated the Tea Party mantra that he represented "common sense conservatism"—and, in a strict sense, he was right. This delusive and dangerous idolatry of the market is very much in the mainstream of American thinking. The New Left cousins of today's libertarian revolutionaries guaranteed Richard Nixon's landmark 1968 elevation to the Oval Office before collapsing into the spiteful, self-destructive violence of the "Days of Rage." With the Paul brand of libertarians launching their own rebellion in a state of unthinking antigovernment rage, we stand indeed on the verge of a whole new wealth-addled Age of Aquarius.

Rich People Thing No. 23

THE IPAD

As it released its latest purring, thin, and sleek app-delivery system, the iPad, Apple Computers, One Infinite Loop, Cupertino, California, also passed a major financial milestone, eclipsing longtime software rival Microsoft in market capitalization, the value of a stock share multiplied by the number of outstanding shares in the market.[1] Apple became second only to Exxon in overall US market capitalization, pushing Microsoft to third place and Wal-Mart to fourth.

The new stock valuation didn't even reflect iPad sales—which seems entirely fitting, since the new gadget seems much less like a new product made by Apple than an advertisement for the Apple brand and lifestyle. For some time, the computing world, and Apple in particular, has been operating on the same basic business model that has stood Mexican cuisine in such good stead for so long: shifting the same handful of basic ingredients around in different formats and employing slightly tweaked delivery systems.

As a slimmer, taller version of the iPhone—the last great status-symbol acquisition for the new millennial technorati—the iPad was hailed mainly by adoring reviewers for its resemblance to already existing rival products. It supplied a more graphically pleasing interface than the Amazon Kindle did as an e-book platform, and its 9.7-inch touch screen could be the salvation of an ailing magazine industry desperately in need of a digital upgrade and the media cachet that would accompany it.[2] (Unfortunately for magazine publishers, such sunny prophecies appear to have fallen flat. After Condé Nast, an early convert to the device's market-boosting gospel, trotted out its iPad edition of *GQ*, the men's fashion monthly logged 365 sales of it over its maiden two months.[3]) Somewhat poignantly, toward the end of the iPad's run through the adoring tech press coverage traditionally accorded to every new Apple product rollout, enthusiasts for the device were reduced to pointing out that the pricey object could double as a PC monitor—a bit like marketing high-priced first-edition books with the pitch that they can help prop your windows open.[4]

But then again, functionality was never the intended measure of the iPad's success. The main point of owning an iPad was to demonstrate that you're the kind of person who can own an iPad—possessed of the proper design tastes, tech savvy, professional-managerial ambition, and the like to regard a stretched-out iPhone as an indispensable lifestyle accessory. And there's apparently no limit to that potential market share. The iPad has broken out from its US fan base to become a global phenomenon, with notoriously snobbish and chauvinistic gadget geeks in places like Japan sleeping overnight outside Apple stores to score one.[5]

The iPad's release also furnishes an occasion to revisit the glyph-like "i" prefix that now brands the company's trendiest new product lines. Back when it was introduced in conjunction with the iMac desktop, the lower case "i" was said to stand for "Internet"—the marketing message circa 1998 being that this was the preeminent device with which to access the graphical interface that was then revolutionizing the global economy. But like all clever product messages, the "i" carried a much more powerful secondary meaning signifying "individual," basically, while also leaving room for allied definitions of "identity." It also carried the more the literal first-person pronoun in lowercased, suitably hip, E. E. Cummings style—an especially apt flourish for an instant-communications medium that essentially rendered capitalization of all kinds elective.

The "i" was meant to signify, in short, everything that technology was said to grimly efface in the early, outmoded twentieth-century jeremiads decrying its dominance in the modern world. Here was liberation, expression, and instant and intimate gratification. This was the sort of interface designed for the mammoth embryo featured in the trippy Stanley Kubrick adaptation of Arthur C. Clarke's *2001: A Space Odyssey*—and as most Apple ads make plain, the ideal user-experience for high-end Apple consumers is that of a child. Hence the sing-songy iPod spots featuring the Canadian folk singer Feist, and the litany of mystically pacifying iPad attributes ticked off in the voiceover of a recent iPad campaign: "It's powerful, it's magical—and you already know how to use it," an oddly grizzled paternal voice intones, as images of the live-action movie "*Where the Wild Things Are*" go speeding by.[6] Such are the lullaby refrains for the sovereign consumer.

With the advent of the iPad, however, the aspiring Whitmanian "i" of the earlier suite of Apple products had withered into a more grasping, complacent, and, above all, status-conscious "me." "I wanted to be one of the first people to get the iPad in the U.K.," went one entirely typical exuberant confession from an overnight Apple store camper, as reported by *BusinessWeek*.[7]

The passive "me" cachet of the iPad extends to the gizmo's content menu as well. By marketing a computer pad full of iPhone apps without an actual phone feature, Apple has sundered its ideal-type product from the last brutish intrusion from the world outside, leaving iPad devotees hermetically encased in user experiences of their own filtered choosing. And since the menu of Apple-compatible software and applications is also rigidly proprietary, the iPad experience tends to divorce users from the messier realm of open-source innovation and hackwork—both of which give users a vivid and direct sense of what's at stake in key computer policy debates, such as Net neutrality, draconian copyright enforcements, and the institution of robust privacy controls. A computing experience outside of such issues is serenely depoliticized—as Apple engineers greatly prefer, since it makes for more frictionless marketing of the company's proprietary content.

The iPad experience is isolating in a far more brutal way as one moves down in the global labor market from the ideal-type Apple consumer to the people who assemble the devices. In 2010, Foxconn, the chief Chinese manufacturer of Apple products—as well as a slew of other electronic and digital devices for other global firms—suffered an epidemic of suicides among its workers, mainly provincial men and women in their teens and early twenties who have been jumping off factory buildings.

Foxconn's production facility in the rural city of Longhua is the largest factory in the world, housing 300,000 workers paid an average of $130 a month. The workers live on site in corporate dormitories, and the shifting population there, combined with punishing twelve-hour workdays often stretching across all seven days of the week, makes for profoundly dissociative working and living routines. Employees aren't permitted to speak to each other during the workday and are often too exhausted to socialize in their narrow margin of off hours, where they're crowded into shared dormitory rooms infested with cockroaches.[8]

Earlier in the year, Chinese journalist Liu Zhiyi published an undercover expose of the routine endured by Foxconn workers. "As they make the world's finest gadgets," he observed, "it seems that while they control the machines, the machines are also dominating them; the parts gradually come together as they move up the assembly line; at the same time, the workers' pure and only youth disappears."[9]

Compounding this chilling depiction is the no-less dramatic alienation that awaits Longhua workers should they adjourn to the nearest major city of Shenzhen, home to one of China's three major stock exchanges and a center of regional high-tech financing. There "workers can envy at people of their own age driving luxury cars and carrying the iPhones they themselves make, but cannot afford," a correspondent in the UK *Telegraph* notes.[10]

Most Western consumers, presented with the image of a multimedia gadget that seems magically to hover far above most worldly notions of privation or social conflict, have difficulty connecting up their luxe consumer experiences in the Apple iSuite with the nineteenth-century working and living conditions that produce their elegant gadgets. That's emphatically not the case for the Foxconn employees. Describing the rigid military-style discipline and the phalanxes of security personnel who keep workers under near-constant surveillance, a nineteen-year-old worker who polishes iBooks explained to the London *Daily Mail* that "we're told that the drilling builds discipline. We need discipline because Apple products are expensive and there are no margins for mistakes."[11]

The eleventh Foxconn suicide of the year came in late May, just a day after the company announced plans to hire on 2,000 psychologists to start addressing mental-health issues among its employees. Apple declined any comment, apart from citing language in its subcontracting agreements intending to confine employee workweeks to sixty hours—agreements that are rarely given much credence in cheap labor regimes such as China's. At any rate, contract language calling for ceilings on work hours must sound more than a little disingenuous coming from a company that gloried in its informal start-up slogan, "90 hours a week and loving it!"[12]

Tech companies have long fed on a self-enabling mythology of blurring the divide between work and leisure, contending that the greater satisfactions of the gadget-enabled life have made obsolete many of the conventional measures of worker productivity, time management, and the like. But such utopian fantasy makes for an awkward fit, to put it mildly, with the intensively managed and soulless work routines on the other side of the globe that render such fancies thinkable for the privileged lords of the knowledge economy. Over at One Infinity Loop, "thinking different" seems to mean little more than the strategic outsourcing of the whole wide social world—in Dickensian, satanic mills and customized product platforms alike.

Rich People Thing No. 24

STEVE FORBES

Whatever the fortunes of the actual American economy, it's never seemed to lack for mogul mascots. Even so, we no longer seem to have one tell-tale titan of commerce who sums up the spirit of our own peculiar commercial age the way that the steel trust king and Treasury Secretary Andrew Mellon did in the 1920s, or that GM chieftain Alfred P. Sloan did during the first flush of postwar prosperity in the early 1950s. Indeed, the signature billionaire of our age is arguably Sam Walton, the founder of the low-wage, union-busting, vertically integrated, and tirelessly rent-seeking retail colossus Wal-Mart—and he's been dead for eighteen years.

Oh sure, other pretenders have had their moment in the sun. There was the Bill Gates heyday of the 1990s, when it seemed that Microsoft would rule every computer platform imaginable, and rival operating systems were so much laughable putty in the monopoly's hands. But one mainly encounters Gates these days as a milksop apologist for the nonprofit charity sector and an opponent of the estate tax's repeal. Rupert Murdoch, Donald Trump, Warren Buffet, Steve Jobs, Michael Bloomberg, and others have all made similar runs at defining the essence of our business civilization, and all have in various ways come up short.

Now that scaling the magnificent heights of American market capitalism has been shown to be virtually synonymous with extortion, fraud, and brigandage, the need for a new financial Napoleon, embodying the business zeitgeist on horseback, has never seemed greater. Fortunately, we have had just the man for the job lurking in our midst all along, biding his time as the lesser free-market ideologues dispatched each other on the field of battle—a tactic that is itself no small indication of true market genius. I speak, of course, of the conquering hero named Steve Forbes.

If Lord Fauntleroy and Leni Riefenstahl could have traveled through time and bent the conventions of fiction to mate, there's little doubt that Forbes would have been the screaming issue. In reality, he is the son of father Malcolm, the sybaritic, motorcycle-bestriding publishing mogul who founded the business monthly that he lovingly graced with the motto "Capitalist Tool" during its Reagan-era heyday. One can only surmise the collateral psychic damage involved in such an upbringing. To cite just one childhood trauma, the elder Forbes compelled Steve and his four siblings to wear kilts to church every Sunday in their youth.[1] But young Steve clearly took the magazine's mission to heart as an invaluable storehouse of life lessons and a roadmap for his own ambitions. His dad mounted two failed runs at the New Jersey governorship, so Steve outdid him by running for president. And if Malcolm half-ironically championed his luxe business magazine as an outlet for free-market propaganda, why then Steve would give his plutocratic readers the real thing.

Because we want any true financial leader to be battle-tested by adversity, we can be heartened by the younger Forbes's resume as an aspiring leader of the free world. True, he lost his 1996 and 2000 presidential runs badly, campaigning on the flat tax, a restored gold standard, and supply-side tax cuts when the American economy was experiencing record peacetime growth, government was operating with budget surpluses, and the dollar was performing well in global currency exchanges. He was, in short, peddling quack remedies for ills that didn't exist in the first place.

He also had a few problems making his unique background resonate with voters on the campaign trail. Forbes's rival business monthly, *Fortune*, published a damning 1996 expose that documented many occasions on which company scion Steve and the magazine's senior ad executives intervened to massage or kill ready-to-publish *Forbes* stories that would likely embarrass firms that advertise in the magazine's pages. "Staffers say that during Steve Forbes's stewardship, they have seen stories changed if a writer turns in a downbeat assessment of an advertiser," *Fortune* reported. "In other words, the magazine's editors are turning downbeat stories into upbeat stories in order to keep advertisers happy—even at the risk of misleading their own readers."[2]

Among the confirmed corporate beneficiaries of this advertiser-osculating policy were AT&T, Georgia Pacific, and Commander Aircraft—the latter company getting an unfavorable story killed outright rather than gussied up in its favor, *Fortune* reported, when the reporter and intervening editor couldn't find enough favorable information with which to gild the wilting lily. While other business press outlets have faced—and caved into—pressure from advertisers, the *Fortune* piece noted that "only *Forbes* systematically allows advertising executives to see stories—and command changes—before they run."

This pay-to-play approach to financial journalism didn't exactly bode well, it's true, for entrusting Forbes with the power to make tough calls on corporate accountability in shaping policy via pivotal appointments at the Federal Reserve or the Securities and Exchange Commission. No less troubling were his ties, via senior campaign adviser Tom Ellis, to the openly racist Pioneer Fund, which had been established in the 1930s by textile magnate Wickliffe Draper, a Nazi sympathizer keen to fund writing and research purporting to demonstrate the genetic superiority of white Anglo-Saxons. Ellis was a former director of the fund in the 1970s and clearly helped ensure that it hewed closely to Draper's aims by issuing grants to Holocaust deniers, to racist college professors, and to the research study that eventually was published as *The Bell Curve*, Richard J. Herrnstein and Charles Murray's discredited 1994 genetic account of alleged black intelligence deficits. While there's no evidence that Forbes himself holds racist or anti-Semitic views, he clearly knew of Ellis's affiliation with the fund. In 1983 Forbes sat alongside Ellis as a Senate committee grilled him on the Pioneer Fund's activities while both men were being confirmed as Reagan appointees to the Board of International Broadcasting, the body that oversees Radio Free Europe and other US propaganda operations. Ellis was forced to withdraw as a nominee over his Pioneer Fund affiliation, but Forbes won his appointment and proceeded to help supervise one of the most corrupt and crony-ridden chapters in the board's history.[3]

Lesser men might have been chastened, or even humbled, by such bruising tours in the public arena. But Forbes's unique brand of wall-eyed hubris cannot be dispatched so easily. He's recently taken to increasing his profile as a publicist of unvarnished free-market idolatry, enlisting co-authors to draft books under his byline that extol the alleged classical virtues of great-man management and ballyhoo unregulated supply-side capitalism as the panacea for a global economic crisis created largely by unregulated supply-side capitalism. He's also flirting openly with Tea Party–branded social conservatism, opening the pages of *Forbes* in 2009 to a roster of creationist contributors and endorsing the insurgent Tea Party Senate candidacies of Marco Rubio in Florida and Rand Paul in Kentucky.[4] Forbes is also on the board of Dick Armey's FreedomWorks lobbying concern, which has furnished a great deal of early financial, organizational, and logistical support to Tea Party protests.

For Forbes, the Tea Party is clearly the most convenient current repository for his uniquely addled brand of free-market dogma. In his most recent book-like object, *How Capitalism Will Save Us*, Forbes and his co-author Elizabeth Ames make a game effort to claim just about every technological innovation of the past thirty-odd years as a direct outgrowth of Reagan-era tax cuts. "The turmoil of the past few years by no means mitigates the explosion of prosperity that has taken place since the early 1980s, when President Ronald Reagan enacted promarket reforms to free the economy from the Carter-Nixon stagnation of the 1970s," they write in a typically misleading thumbnail portrait of recent economic history. But wait, there's more: "Those reforms—lowering tax rates and loosening regulations—unleashed job-creating capital. The result: a roaring economy that produced a flood of innovations—from personal computers and cellular phones to the Internet. Indeed, we may one day look back on the period of 1982 to 2007 as an economic golden age. Many conveniences we take for granted today—from automatic teller machines and DVD players to home computers and CAT scans—did not exist or were not widely used as recently as the 1970s and early '80s."[5]

Never mind that most of these products were in development long before Reagan ever cocked his head backward confidently from his debate lectern to proclaim government was the problem, not the solution (an aphorism that, of course, never prevented government from continuing to grow during the deficit-happy Reagan years). Never mind, in addition, that the chief defining innovation of our age—the glorious Internet—was entirely funded in its crucial development stages on the taxpayer's dime, as a product of the Defense Advanced Research Projects Agency.

Consider instead the simple truth that the bulk of Reagan deregulatory and tax-cutting policy didn't benefit scientific research and development efforts—the long-term outlays of capital indispensable to produce breakthrough technologies—in either the public or private sector. The leveraged buyout craze fueled by the deregulation of the financial sector and the dramatic Reagan-era reductions in corporate tax rates claimed company R&D divisions as a principal casualty. As Haynes Johnson writes in his chronicle of the Reagan years,

Sleepwalking Through History, since most new company owners were financing their takeover bids with low-interest loans, "They sold or eliminated entire divisions. Among the first to be cut were industrial research laboratories producing basic corporate research and development for the future. They produced no current income, so they went."[6] Johnson cites a National Science Foundation study of the corporate R&D spending in the 1980s finding that "in the first half of the decade R&D expenditures had increased by 5.5 percent. In the closing years of the decade those expenditures were more than cut in half."[7] Nor was government R&D funding taking up the slack. During Reagan's second term, federal spending accounted for less than half of overall R&D expenditures for the first time since 1953.[8]

The only case one could make for the Reagan administration as an engine of innovation might be the argument that inventors felt an especially urgent need to rush their innovations out the door before their grants were cut, or their host company carved into bits by an S&L-financed arbitrageur. Yet this is the capstone argument Forbes and Ames advance in favor of unregulated free-market policymaking. Their other central talking points are that the global mortgage meltdown was chiefly the handiwork of "government-created behemoths Fannie Mae and Freddie Mac" and the outlandishly high costs of health care are due mainly to "the mammoth impact of government insurers Medicare and Medicaid."[9]

Both claims are equally delusional, but, to start at the beginning, just examine the carefully worded appositive for the Fannie and Freddie "behemoths"—they are "government-created" in Forbes and Ames's telling. This is technically true because they are in fact government-created private-sector enterprises tasked with showing a profit at the time of the 2008 collapse. (Like many other firms brought to the brink then, they are now in government receivership.) The two agencies are, in the official Washington argot, "government-sponsored entities"—that is, created by federal statutory authority, but operating on the same market playing field as other lending concerns.

It's true that part of their statutory mission is to consolidate home-owners' debt so as to keep lending costs affordable. But that mission just means that as the crisis plunged to rock bottom, Fannie and Freddie were holding disproportionate amounts of lousy scrip. This made it easy for lazy propagandists to shriek that the mortgage mess was all their sinister doing, a claim about as logically persuasive as fingering Poland as the cause of the Second World War.

Meanwhile, the claim that Medicare and Medicaid are the principal authors of the crisis in health-care affordability is so manifestly ludicrous that even congressional Republicans have stopped trying to make it. While GOP opponents of the 2010 health-care reform law used its proposed Medicare cuts as a convenient political cudgel to frighten senior voters into opposing the plan, they nevertheless also wound up conceding in the process what has long been an evident political and economic truth—that government insurance is an efficient way of securing affordable health care for Americans of limited means, such as Medicare recipients. In fact, the covert bid to gradually privatize the program within the 2005 Bush administration Medicare reform law winds up making that point with admirable clarity. "Medicare Advantage," a pet project of free-market GOP ideologues that compels providers of the plan to purchase coverage for the elderly from private insurers, has driven prices 14 percent higher than publicly funded Medicare plans, and so came in for more than $150 billion in cuts under the 2010 reform law.

One is tempted to reply to Forbes's economic broadsides by paraphrasing the words that famously goaded Lillian Hellman into suing Mary McCarthy: Every word he writes on the subject is a lie, including "and" and "the." But that's precisely why the empiricism-challenged, woolly-minded, politically manipulative mogul is the perfect symbol for our age. He's never had to hold down a real job. He preaches the unassailable virtues of the sovereign free market from a media platform he controls by virtue of inheritance. He successfully packages corporate propaganda to flatter the self-image of the highest bidder;

he defines contradictory evidence out of the picture in pursuing a blinkered dogmatic worldview; and he's none too careful about the kind of bigoted company he keeps. If we can't anoint Goldman Sachs's Lloyd Blankfein for the role on grounds of his awkward brushes with the law and public infamy, and if Countrywide's erstwhile high-rolling CEO Angelo Mozilo isn't available for much the same reason, then Forbes should plainly be elected—for something, at last.

Rich People Thing No. 25

ALAN GREENSPAN

Of all the spectacular falls from grace we've witnessed in American public life, Alan Greenspan may be in for one of the greatest in modern memory. Back when the markets ruled all, the Reagan-appointed former head of the Federal Reserve was treated as their unparalleled seer during his nearly two-decade tenure. Once touted as "The Maestro" of the US economy by no less a practiced sycophant than Bob Woodward, and the subject of countless adoring financial columns and magazine profiles, Greenspan is now openly derided as the great enabler of the 2008 mortgage meltdown.

And the evidence is quite damning. As his tenure was winding down in 2006, Americans were showing a negative savings rate—the first time the country passed this milestone since an epidemic of bank failures crippled the financial system in 1933. Fueling this casino-style debt binge was the hectic overvaluation of housing prices—which made it seem not only worthwhile, but also downright savvy, for mortgage holders to take out second and third loans on their mortgage nest eggs.

This was not mere coincidence. "If anyone could be held directly and immediately responsible for the record level of America's foreign and domestic debts, it was Alan Greenspan," write Bill Bonner and Addison Wiggin in *Empire of Debt*.[1] While the Fed chairman raised hawkish alarms about the prospective increase of federal indebtedness during the Clinton years, the Potemkin boom of the aughts had an intoxicating effect on the man's policy thinking. In early 2004, he urged US homeowners to take out adjustable rate mortgages (ARMs), since "overall, the household sector seems to be in good shape," and "American consumers might benefit if lenders provided greater mortgage product alternatives to the traditional fixed-rate mortgage."[2] ARMs are now the gruesomely efficient delivery systems of toxic debt stoking the great wave of foreclosures across the country as American consumers learn to their woe that the mortgage-fueled engorgement of the US economy was not to their benefit at all.

Greenspan's daft 2004 pronouncement sealed the debt-binging turn that began when Greenspan essentially said "oh, what the hell" and decided to anoint the first Bush tax cuts of 2001, even though there was nothing on offer in the Bush economic program that remotely resembled the fiscal discipline the Fed chairman extracted from the Clinton White House. And as the government swooned into a sea of red ink, so went the American consumer in its wake. Mortgage debt increased from $6 trillion in 1999 to more than $9 trillion in 2005.[3] Average household debt levels increased nearly fourfold between the start of Greenspan's tenure in 1987 through 2005—from $28,892 to $101,386.[4] As Stephen S. Roach, one of the only economists prescient enough at the time to see the calamity ahead, noted back in 2005, "over the last four years, debt accumulated by US families was 60 percent larger than overall US economic growth."[5]

Roach also noted that the debt explosion helped mask the anemic nature of the real economy's "recovery" in the wake of the 2001–02 recession—a recovery that looked more like a sick joke to most working Americans. "Lacking in job creation and real wage growth, private sector real wage and salary disbursements have increased a mere 4 percent over the first 37 months of this recovery—fully ten percentage points short of the average gains of more than 14 percent that occurred over the five preceding cyclical upturns. Yet consumers didn't flinch in the face of what in the past would have been a major impediment to spending. Spurred on by home equity extraction and Bush administration tax cuts, income-short households pushed the consumption share of US GDP up to a record 71.1 percent in early 2003 (and still 70.7 percent in 4Q04)—an unprecedented breakout from the 67 percent norm that had prevailed over the 1975 to 2000 period."[6]

Throughout all these worrisome trends, Greenspan looked placidly on and did nothing. Waving away concerns about a building mortgage bubble in 2003, he announced that the mortgage market was insulated from the "type of buying and selling frenzy that often characterizes bubbles in the financial markets." He added that since "there is no national housing market in the United States," a bubble, should one occur, would be confined to regional economies: "Home prices in Portland, Maine, do not arbitrage those in Portland, Oregon. Thus any bubbles that might emerge would tend to be local, not national, in scope." Home prices looked to be on course "to rise relative to the general price level in this country"—and so, joy of joys, "a sharp decline, the consequences of a bursting bubble, seems most unlikely."[7]

You don't say. In part, Greenspan was able to peddle this bald fiction by virtue of an obscure technical manipulation of housing data: The Fed uses the outmoded "Owners Equivalent Rent" measure of home values in computing the Consumer Price Index. But one side effect of a housing bubble is that it keeps rental prices artificially low—a natural result of more money flowing into the real estate market. Using the more accurate Case-Schiller measure of home values, the Fed would have noticed a huge discrepancy between home valuations and the overall Fed Funds Rate—8 percent and 4 percent, respectively, at the height of the bubble in 2005.[8]

Greenspan's oversight clearly partook of a more fundamental and ideological blindness. A former editor of the Randian *Objectivist Newsletter*, Greenspan stubbornly hewed to the quasi-libertarian conviction that markets possessed a near-mystic capacity for self-regulation. Hence his Fed heartily endorsed the central Clinton-era measures deregulating the mortgage and financial markets—the 1999 Gramm-Leach-Bliley Act repeal of the Glass-Steagall Act erecting strict industry firewalls between commercial and investment banking, and the 2000 Commodity Futures Modernization Act, which loosed the surly regulatory bonds on the over-the-counter derivatives market and thereby unleashed a new era of securitized mortgage debt, via collateralized debt obligations and credit default swaps. As he later confessed to the House Committee on Government Oversight and Government Reform, Greenspan "found a flaw" in his operating assumptions about the organic capacity of markets to rein in their own excesses. "I don't know how significant or permanent it is. But I'm very distressed by that fact."[9]

"Those of us who have looked to the self-interest of lending institutions to protect shareholders' equity, myself included, are in a shocked state of disbelief" in the wake of the epic 2008 collapse, he admitted.[10] They shouldn't have been. For one thing, Greenspan's Fed regularly heard the pleas of community activists from inner-city neighborhoods desperately trying to get the agency to curb the explosion in abusive subprime lending practices they were seeing on the ground. Just as regularly, Fed officials ignored the appeals. "Under a policy quietly formalized in 1998," writes *Washington Post* reporter Binyamin Appelbaum, "the Fed refused to police lenders' compliance with federal laws protecting borrowers, despite repeated urging by consumer activists across the country, and even by other government agencies."[11] Greenspan defended this look-the-other-way posture by claiming subprime oversight would be too complicated a regulatory undertaking and by asserting that the Fed's involvement might give borrowers a false sense of security. The latter claim is laughable on two levels. Greenspan was plainly envisioning a cursory-sounding approach to oversight at best. More fundamentally, the Fed chairman seemed to tacitly concede that the subprime market was on shaky ground if he was worrying that his agency's imprimatur was supposedly going to prop up a suspect business model.

Nevertheless, in the cult of the Greenspan Fed, when the Maestro speaks, policy is settled, and so the toxic subprime concatenation of non-banks, bank affiliates, and assorted other mortgage operators kept shoveling subprime loans into the maw of the securitized debt industry without benefit of any meaningful federal oversight.

The subprime fiasco was just one of countless opportunities to intervene that Greenspan's Fed declined to follow up on. Greenspan's successor Ben Bernanke professed astonishment that so many banks that began failing in 2007 had been backed by the Federal Deposit Insurance Corporation, which is supposed to limit risk exposure in the banking industry by enforcing minimal capitalization requirements to cover outstanding loans and debt obligations. But in reality, Fed banking overseers weren't able to discern when such institutions ventured too far into risky subprime markets—again, because they declined to pursue independent reviews as "a matter of philosophy," Appelbaum reports. "Rather than scrutinize banks directly, the Fed decided to push them to appoint internal risk managers who imposed their own checks and balances. Regulators focused on watching the watchmen." As Greenspan "put it bluntly in 1994, self-regulation was increasingly necessary 'largely because government regulators cannot do that job.' "[12]

Greenspan toed the same dogmatically antiregulatory line on derivatives trading, even as market boosters such as Warren Buffett were raising alarms about the speculative harm they could do. In 2002, when the Senate was weighing whether to enact some modest curbs on the frontier-style derivatives market created by the 2000 deregulation law, Greenspan rushed to join forces with Bush White House economic officials to smite the notion. Derivatives, they explained in their joint letter to the Senate, "have been a major contributor to our economy's ability to respond to the stresses and challenges of the past two years," so it stood to reason that any regulatory effort to tamp down their lubricating wonderment could increase "the vulnerability of our economy to potential future stresses."[13]

Greenspan and his chorus of Bush allies were even more adamant the following year, when a similar proposal was floated again in the Senate. Look here, the letter said: "Businesses, financial institutions and investors throughout the economy rely on derivatives to protect themselves from market volatility triggered by unexpected economic events. The ability to manage risks makes the economy more resilient, and its importance cannot be underestimated. In our judgment, the ability of private counterparty surveillance to effectively regulate these markets can be undermined by inappropriate extensions of government regulation."[14]

Greenspan's smitten view of the derivatives market is especially puzzling when one recalls how he was compelled to violate just about every sacrosanct Randian theory of how private markets should operate by orchestrating the 1998 bailout of the Long-Term Capital Management Fund, a hulking hedge fund undone by some truly lousy derivatives trades. That effort—which permanently introduced "Too Big To Fail" into the lexicon of our political economy—should have provided the opportunity for even a confirmed free-market ideologue like Greenspan to engage in a bit of long-overdue introspection. Perhaps, after all, the purveyors of instruments all but synonymous with financial risk aren't the best candidates for eliminating dangerous volumes of that risk from financial markets. But quite to the contrary, writes Roger Lowenstein in his excellent chronicle of the LTCM debacle, *When Genius Failed*: "Greenspan's more consistent and longer-running error has been to consistently shrug off the need for regulation and better disclosure with regard to derivatives products. Deluded as to the banks' ability to police themselves before the crisis, Greenspan called for a less burdensome regulatory regime six months after it. His Neolithic opposition to enhanced disclosure— which, because it allows investors to be their own watchdogs, is ever the best friend of free capital markets—served to remind one of the early Greenspan who (in thrall to Ayn Rand) once wrote, 'The basis of regulation is armed force.' "[15]

Indeed, Lowenstein writes further, "If the Long-Term episode proved anything, it is that the system of disclosure that worked so well with regard to traditional securities has *not* been able to do the job with respect to derivatives contracts. To put it plainly, investors have a pretty good idea about balance-sheet risks; they are completely befuddled with regard to derivatives risks . . . . Why, then, does Greenspan endorse a system in which banks can rack up any amount of exposure that they choose—so long as that exposure is in the form of derivatives?"[16]

As Lowenstein well knows, the only real answer to that question is the terse little Randian shibboleth he quoted earlier: The basis of regulation is armed force. When we grant ultimate economic authority to someone with that harebrained notion rattling around in his head, we shouldn't be surprised by anything—except, perhaps, by a journalistic-political culture that dubs him a maestro.

Rich People Thing No. 26

THE SPORTING LIFE

There are few articles more treasured in the American civic faith than the notion that competitive sports build character. Major sporting leagues teach their youthful fan base invaluable lessons about the quest for individual excellence, the virtues of self-discipline, and respect for one's adversaries on the field of competition. And individual sports heroes serve—whether they want to or not—as role models for their young fans, yardsticks against which they can measure their own achievements and still-developing characters.

Well. It's scarcely shocking, at this advanced stage of our decadent sports culture, to report that all these sturdy virtues have been systematically hollowed out from the contemporary sports experience to make way for an avalanche of cash. The players still give their all (often with some selective pharmaceutical enhancements); fans still hotly debate individual and team performance records; host cities still go through the motions of home-team boosterism—replete with gargantuan, publicly funded stadium giveaway deals. But the modern sporting franchise is above all a rich person's plaything—from the upward spiraling superstar salaries and ticket prices to the merchandising deals to the elite skybox culture of the only fan base remotely equipped to support such excess over the long haul.

The vulgar materialist view of professional sports has long been that they are bread-and-circus spectacles, another in the long line of sinister plutocratic distractions cooked up to keep the toiling masses pacified and docile. But that view of things makes no allowance for the far more universal and insidious reach of the sports-merchandising complex—and for the way that modern sports faithfully mirror the crony-capitalist model of virtually every other financial and commercial fiefdom in the bailed-out American economic scene. Far from claiming the leading edge in elevating the virtues of individual achievement and teamwork, sports are now little more than a lagging repository of cash in a deeply entitled culture of moneyed vanity.

The scandal of professional sport is by now an everyday feature of the news cycle, so much so that the scale of the thing simply fails to register with most casual followers. Whether it's the heroically adulterous exploits of Tiger Woods, the date rape allegations against Ben Roethlisberger, the pay-to-play graft showered on supposed amateur college athletes like former Heisman football standout Reggie Bush, or the numbing march of reports of steroid and human-growth-hormone abuse among once-glorified baseball stars, athletic distinction now serves as a kind of a parodic gloss on the gospel of American success. The idea is no longer to test one's character against the standard set in a long tradition of impersonal contests of glory and excellence, but rather to cash in to the maximum degree on the fat years of one's playing careers.

In this respect, the pharmaceutical enhancement of individual performance is an entirely rational economic decision, promising to boost an athlete's earning potential by tens of millions of dollars a year. In professional baseball—the sport with the deepest and most damaging tradition of steroid abuse—the sport's staggeringly corrupt and conflicted commissioner Bud Selig (the first former franchise owner to serve as commissioner, and certainly the only major sports commissioner to take office after arranging a palace coup to oust his predecessor, Fay Vincent, for pursuing charges of collusion pertaining to Selig and his team, the Milwaukee Brewers) essentially instituted a "don't ask, don't tell" approach to the performance-enhancing drug (PED) epidemic until Congress forced his hand with its 2005 hearings into the steroid scandal.

As Larry Starr, a thirty-year veteran Major League Baseball trainer, recalled, the question of widespread PED abuse first surfaced in the late 1980s, when Selig had just begun his tenure as commissioner. "At one of those [offseason] meetings, a team physician stood up and said, 'We have a problem, and the problem has to do with possible drugs that are being used by athletes and players, and the only way we can deal with this problem is through testing,' " Starr told ESPN reporter T. J. Quinn. "The basic feedback from that meeting and subsequent meetings for a number of years after that was, from the owner's group, 'We agree: We need to do testing. But the Players Association won't let us.' Players Association would say, 'We agree: Most of my members would say testing would be fine, but we don't trust the owners.' "[1]

In truth, neither constituency felt any strong incentive to force the issue, since chemically enhanced performance juiced up baseball's box-office draw—particularly after the 1994 players' strike, which grew out of still more collusive intransigence from Selig's client base of owner-cronies, badly damaged the popular appeal of America's pastime. PEDs were technically illegal if obtained without a prescription, but they weren't formally barred by the MLB's collective bargaining agreement. So players and owners did what the sports ethos of the age dictated: They followed the money.

This litany of venal abuse—which can be repeated, with mild variations, in every other major American sports league—excites no great public outcry largely because no one really believes any longer that a professional athletic career unfolds without a heavy outlay of graft and cheating. The best hope for unsullied sporting competition, the broad consensus holds, is the integrity of amateur competition—the kind of ideals upheld in the Olympic Games.

The international Olympiad is indeed held forth as the last best hope for the spirit of true athletic competition. It's not merely a venue where the triumph of meritocratic virtue is foreordained, so the story goes, but also a forum for international rivalry promoting broader peace and understanding among the nations. Every four years, the Summer Olympic Games captivate the world's attention, as amateur athletes congregate to test their mettle before impartial judging panels. If this event can't serve as the limit-case of sporting excellence, then all is lost.

Well, in that event, prepare to kiss it all good-bye. Since the modern Olympics recovered from its own PR debacle—the US-boycotted Moscow Games of 1980—the chief benefactor of the International Olympic Committee (IOC), Adidas mogul Horst Dassler, fatally set about reinventing the spectacle as a great sluice for broadcasting, endorsement, and merchandising revenues. And to bring the Olympics tradition into its internationally branded prime, he recruited Juan Antonio Samaranch, a loyalist to the bitter end of Francisco Franco's fascist government, who'd successfully lobbied to get Spain to break the Western boycott of the 1980 Games while serving as Spain's ambassador to Moscow. The new secretary general of the IOC was apparently the sort of official who—as it was famously said of Maurice Chevalier—would sing for whatever troops happened to be in town.

As such, Samaranch used the perquisites of his office to reward like-minded world leaders. He bestowed the coveted honor of the Olympic Order not only on his chief corporate sponsor Dassler, but also on Romania's murderous former President Nicolae Ceausescu and onetime South Korean President Roh Tae-woo, who led the infamous 1980 Kwangju Massacre that killed nearly 200 students in Seoul and was a chief bagman in a $650 million corruption scheme that eventually landed him in jail.

Samaranch stocked the directorate of the IOC with just about every sort of corrupt government official on offer—a bitter kind of mockery of the uplifting brotherhood-of-man propaganda trotted out for every quadrennial Summer Games competition. To take but one especially gaudy example, Anwar Chowdhry, the Pakistani head of the IOC's Boxing Commission, presided over the now-notorious

1988 Seoul contest where Park Si Hun was awarded the gold medal over American boxer Roy Jones, who had landed eighty-six punches compared to Hun's mere thirty-two. The judging was so clearly mishandled that Hun pronounced himself "ashamed" by the outcome, and lifted Jones in the air after the bout to signal that the American was the rightful winner. (Muckraking British journalist Andrew Jennings, who has furnished most of this edifying detail in his trio of books on the Olympics spectacle, has since uncovered evidence in the East German Stasi archives that a Korean millionaire had paid the judging panel to fix the bout on Hun's behalf.[2]) Chowdhry's crew pulled essentially the same stunt in the 1999 off-year Havana competition, denying the title to the clearly victorious Cuban light featherweight Juan Hernandez, triggering the first protest walkout by a national team in Olympic history. (Hernandez was later given the title, and four of the panel's judges were suspended for "gross and blatant divergences.")[3]

Samaranch retired in 2001 and died in 2010, but his appointees still make up 70 of the 112 sitting members of the IOC, by Jennings's count.[4] And they are notoriously alert touches for bribes from city officials desperate to host the Games—more than $1 million went into the pockets of 24 IOC members from the organizers of the Salt Lake City Winter 2002 bid alone. Samaranch's personal assistant had the civic boosters of Anchorage, Alaska, hire on Samaranch's son for a $120,000 "bid consultant" fee, even as the enterprising lad was on the payroll for other cities bidding for the IOC's favors, according to former *Anchorage Daily News* reporter David Postman.[5]

Generous amounts of boodle earmarked for the IOC elite are written into the already-bloated budgets that the successful host city produces to host the heaving media spectacle. Prior to the 2000 Sydney Summer Games, no less than $47 million was set aside to provide some 4,000 senior Olympic officials—the IOC and their families, along with National Olympic Committees' retinues and various other favored officials—with a fleet of 1,800 limousines. When the deal became public, that armada was downgraded to a contingent of loaned vehicles from an area Mercedes dealership.[6] It's sobering to consider the degree to which the present debt crisis in Greece was compounded by the $12.8 billion Athens paid for the dubious privilege of hosting the 2004 Summer Games. The next summer host city, London, is already on the hook for some $17.6 billion—a fourfold increase from the amount projected when it won the bid in 2005, and a total that's almost certain to keep ballooning as the opening ceremony draws near. (Moreover, that sum presumably doesn't include the reserve of extra-official bribes that a BBC film crew exposed when they posed as business consultants tendering bribe offers to representatives of IOC members.[7])

Samaranch's successor, former Belgian IOC member Jacques Rogge, has pledged to move beyond the committee's fragrant past. He got off to a rocky start, however, when his vice president—another gloriously corrupt Samaranch recruit from South Korea named Kim Un-Yong—was forced to resign his post in 2004 in order to serve a prison sentence on embezzlement charges in his home country. The disgraced vice president was notorious in Olympic circles for arranging performances for his daughter, an aspiring classical pianist, in host cities for the games. The young musician's concert CV doubles as a travelogue of recent Olympic glory, with gigs in Salt Lake City, Melbourne, Atlanta, and Sydney to her credit.[8] It's hard to see how to reform an Olympic regime that has all but enshrined the principle of open graft in soliciting multiple bids from aspiring host cities in the first place. It's true that Rogge has forbidden IOC members to visit cities in contention, and has inaugurated public presentations to the members en masse in a neutral location. But it's also true that Spain's seat on the IOC is now occupied by one Juan Samaranch Jr.

In global amateur competitions, as well as their far gaudier professional US counterparts, all you have to do to chart the triumph of the money culture is to follow the bouncing ball.

Rich People Thing No. 27

FRANK GEHRY

Even before becoming the object of Ayn Rand's unseemly affections, the figure of the modern architect was a key culture hero of capitalist enterprise. Here, after all, was someone who hewed a primal vision of urban economic achievement out of the raw materials of the earth, stamping the very skyline with monuments to corporate-mogul vanity. Okay, so maybe Philip Johnson had a soft spot for the Nazis; so Washington's landmark Watergate complex was designed by the unrepentant Mussolini toady Luigi Moretti. Artists have always had their quirks, and these were just the passionate excesses we had to tolerate so as to be graced with the visions of our great modernist masters of concrete, steel, and granite.

Nevertheless, these were the architectural strongmen of the last century. The more improvisational, just-in-time ethos of information-age capitalism now calls for a different sort of architectural overlord— someone who combines the laid-back mien of our digitized culture industry with the imperial self-regard of a new global knowledge elite. It requires, in other words, LA's great impresario of the folded building, Frank Gehry.

Gehry is a slouchy Howard Roark of the postindustrial era, favoring black T-shirts and jeans and cultivating a suitably *Wired*-inflected image of himself as a perennial outsider, tweaking the taste establishments and upending the ossified hierarchies of his profession. "Whatever this fame thing is, it's only come in the last 15 years," Gehry announced to *Departures* magazine scribe Raul Bereneche, in one of the countless adoring Gehry profiles that glossy monthlies order up with the same monotonous regularity that explosions stud Michael Bay films. "And because it happened late in life, I don't believe in it. It's not real to me. It's nice when people ask for my autograph, but I'm still Joe Schlepper." Summing up a recent project—a Miami arts center commissioned by New World Symphony director Michael Tilson-Thomas, consisting of overlapping rehearsal rooms and performance area, flanked by an outdoor video projection facility—Gehry again sounds a demotic refrain. "It's not about getting all dressed up to go to the Philharmonic. People can drift over with their Bellinis or whatever. Artistically it's exquisite and impeccable, but from the user standpoint it's cozy and accessible." There is, of course, a world of presumption in this rumpled celebration of the casual bourgeois spectator—and not a little condescension, for someone calling himself Joe Schlepper. In this vision of how his work communicates to its public, beauty isn't a sublime or edifying experience, but a comforting spectacle, a Bellini-fueled foray into a "cozy and accessible" space designed to flatter a cultured boulevardier's taste preferences. And it's best that way, apparently, since not even Gehry's clients can be counted on to grasp the hectic import of the aesthetic statements they're paying top dollar for. "I'm taking your language [and] making it into something better," Gehry says he tells clients. "I'm taking your junk and making something with it."[1]

The great triumph of the Gehry aesthetic is, of course, the Guggenheim museum he erected in the Basque city of Bilbao. The Bilbao project has received every imaginable architectural laurel, and was recently named the greatest building of the past thirty years by a panel of architects polled in *Vanity Fair*. And in formal terms, the Bilbao structure is indeed impressive—a titanium-wrapped, kinetic explosion of shiny silver and glass on an expanse of waterfront that's been variously likened to a fish, a floral invasion, a tower of Babel, and a resurrected Marilyn Monroe.

But while Gehry's Bilbao is something of a real-world infomercial for the shock of the new, it's also difficult to overlook the broader civic vacuum that it occupies. It's true that postmodern expression in all fields has drifted steadily away from nonironic use values, but it's also true that architecture, by definition, possesses a unique public dimension; the end-product of any given architectural vision is a structure that people will inhabit, work in, and come to incorporate—for better or worse—into their own sense of urban place. As that cranky modernist Louis Sullivan famously insisted, form follows function, and amid all the hosannas lavished on Gehry's work, it's fair to ask what purpose a Gehry building really serves.

In this regard, the Bilbao project is a perfect summation of the Gehry problem. Shortly after its debut in 1997, the structure inspired critics and theorists to enthuse over "the Bilbao effect"—the strategy of using superstar architects and sculptors to reconfigure a central building project and thereby revive a hard-luck city's economic fortunes. The theory, roughly speaking, is to adapt the economic model of the destination wedding to urban revival—create lavishly praised, high-concept structures in decaying industrial cities, and presto: A rising titanium tide will lift all boats.

But the feverishly hyped "Bilbao effect" has always been something of a mirage, even in Bilbao itself. A long-depressed former mining center and seaport, the Basque capital spent the last half of the twentieth century losing population and fending off brutal political violence of the ETA, the terrorist group spearheading the Basque separatist movement. (Indeed, the ETA famously agreed to a year-and-a-half truce in its terrorist campaign so as to enable the Guggenheim project to be completed on schedule.) The city's political leaders endorsed the Guggenheim project in the late 1980s, as part of an ambitious citywide facelift, including a new subway system, an airport and several other freshly commissioned public structures, all designed by marquee names on the international architecture scene. The roughly $100 million Guggenheim project translated into less than 10 percent of the city's dramatic $1.5 billion overhaul. And while the museum has proved itself a major tourist draw, Bilbao's concerted and costly civic overhaul—paid for chiefly from the city's public fund—is what's kept visitors returning. No less an authority than Gehry himself has pronounced the Bilbao effect "a bunch of bullshit," again stressing the far more comprehensive makeover of the city's infrastructure.[2]

But amid all the Bilbao hype, a far more fundamental feature of the Gehry aesthetic has gone unnoticed: Its historic alignment *against* the idea of an inclusive public sphere in the first place. As Gehry was building his reputation in Los Angeles with a series of big quasi-civic contracts, this motif was hard to overlook—though of course most of his adoring champions in the architecture world did just that. In *City of Quartz,* his chronicle of the gradual "militarization" of LA's built environment, Mike Davis noted Gehry's curious contribution to the process: "a nostalgic evocation of revolutionary constructivism and a mercenary celebration of bourgeois-decadent minimalism."[3] For Davis, the signature Gehry project is Hollywood's Frances Howard Goldwyn Regional Branch Library, which resembles a prison guard tower more than a book depository; as Davis notes, it draws many of its core design elements from Gehry's high-security design for the US Chancellery in Damascus. Boasting fifteen-foot concrete stucco exterior walls, the library is fortified by anti-graffiti barricades of ceramic tile, ten-foot steel stacks and a pair of sentry boxes flanking the sunken entrances. Since arsonists destroyed an earlier version of the library, the new structure's backers in the Goldwyn Foundation placed a premium on "vandalproof" and security-conscious design that Davis properly describes in clinical terms: "The Goldwyn Library relentlessly interpellates a demonic Other (arsonist, graffitist, invader) whom it reflects back on surrounding streets and street people. It coldly saturates its immediate environment, which is seedy but not particularly hostile, with its own arrogant paranoia."[4]

The economic power of the "Bilbao effect" is debatable, but the social message of the Goldwyn Library—what might be called the "Angeleno Gehry effect"—is quite straightforward. And, as Davis notes, the rallying cry it represents for the private developer is much more stirring than all the loose talk of adopting accordian-style museum plans as the new model of twenty-first-century urban revival. Hollywood developers have expertly gamed eminent domain laws to ramp up block-busting projects that have forced Central American immigrants out of the neighborhood surrounding the Goldwyn project in order to brand the neighborhood more effectively as— you guessed it—a destination for international cultural tourists. As Davis observes, the economic logic here is very much the photographic negative of the sort of public-private cooperation that city boosters cheerily hail in their high-Bilbao reveries: "Within this strategy, the Goldwyn Library is a kind of architectural fire-base, a beachhead for gentrification. Its soaring, light-filled interiors surrounded by bellicose barricades speak volumes about how public architecture is literally being turned inside out, in the service of 'security' and profit."[5]

And now that Gehry is a bona fide, Bilbao-branded superstar, that same shiny and brutalist dynamic has only gained further prominence in his portfolio—though again, with virtually no notice from the swoon-on-demand, developer-appeasing architectural press. Gehry was among the lead architects recruited for the now-infamous riot of postmodern construction on Saayidat Island, in the Arab oil fiefdom of Abu Dhabi. He is again working out another swooping titanium Guggenheim facility, though the project has been waylaid, along with a vast array of other superstar-branded works-in-progress in the oil-money resort, by Abu Dhabi's recent brush with bankruptcy.

Gehry's Abu Dhabi project certainly didn't involve any labor-related cost overruns. In a 2009 report, Human Rights Watch singled the

Guggenheim site among the Abu Dhabi projects guilty of "abuse and severe exploitation" of immigrant workers whom the feudal monarchy essentially treats as indentured labor, withholding their passports and assessing steep fines for nugatory—and in most cases, unofficiated and unproven—violations of workplace protocols. Workers on the Saayidat compound—named "The Island of Happiness" in a mordant monarchial jest—made an annual salary lower than $2,600, far below the kingdom's annual average $30,000 income. Employers also assessed steep company-store charges against staples like food and toiletries, so that by many accounts, laborers in the projects were unable to realize any savings, instead just working so as to retire the outstanding credit owed to their contract bosses. Workers are also denied transportation to central Abu Dhabi any day other than Friday, when the kingdom's Shari'a courts are closed, so they also toil without any mechanism of grievance—even though, as is the case with most victims of human trafficking, they were typically lured to their jobs on fraudulent grounds.[6]

Back on the stateside front, meanwhile, Gehry has lately been upgrading his urban-paranoid Angeleno aesthetic for New York consumption. In 2007, he unveiled a curved-yet-hulking glassy "tower of light" to serve as the New York headquarters for Barry Diller's IAC entertainment-industry complex. While critics hailed it as a triumph of "lightness" on the Manhattan skyline, IAC recapitulates the same hostility to integrated public use that stands out in Gehry's LA portfolio. Diller indeed commissioned the structure with the request that it resemble a yacht—or better yet, interlocking forms that "pull apart to suggest a hiked dress or gently parting legs," as Diller's 75-year-lease on the place stipulated.[7] The civic statement made by the IAC structure, in other words, was the same message that weary Manhattanites had been force-fed throughout the Bloomberg years: that their metropolis was being reconfigured into a theme park for the overlords of the finance and entertainment sectors.

That's also very much the message of Gehry's other major New

York commission, a nearly completed downtown skyscraper billed as the city's "tallest luxury residential tower." The upward-curving spires of the structure suggest the implacably upward flow of urban privilege in a sleek, reflective funnel cloud. It's the sort of vision that would warm the heart of even the most jaded Abu Dhabi royal—or inspire the devotion of the Wall Street brokers and bankers all casting their own rivulets of cash skyward, just around the corner from the Gehry tower's address at 8 Spruce Street.

Nevertheless, in the adulatory critical notice that must, seemingly by law, accompany the appearance of a new Gehry building, *New York Times* critic Nicolai Ouroussoff quite witlessly hailed the luxury settlement as a "stirring" embodiment of Gehry's message: "to reassert the individual's place within a larger social framework. [Gehry's] interest lies in the clashing voices that give cities their meaning; it is democratic at heart."[8]

Yet, as Ouroussoff goes on to explain in the body of the review, the luxury development—financed by real-esate mogul Bruce Ratner and formerly known as Beekman Place—sits awkwardly atop some public facilities, in a configuration dictated by Manhattan's political zoning wars. At the structure's base is a six-floor public school, decked out in standard-issue institutional orange, while a floor above is a hospital. In an unselfconsciously feudal disclaimer, Ouroussoff notes that in view of the social chasms separating the two divergent sets of tenants, "not surprisingly, the two groups won't be mixing. Residents will enter through a covered drive that cuts through the block along the building's western side. Framed by massive brick pillars and a glass-enclosed lobby, the space's generous proportions will accommodate taxis and limousines ferrying people in and out of the building, making it feel more like a luxury hotel than a classic Manhattan apartment building."

The "democratic" ethos at the project's "heart," in other words, clearly doesn't extend to the shuffling public-sector wards serving time in the classrooms downstairs. In a yet more obtuse aside that he evidently mistakes for humor, Ouroussoff writes that "Gehry did not design the interiors of the school, which is still under construction, and students may ask why the pampered young professionals living above them get to live in apartments designed by an architectural superstar."

In reality, of course, the students downstairs will likely simply be grateful to attend a school with a new physical plant that may not produce grotesque classroom overcrowding. And they'll probably count themselves lucky when they realize that, unlike many of their peers, they don't have to go to classes in a building still heated by a coal furnace. They're also unlikely to marvel at the handiwork of the "architectural superstar" in the apartments overhead, since they're likely to get apprehended and/or tasered before they come anywhere near the entrance to any of these posh high-rise residential units.

One can be forgiven, in the face of such disparities of access and wealth inscribed within the same architectural footprint, to greet Ouroussoff's burbling pronouncement that "the building's endlessly shifting surfaces are an attack against the kind of corporate standardization so evident in the buildings to the south and the conformity it embodied" with a hearty horse laugh. And one will likewise be well advised to take several deep breaths and probably a drink of water in the wake of the chortling fit certain to be brought on by this: "He aims, as he has throughout his career, to replace the anonymity of the assembly line with an architecture that can convey the infinite variety of urban life."

The expressive aims of "infinite variety" presented in a social context where "not surprisingly, the two groups won't be mixing" unwittingly sum up the remorseless class segmentation at the dark heart of Gehryism. Of course, the lords of finance tooling home in the limo lane at the rear of the school complex can afford to ponder life's capacious variety, and their very own soulful individuality at the foundation of it all—so long as they needn't mix with the publicly subsidized patients and students at the other end of the building. In this regard, the design of the great downtown residential tower makes perfect sense: Probably the most important lesson that public school kids can learn in downtown Manhattan is that they will never have a place in Frank Gehry's vision of New York.

Rich People Thing No. 28

THE SOCIAL MEDIA

For all the convulsive creative destruction that's supposed to besiege the American social scene, the basic myth of New World mobility is remarkably static. There is always an entrenched elite on the Eastern seaboard, and there is always an insurgent formation of brave new thinkers poised to topple the ancien regime's hold on the institutions of privilege. This was the story that the literary radicals of the 1920s told themselves as they overthrew the puritanical "genteel tradition" in American letters. It's also the story that Nicholas Lemann recounts in *The Big Test*, his history of Harvard's effort to topple its own old-money WASP hierarchy with the magical solvent of standardized testing. And it's the paint-by-numbers script of *The Social Network*, Aaron Sorkin's Oscar-winning cinematic fable of digital-media success.

In purporting to depict the origins of Facebook, the social-media empire that sprang from Mark Zuckerberg's tour at Harvard, Sorkin invented much of the script's dramatic interest from whole cloth, from the depiction of geek culture's innate sexism to the What-Makes-Sammy-Run schematics of Zuckerberg's character. The question of the movie's distinctly shabby fidelity to the narrative truth of Facebook's founding is ultimately far less interesting, however, than its echt-Hollywood conception of what makes for social ambition in the digital age. In Sorkin's version of the Facebook gospel, Zuckerberg (Jesse Eisenberg) is a fast-talking robo-geek programmed to upend established hierarchies—here twitting the university's disciplinary board, there outwitting the old-money Winkelvoss twins, and there again delivering impassioned defenses of his solitary genius during depositions in multiple lawsuits over the ownership of Facebook. At the same time, of course, like any other computer geek, he's perpetually scheming to belong—positioning himself for entry into one of the school's exclusive social clubs, smarting from the rejection of his freshman girlfriend, courting the hipper Silicon Valley favor of onetime Napster impresario Sean Parker. We are meant to savor the profound irony of the movie's closing "Rosebud" moment, when Zuckerberg declines a dinner invitation from the hard-charging and fetching intellectual property lawyer who's been deposing him to check the updates on his long-lost girlfriend's Facebook page. At the end of his long, upward-striving odyssey, the arch purveyor of social connectedness on the Web is as alone, and misunderstood, as ever. Insert sad-face emoticon here.

The curious thing about the rampant psychologizing of *The Social Network*'s protagonist, however, is that the movie takes the larger import of the Facebook revolution simply as a given: Zuckerberg could just as well be a commodities trader, or a meth dealer, or a high-flying ad executive. For all the film's breathless evocations of the ambiance of start-up business culture, all we see of the fabled social architecture of the Facebook site are some fleeting glimpses of code-crafting all-nighters, which typically segue into more cinematic debauches involving drugs, alcohol and very heavy petting.

In this regard, Sorkin's screenplay is entirely representative of the American consensus on the social-media revolution: It's a fixture of our online lives that exists without apparent acknowledgment of the work or social conflict that makes up either the offline world—or the mediated digital one itself. There's a weird circularity to the tacit logic of this asocial dispensation: Facebook is wildly popular because it simplifies our sense of digital connection—and we crave a constant sense of digital connection because we're on Facebook so very much of the time. Likewise, Twitter, the ubiquitous microblogging site, delivers an absurdly foreshortened version of human interaction— typically delivered in high-school classrooms, workplaces and super- market checkout lines—yet it's credited with all-but singlehandedly toppling authoritarian regimes in the Middle East. In the end, the social power we ascribe to social media says far less about the actual course of mass revolts abroad than it does about the privileged West- ern vision of social change—hatched in Harvard dorms and incubat- ed in venture-capital boardrooms rather than in the ranks of Tunisia's dissident community or Cairo's labor movement.

That's why Sorkin is so eager to frame *The Social Network* as a Harvard secession tale: Facebook *must* channel the inchoate urg- ings of the General Will—why, just look what it did to those snob- bish Winkelvoss twins, after all! But on closer inspection, the social network—either in its cinematic or quasi–real world incarnations— doesn't really have much of a social there there. What does it mean, really, to say, as Sean Parker's character giddily declares in the film, "We lived on farms, then we lived in cities, and now we're gonna live on the Internet"?

Well, among other things, it involves an enormous condescension toward people who continue to live in farms and cities—that is, the vast majority of the world's population. Nor is this an idle theoreti- cal objection: For all the ballyhooed use of Facebook as an organiz- ing tool in mass uprisings in Egypt and Tunisia, the site is just as frequently apt to close off access to social causes that it possesses no direct commercial stake in.

To take just one example, Zuckerberg's company pulled the plug on a group maintained by a Moroccan activist named Kacem El Ghaz- zali, which simply promoted discussion about secular education in the theocratic country. When El Ghazzali emailed site engineers back in the Facebook home offices in Palo Alto requesting an explanation, they deleted his own personal profile on the site for good measure. Eventually, a wave of adverse press attention in the West prompted

Facebook to relent and restore the education site—but El Ghazzali was left to painstakingly rebuild his own Facebook site on his own. And needless to say, there's no way of knowing how many other dissidents have faced similar commercial censorship from an Internet giant that has no rooting interest in disputes over free expression in countries that don't make up a significant share of its market. Hence, as Evgeny Morozov observes in his indispensable study, *The Net Delusion*, "contrary to the expectations of many Western policy makers, Facebook is hardly ideal for promoting democracy; its own logic, driven by profits or ignorance of the increasingly global context in which it operates is, at times, extremely undemocratic."[1]

The great premature Twitter revolution—the 2009 postelection protests in Iran—are also an instructive case study in the limited reach of Tweeted social upheaval, and the all-but inverse Western penchant to see our own preferred modes of digital activism in a distortion-mirror version of postcolonial revolt. Morozov, by contrast, patiently unpacks the ways that American Twitter champions ludicrously overestimated the technology's impact. Just over 19,000 Twitter accounts were registered in Iran prior to the uprising, he notes—meaning that roughly 0.027 percent of Iran's population could have plugged into the Twitterfied protests. What's more, many of those accounts belonged to expat Iranians, such as the blogger "oxfordgirl," who supplied crucial updates and aggregated news roundups on the protests—but from her perch in the British countryside.[2]

Many Westerners, though, were plugged into the events in Iran via Twitter, and the whole thing felt extremely significant to them—so much so, in fact, that a Bush administration undersecretary of state named Jared Cohen wrote to the social-media company's executives requesting that they postpone a scheduled site maintenance lapse in service so as to keep Iranian dissidents online at a critical juncture in the Tehran demonstrations. That was all that leaders in rival authoritarian states needed to hear in order to justify their own crackdowns on social media: Twitter may not have launched the anti-

Ahmadinejad rebellion, but in one fell diplomatic swoop, the world's dictators saw cause to repudiate it as a tool of the neoconservative Bush White House. This, Morozov writes, was "globalization at its worst: A simple email based on the premise that Twitter mattered in Iran, sent by an American diplomat in Washington to a parent company in San Francisco, triggered a worldwide Internet panic and politicized all online activity, painting it in bright revolutionary colors, and threatening to tighten online spaces and opportunities that were previously unregulated. . . . The pundits were right: Iran's Twitter Revolution did have global repercussions for authoritarian regimes everywhere. They were, however, far from positive."[3]

This is not, however, a distinction you're apt to encounter in the vast literature of cyberutopian theorizing about the social-media world. For a Net 2.0 prophet like Clay Shirky, the Iranian uprising was nothing less than "the big one . . . the first revolution that has been catapulted onto a global stage and transformed by global media.[4]

Such raving fits in perfectly with Shirky's totalizing argument that the capacity of social media to streamline global communication and upend former hierarchies of professional content generation means that digital media is always and everywhere a great democratizing engine of social generosity. As Shirky argues in his counterempirical tract *Cognitive Surplus*, the new information age has enabled the globe's population to pool its collective storehouse of free time—a shared social resource of nothing less than one trillion hours, he calculates—while the Web's ethos of free reproduction and publication means that the costs of social generosity has plummeted basically to zero. And so we have a magical new version of the social contract, Shirky insists—one that rewards virtue and charity, and punishes old-line hierarchies of reward and copyright in just the same way that Mark Zuckerberg sent the Winkelvii packing. "The ability for community members to speak to one another, out loud and in public, is a huge shift," Shirky writes, "and one that has value even in the absence of a way to filter for quality. It has value, indeed, *because* there is no way to filter for quality; the definition of quality becomes more variable from one community to the next than when there was broad consensus about mainstream writing (and music, and film, and so on)."[5] To drive this nonsensical point home, Shirky insists that the Web's lack of filtration is a virtue because it allows our truly generous natures, at last, to overcome the old pre-digital conceptions of self-interest as the root of all human behavior. As his prooftext, he cites a famous experiment in social psychology called "The Ultimatum Game," in which researchers give test subjects $10 and instruct them to strike a bargain to divide it between them. Rational self-interest would dictate that the chief bargainer keep $9 and give away the minimum $1 to keep his bargaining minimally appeased, but in test after test, the exchanges cluster in the center spread, since a 50-50 split seems more intuitively fair—even when the stakes in the experiment are raised tenfold, to $100. The inescapable conclusion, Shirky writes, is that, contra economic theory, markets and selfish behavior correlate

> in the opposite way you might expect. Markets support generous interactions with strangers rather than undermining them. What this means is that the less integrated market transactions are in a given society, the less generous its members will be to one another in anonymous interactions . . . exposure to market logic actually increases our willingness to transact generously with strangers, in part because that's how markets work.[6]

In classic Malcolm Gladwell fashion, Shirky tries to extend this dictum across a range of didactic vignettes drawn from digital culture. There are, naturally, the standard encomia to open-source computer-engineering collaborations such as the Linux operating system and the Apache server software. But he also finds stirring samples of digitally enabled generosity in a volunteer-run charity that sprang up on a Josh Groban fan discussion board, a vast online exchange of

J. K. Rowling–inspired fan fiction, and PickupPal.com, a site that began life by dispensing contact information for would-be Canadian carpoolers (which, wouldn't you know it, was the subject of an iron-fisted shutdown campaign from statist Ontario bus carriers).

What emerges from all these parables of the information marketplace is a vision of a gloriously uncoerced social order, all within reach of any suitably wired and enterprising soul inclined to donate some of that unfathomably huge surplus of time to this or that crowd-sourced task. This being the general drift of our social destiny, Shirky impatiently waves away the old-school leftist critique of crowd-sourced content as "digital sharecropping" as so much "professional jealousy—clearly professional media makers are upset about competition from amateurs." And what's more, such critics are guilty of a category error, since "amateurs' motivations differ from those of professionals." What if the dispensers of free user-generated content just "aren't workers?" Shirky asks. "What if they really are contributors, quite specifically intending their contributions to be acts of sharing rather than production? What if their labors are labors of love?"[7]

What, indeed? Well, let's retrace the argument a bit here. To back up to the original Ultimatum Game that furnishes the creation myth for so many of Shirky's trippy speculations, its basis for a new market-enabled theory of human nature thins out considerably when one realizes that the players are bartering with unearned money. They aren't dividing proceeds that "belong" to either player in any meaningful sense. All one has to do is consult virtually any news story following up on a lottery winner's post-windfall life —to say nothing of the well-chronicled implosion of the past decade's market in mortgage-backed securities—to realize that playing games with other people's money has a rather deranging effect on many human characters.

In this respect, the Ultimatum Game is an all-too-apt case study to bring to bear on the digital economy—but to paraphrase Shirky, in the opposite way that one might expect. For despite all the heady social theorizing of Shirky, Chris Anderson and the *Wired* set, the

Web has not, in fact, abolished the conventions of market value or rewritten the rules of productivity and worker reward. It has, rather, merely sent the rewards further down the fee stream. It's a sad truth that in Shirky's idealized market order, some people's time remains more valuable than others'—and as is the case in that gray old labor-based offline economy, the actual producers of content routinely get screwed.

As for the "labor of love" business—Shirky of course primly reminds us that the term *amateur* "derives from the Latin *amare*, 'to love' "[8]—the governing metaphor here wouldn't seem to be digital sharecropping so much as the digital plantation. For all too transparent reasons of guilt sublimation, patrician apologists for antebellum slavery also insisted that their uncompensated workers loved their work, and likewise embraced their overseers as virtual family members. This is not, I should caution, to brand Shirky as a latter-day apologist for slavery, but rather to note that it's an exceptionally arrogant tic of privilege to tell one's economic inferiors, online or off, what they do and do not love, and what the extra-material wellsprings of their motivation are supposed to be. To use an old-fashioned pre-Facebook construct, it's at minimum an intrusion into a digital contributor's private life—and the just and proper rejoinder to any propagandist urging the virtues of uncompensated labor from an empyrean somewhere far above mere "society" is, "You try it, pal." And oddly enough, it is nowhere recorded that Shirky has sought to extend the magical spirit of Web-based generosity to abjure fees from his lucrative sideline of offering digital marketing counsel to Nokia, News Corp., Proctor and Gamble, the BBC, the Lego Corp., and—perhaps most distressingly—the US Navy.

Then again, that's largely the point. In an age when respected social commentators can miniaturize the social dynamic of generations of democratic resistance into a Facebook entry, or a 140-character Tweet, the hard slog of comprehending economic conditions as they actually exist in the world is a gratuitous offline distraction. And needless to say, there's even less of a point in exhuming the social legacies of the dead pre-digital past. Once you start down that path, there's no telling where things might end up. You might even find yourself wondering just what Mark Zuckerbeg, perennial social underdog and digital zeitgeist on horseback, was doing at Harvard in the first place.

Rich People Thing No. 29

.TAX CUTS

Much as medieval cosmologists believed that the earth was balanced on the back of a turtle, Americans are in thrall to the great theological superstition known as the tax cut. It matters not which major party holds power in Washington, and it matters even less what the objective condition the economy or the federal budget may be in: The solution to our ills always boils down to further reductions in the marginal tax rate. In the wake of the Obama administration's craven postelection caving on the extension of George W. Bush's tax cuts to the wealthy, the United States had the lowest rate of effective taxation since the Truman administration. Nevertheless, in our Banana Republic of dull-witted neoliberalism, the only conceivable way to address the funding priorities of the public sector at any level is by proposing tax cut after tax cut.

The ideological adulation of the tax cut hearkens back, of course, to the deficit-bingeing administration of Ronald Reagan, which built its financial legacy on such fantasias of supply-side policymaking as the aptly named Laffer Curve. This theory—literally scrawled on a cocktail napkin—held that if only lawmakers managed to cut tax rates steeply enough, the resulting business growth would ultimately only increase the flow of revenues into federal coffers. This has nowhere proven to be true, any more than one can claim to have cured cancer with a feather duster.

Indeed, despite the ritual incantations of the supply-side faithful, actual economic history tells the opposite story. Stripped of all its rhetorical fanfare about government being the problem, the economic growth that occurred during the Reagan years came about via the classic Keynesian tactic of priming the pump with deficit spending: Having cut taxes, Reagan embarked on a giddy bout of sharply increased defense spending—which, in the structural terms of fiscal policy, was no different from how FDR presided over the heyday of the New Deal. The only real difference was that Reagan was commissioning new bomber contracts—and launching a whole daft cottage industry in "Star Wars" defense-shield research—while Roosevelt, silly free-spending Democrat that he was, sought to revive the nation's moribund credit market and the Depression-battered jobs economy. What's more, when the results of his short-sighted financial management became clear, Reagan was forced to enact tax increases to prevent the federal budget from turning into a wind tunnel of fast-receding cash; after his much-touted 1981 tax cut, he proceeded to raise taxes no less than eleven times, recouping about half of the value of the initial cut in a belated effort to simulate the behavior of a responsible government.[1] At the end of the day, Reagan was squarely in the average range of modern Oval Office tax collectors, gathering up a little more than 18 percent of the nation's GDP in revenues, while well eclipsing the comparable 20 percent average for federal outlays, with government spending accounting for more than 25 percent of the GDP on his watch.

So much, in other words, for the "Reagan Revolution." None of these empirical embarrassments really mattered, though. An uncritical press continued hewing to the Reagan White House's foundation myth of stoking economic growth by using tax cuts to unleash the talismanic power of the private sector. So in election cycle after election cycle, tax cuts became a magical incantation of what the first George Bush derisively called the "voodoo economics" crowd. Proposing tax cuts was a shorthand way for a candidate to say, "I trust the ingenuity and efficiency of yon Average American Citizen over your standard-issue government bureaucrat or union boss." And needless to say, the idea of raising taxes became a no-less-potent form of box-office poison. When Reagan's 1984 opponent Walter Mondale decided that it was time to level with the American people and inform them that he'd set about increasing taxes if they voted him into office, he was duly crushed in the greatest reelection landslide in US history. From then on, Democrats, too, started closely heeding the lesson of the GOP playbook: You might actually raise taxes once in power, but for God's sake, under no circumstances could any candidate for national office approach the American people as if they were sober adults capable of seeing their financial interests in a long-term collective light. And it's even more futile, of course, to let any remote issue of fairness or equality of access to social goods enter into the picture—that's liberalism, of the most transparent "tax and spend" variety, and hence never to be spoken of in public, let alone to be entertained as a serious option for economic policy.

As a result, ever since the delusional heyday of Reagan, it's mattered little which major party has made the critical call on how taxation works to reward certain economic actors and punish others. To paraphrase the old maxim about the dead but never discredited John Maynard Keynes, they're all tax-cutters now. In his staggeringly business-appeasing administration, Bill Clinton trotted out a long string of "targeted middle-class tax cuts" to create incentives for the soft-focus quality-of-life reforms, such as Family and Medical Leave Act, that are now the calling card of the New Democratic party—even as his administration was able to pay for such campaign-friendly overtures to affluent voters by slashing at direct subsidies to sub-middle-class Americans, such as Aid for Families with Dependent Children, the Pell Grant program and the all-but-hollowed-out system of federal subsidies for affordable housing.

Likewise, when the Obama White House decided it was unable to make good on the pledge to retire the Bush tax cuts to the nation's wealthiest citizens, it didn't find the bulk of its offsetting costs in the raft of corporate and paper-economy tax breaks crafted by a generation of financial industry lobbyists. No, it followed the counsel of the president's laughably partisan and plutocratic "debt commission," and proceeded to float proposals to hack away at "entitlements" such as Medicare and Social Security—even though the latter program consistently operates with a surplus, and the former, while prey to insurance industry and physician fraud, is one of the only universal social welfare programs left standing, and a critical bulwark of affordable health care as a generation of boomers whose home values and retirement accounts have been pillaged by Wall Street start to exit the work force. For good measure, the Obama White House elected, in the dead of winter, to announce plans to cut the budget for LIHEAP, the federal energy assistance program for low-income Americans, nearly in half, from $5.5 billion to $3 billion. Such symbolically punitive yet fiscally nugatory budget cuts, like the pledge to get tough on "runaway" entitlement spending, are a badge of Great Beltway Seriousness in fiscal matters. Meanwhile, of course, the extension of the Bush tax cuts to the wealthy blew nearly a $900 billion hole in the federal budget—and for all the frothing complaints from the business right of the failure of government stimulus efforts to create jobs, these tax cuts are the genuine "job-killing" article, since they do nothing to stimulate consumer demand for essential products, as is true of far more efficient direct government payments, ranging from food stamps to LIHEAP payments to unemployment benefits.

This is to say nothing of truly unconscionable tax cuts, such as the steep reduction in the estate tax—an excise, which for all the desperation of the Chamber of Commerce and others to depict as a heroic safeguard of the struggling family farm, applies now only to individual estates valued north of $5 million, or couples' joint estates of $10 million or more. When adherents of the prostrate bipartisan Washington consensus on tax cuts failed utterly to address the simple challenge of taxing lavish estates—a process that, by the way, gives no trouble whatsoever to any other developed Western country—plutocrats who passed on to their final reward during the blessed 2010 "moratorium" year didn't have any federal taxes assessed on their estates whatsoever. So, for instance, George Steinbrenner, the venal character assassin who debauched the national pastime of baseball into a garish spectacle of proprietary cable fees, skyboxes and bloated free-agent salaries, left a $1.1 billion estate, which under pre-Bush-era estate tax rules would have produced $500 million in revenues for the federal government—or for those of you keeping score at home, about one-fifth of the funds the Obama White House purloined from Americans too poor to pay their own heating bills. (Baseball fans determined to cling to the principle of karma in this earthly vale of tears were left to console themselves with the thought that Steinbrenner's legacy still wasn't enough to purchase a competent staff of starting pitchers.) Likewise, natural gas tycoon Dan Duncan left a tax-free estate of more than $9 billion to his heirs when he died the same year—a payday that was almost twice the sum the Obama White House took from LIHEAP in its swaggering big-man display of budget austerity.[2] Team Duncan defeated Team Steinbrenner by a healthy eight-to-one margin, in other words, with the US government senselessly and repeatedly forfeiting on the sidelines.

The Obama White House defended its capitulation on the extension of the Bush cuts for the wealthy in the same fashion that all spineless Democrats have rationalized their giveaways to the privileged class since the age of Reagan: It claimed to be hostage to adverse political circumstance, with an incoming GOP majority in the House of Representatives certain to offer less generous concessions on a grand tax bargain than the 2010 lame-duck session of the Democratic-run House could. In a classic ignore-the-potbellied-plutocrat-behind-the-curtain feint favored by earlier Democratic appeasers in the top-down class wars, these quisling politicos pointed to the brewing threat among House Republicans to deny a proposed thirteen-month extension of unemployment benefits unless the American overclass could cling to its accustomed portions of pelf for another two years. And showcasing the usual New Democratic eagerness to make the whole messy economic question simply go away, White House flacks set about trying to brand the GOP-coerced bargain as a "middle-class" tax cut deal, and a general boon for working Americans.

But of course there were several grievous category errors in this hastily sketched line of argument. For one thing, it's a mistake, especially in the teeth of a job-challenged recovery, to characterize jobless benefits as some sort of luxurious outlay for a special interest, to be offset by budget-busting concessions to the political opposition. Unemployment benefits are in fact a stimulus—since their recipients have little choice but to spend them promptly and stoke broader economic demand. Given the general run of competitive hoarding behavior in the successor generations of affluent families, there's nothing like a comparable macroeconomic bang for the buck in slashing estate tax rates, let alone waving the Steinbrenner and Duncan fortunes unmolested through the customs line. And bitter experience should have taught us by now that granting lavish federal bailouts to the overleveraged lords of the paper economy can achieve many short-term bonus spikes for Wharton-trained investment bank partners, but only the most diehard libertarian theorist (and/or the most ardent of opium eaters) would characterize TARP expenditures as a gain to the wider productive economy. In other words, to permit jobless benefits to become this sort of a provisional Beltway bargaining chip in the first place is worse than a political miscalculation—it's an unmitigated failure of analytical thinking, and a still greater bankruptcy of the moral imagination.

What's more, leaving aside the policy case for extending jobless assistance in a recession, helping out the victims of a Wall Street–authored economic collapse is simply the decent human thing to do. If congressional Republicans wish to take the opposite view in House floor debates, by all means let them—even if they end up carrying the day in the chamber, they will still be convicted in the court of public opinion, and maybe, *just maybe*, there wouldn't then be such a thing as a Speaker Boehner and an incoming House GOP majority for New Democrats to exploit as a rhetorical foil for their invertebrate policy-making in the first place.

Washington's nondebate on the Bush tax cut extension also gave the lie, as so many tax questions in our age have, to the great enabling fiction of the "middle class" as the beneficary-cum-rationale for all economic policymaking. Indeed, in a little-noted bit of lawmaking legerdemain during the Bush tax-cut debate, the Senate blocked the extension of the 2009 stimulus law's "Making Work Pay" tax break aimed at individual earners making $75,000 or less, and couples in the $150,000 and under income bracket; in its place, lawmakers substituted a two-year payroll tax holiday that costs the Treasury twice as much while overwhelmingly benefitting higher earners.[3] This is the sort of strategic gaming of the system that goes on all the time on Capitol Hill, where corporate lobbyists are essentially empowered to draw up their own preferred version of the tax code. But it comports quite badly with the Obama administration's increasingly shrill insistence that it is acting to preserve the foundations of middle-class prosperity.[4] If the Democratic capitulation on tax cuts is merely yet another specimen of tough-minded political realism, as these self-same flacks are so fond of insisting, then critics of the administration's economic priorities are well entitled at this late date to ask "Realism for who?"

The tax-cut consensus, as we have come to wearily know and succumb to it, certainly bears no resemblance to political reality—at the height of the congressional debate over extending the Bush cuts for the wealthy, polls showed Americans opposed the proposal by a two-to-one margin, a level of popular approval nowadays only reserved for NASCAR and motherhood. And as a reckoning with the empirical state of the US economy, bipartisan backing for tax cuts is yet more delusional. Its own inherent logic can only produce a future calamitous crisis for the already anemic American welfare state—which will in turn produce a very serious downgrading of the US quality of life. As Bloomberg columnist Simon Johnson—certainly no fire-breathing socialist—has observed, tax cuts always work to squeeze federal revenues, and

> the U.S. government doesn't take in much tax revenue—at least 10 percentage points of GDP less than comparable developed economies—and it also doesn't spend much except on the military, Social Security and Medicare. Other parts of government spending can be frozen or even slashed, but it just won't make that much difference. That means older Americans are going to get squeezed, while our ability to defend ourselves goes into decline. Just because there's a bipartisan consensus on an idea, such as tax cuts, doesn't mean it makes sense. Today's tax cutters have set us up for tomorrow's fiscal crisis and real damage to U.S. national security.[5]

As is the case with so many other dreary social prospects, California offers a preview of what our cheerfully tax-cutting lawmakers are laying in store for the nation at large. Ever since the great property tax revolt that won passage of Proposition 13 back in 1978, California's public sector has been starved for revenues and the requirement that state budgets win two-thirds majorities in the legislature has ensured no meaningful budget reckoning can ever issue from the authors of a state budget now $24 billion in the red. Corporate profits in the state grew by a whopping 557 percent between 2001 and 2005, while individual income in the same period rose by a negligible 22 percent. And as throughout the federal system, the heaviest tax burden falls disproportionately on the state's poorest filers, thanks to various individual exemptions and legislative tax breaks.[6] As the California Budget Project noted in 2007, this results in a state taxation system skewed ludicrously toward the top. "Over the past two decades, the cost of funding state services has shifted from corporate to individual tax payers. Forecasters estimate that personal income tax receipts will provide 54.9 percent of General Fund revenues in 2008–09, up from 35.4 percent in 1980–81. Corporate tax receipts are expected to provide 11.6 percent of General Fund revenues in 2008–09, down from 14.6 percent in 1980–81. New, increased and expanded corporate tax breaks and the 1996 corporate tax rate reduction are responsible for the decline in the share of state revenues provided by the corporate income tax. Tax cuts have limited growth in state revenues as a whole, with tax cuts enacted since 1983 reducing 2007–08 revenues by an estimated $12 billion."

The political upshot of all this state-sanctioned inequality is now painfully obvious: Even newly elected Democratic governor Jerry Brown has begun slashing away at education and social services, while proposing a 10 percent across-the-board cut in salaries for unionized state workers. He has claimed to support a five-year extension of provisional tax increases enacted in 2009—but has cynically proposed putting those hikes forward in a referendum vote by a notoriously tax-averse California electorate, whose 1978 mad-as-hell Proposition 13 tantrum largely landed the state in its insoluble budget crisis in the first place.[7]

At least there's a certain moral symmetry in Brown's grandstanding move. On the national scene, there's only a ceaseless and deferential obeisance to every imagined whim of the moneyed set, which almost always segues directly into more and steeper cuts to federally funded income supports, education grants, and housing assistance. And that, ineluctably, bolsters the political dynamic for the *next* round of tax cuts, since political leaders all too plainly see that there's no percentage for them in sustaining the effort to fund universal social goods in an electoral system driven by corporate campaign donations that gives less fortunate voters a steadily diminishing stake in political participation. One desperately awaits the arrival of a latter-day Jonathan Swift, who can highlight the expropriative absurdity of the something-for-nothing fantasia known as federal tax policy by gently ratcheting up the terms of its daft flight from sanity. Perhaps this gimlet-eyed satirist can propose a regressive tax on the oxygen that poor people consume, or a terraform system of outer-space workhouses, or a program to house the unemployed in the tunnels of the large Hadron collider. Then again, satire seems wasted on a subject as fundamentally deranged and as fatally unserious as the American consensus on tax cuts.

Conclusion

THE LANGUAGE PROBLEM

If markets truly do possess "tipping points"—those storied moments when they spontaneously rearrange themselves in mystical accordance with the general will—then our recent economic calamity should have produced a revolution in our common tongue. For the argot of economic specialization has long been an almost perfect inversion of how we actually live our productive lives. In the late years of the aughts, we've seen no end of billowing, multisyllabic abstractions take on lethally precise traits of social destruction. Collateralized debt obligations, credit default swaps, mortgage-backed derivatives, securitized risk—all these concepts, and (just as important) the words used to characterize them, seem in retrospect to be the kind of incantation worthy of the great *Harry Potter* villain Lord Voldemort, an evil force far too potent to have his name spoken aloud.

And so it is, one might argue, with the forces that have so deeply deranged our common life. As the investment economy laid siege to the American moral imagination in the past twenty-odd years, we seemed instinctively to realize that there was something dangerous in saying outright just what the thing was actually doing. And so we entered a true golden age of bloodless euphemism, affixing no end of harmonious social modifiers to the term "economy" as a bold sort of speech-act—"new information," "knowledge," "digital," and "soft." We often used such terms interchangeably to mean, roughly, "postindustrial" and always employed them with the same reverent certainty that accompanies the more familiar catechisms of the High Church.

As with the older spiritual acts of prayer, the great age of post-productive euphemism has been an exercise in perfecting word formations in the pure conviction that the wishing would make it so. The ideas that bound us to the old industrial order—the site of so much social conflict and gray ideological neurosis—were suddenly melting into air, and new ways of thinking now had to summon forth an entirely new way of being in the world. In time, even the notion of an "economy" seemed inadequate to describe the great social transformations we were living through. One heard of "telecosms," "the long boom," "big sorts," "long tails," and "the wisdom of crowds"— even, lo and behold, the endlessly comforting notion that "everything bad is good for you," as one popular work of cultural theory had it at the height of millennial-boom culture. Social virtue had become a frictionless software application, and the economy was delivering fundamental change at a clip far faster than our meager Industrial Age brainpans could assimilate it all.

However, for the people still actually working in the American economy—those who had been denied these wondrous powers of social prophecy—things looked very different indeed. Social inequality, measured by the gap between the highest and lowest percentiles of income earners, sharpened throughout the Clinton years, the moment when we were vouchsafed most of these soothing visions of the New Information Valhalla. And things got implacably worse during the Bush years, with extremely prejudicial tax cuts redistributing wealth upward, as the speculative paper economy not only crowded out conventional productive enterprise, but also hollowed out the financial foundations of our homes. The Bush years saw the first five-year period of economic expansion in modern US history that produced no increase in median wages. Instead of recognizing this for the distressing structural defect that it plainly was, Bush economic officials rallied to find inventive new ways of appeasing the investor class. In 2005, for instance, SEC chairman William Donaldson was effectively cashiered for advocating unpleasant levels of transparency, for share-holders and financial markets alike. His replacement, former Califor-nia Republican Representative Christopher Cox, was overtly tasked with keeping the great Wall Street barbecue going. Housing prices and derivatives markets continued soaring upward, until they, well, didn't.

What's most striking about the long unwinding of this speculative nightmare is the still-impoverished vocabulary we are condemned to use in our efforts to explain just what's happened to us. The usual storehouse of red-faced business-press expressions such as "down-turn" and "recession"—and even their more-robust variants such as "collapse" and "meltdown"—seemed like so much pallid, inadequate phrasemaking compared to the scale of the disaster upon us. Faced with the prospect of the full-tilt collapse of global financial capitalism, we were left with terms almost solely of the government's devising—expressions such as "too big to fail," "troubled assets," "frozen credit," and "mark to market."

In this atmosphere, many sturdy advocates of plutocracy are still protesting the expression "predatory lending"—which seemed, under the circumstances, a fairly generous way of putting things—as an over-ly loaded phrase that in any event couldn't possibly describe an actual market phenomenon. People entered into ARMs and nothing-down loan arrangements voluntarily, after all, and the merchants of capital were furnishing them with unprecedented access to credit. Couldn't they be a little more grateful, for God's sake? As mortgage economist Arnold Kling harrumphed over Congress's plan to institute a modest Consumer Financial Protection Agency, "The idea of predatory lend-ing is to saddle the borrower with an expensive mortgage so you can foreclose on the property and sell at a profit." Disbelievingly, he asks, "Have you read of a single instance in the past three years when the bank made a profit on a foreclosure?" It therefore follows, of course, that while poor people may be worthy of some abstract pity "because of their poverty . . . I cannot feel sorry for somebody who was given a basically free option on a house and the option didn't happen to come into money."[1]

All socially acceptable talk of predation, bizarrely enough, has been reserved for the poor saps trying to hang onto criminally over-valued mortgages in the wake of the great '08 reckoning. Consider the famed on-air outburst of the petty and indignant CNBC market correspondent Rick Santelli—speaking on the floor of the Chicago-based futures exchange, the CME Group. This moment served as "the founding document of the Tea Party movement," in the judgment of conservative political writer Michael Barone. And like that move-ment's entire antigovernment platform, it is a staggering display of incoherent socioeconomic entitlement. "This is America!" Santelli egged on his cheering on-camera audience of brokers. "How many of you want to pay for your neighbor's mortgage that has an extra bathroom and can't pay the bills?"[2]

No one—least of all the putative economic correspondent and his admiring retinue of traders—paused to reflect that, in the vast ma-jority of cases, those mortgage holders were the least consequential players in a global chain of securitized debt that ran into the trillions of dollars. Far less did anyone on the CME floor interrupt to mention the kinds of domestic improvements that they had managed to fund, free and clear, via the upstream fees they collected on mortgage-backed derivatives. The spectacle of Santelli's staged "rant" was very much like seeing a room full of arsonists, reeking of flame accelerants, blaming a citywide conflagration on a single defective fire hydrant.

But it's an awkward business, owning up to the way the model of one's profession is founded on what amounts to a long-term formu-la of financial ruin. Better, by far, to summon the sinister wheezing specter of communism. "Cuba used to have mansions and a relatively decent economy," Santelli huffed. "They moved from the individual to the collective and now they're driving '54 Chevies—the last great car to come out of Detroit." (Because, you see, it's not sufficient merely to demonize the mortgage holders tricked out of their unrecoverable nest eggs by the financial industry; no, to do the job right, one has to work in a gratuitous attack on the heavily unionized American auto workforce.) By the time he was winding down, Santelli was summoning the spirit of the Founding Fathers—"What we're doing now in this country would make them roll over in their graves"—and announcing that, yes, "We're thinking of having a tea party in Chicago this July."[3]

It's bracing, in the face of such vicious, analytically empty showboating, to recall that things were not ever thus when American citizens contended with the wreckage of a money culture. When notions of economic justice and equality still figured prominently in our political debate, past financial abuses were described openly as treasons, infamies, or crimes. Indeed, the postbellum Greenback Party adopted as its rallying slogan "the Crime of '73"— referencing the retirement of wartime paper currency in favor of the gold standard. As a straightforward description, it was entirely apt, considering the swiftness with which the resumption of gold dispatched an entire generation of farmers, small producers, and laborers into debt peonage. The perpetrators of these fleecings, meanwhile, were graced with vivid—and usually spot-on—descriptors that combined moral assessments of their deficient characters with a visceral sense of the damage they'd wrought on the republic. They were "bloodsuckers," "plutocrats," "brigands," and "robber barons." When nineteenth-century orators were feeling more philologically minded in their abuse, the lords of commerce would be described as "Croesuses," "Judases," "Caesars," "Neros," "Pharaohs," and "the pagan worshipers of Moloch."

Admittedly, when this rhetorical fire was trained on bankers and speculators of the age—the Rothschilds, most especially—it could curdle into ugly anti-Semitic bile. That was regrettably the case as the Populist movement sank into its terminal political decline, with rabid and irrelevant veterans of the Populist uprising substituting distant ethnic scapegoats for the more obdurate and powerful enemies who were actually despoiling the land and robbing workers of their just day's wage.

Despite this unconscionable drift into bigotry, this earlier vocabulary of financial crime was a crucial orienting device. It permitted its users to envision the otherwise harsh and impersonal workings of the market as a reflection of fallen human nature, as opposed to a remorseless, undeviating natural law. When the socialist reformer Henry Demarest Lloyd wrote of economic exploitation in his classic 1894 treatise *Wealth Against Commonwealth*, he pinpointed the way that excess and greed disfigured not merely our public institutions, but also our innermost characters. The effect, as he described it, is a state of willed social delusion—a sundering of the most vital connection that one person can feel for another in a community of shared moral interest. "Our size has got beyond both our science and our conscience," he wrote. "The vision of the railroad-stockholder is not far-sighted enough to see into the office of the General Manager; the people cannot reach across even a ward of their city to rule their rulers; Captains of Industry 'do not know' whether men in the ranks are dying from lack of food and shelter; we cannot clean our cities nor our politics; the locomotive has more manpower than all the ballot boxes; and millwheels wear out the hearts of the workers unable to keep up beating time to their whirl."[4]

It's quite easy—and has long been the fashion in academic histories—to dismiss such rhetoric as the misplaced longing of a small-town, patrician, bourgeois class of reformers for a simpler time when the blind laws of the concentration of industrial power were tempered by the sentimental moralism of the busybody (and usually evangelical) provincial reformer. Yet that is its own kind of moral obtuseness—substituting the fiction of an expansive, upward-tending market order operating under its own impersonal momentum for a universe where people can and should apprehend the consequences of their own actions and uphold mutual obligations that stretch across and beyond the social conventions of property. To realize that the negligent Captain of Industry who "does not know" the condition of the laborers under his dominion is consigned to a state of moral idiocy—idiocy, in its strict Greek derivation, being the condition of existing without a public life—is to be able to hold fast to the most crucial questions that are really at stake in our productive lives. Likewise, to see that blindness as of a piece with the civic isolation of a railroad stockholder or an urban citizenry disenfranchised by a graft-ridden machine politics is to give voice to a distemper in normal business affairs far deeper than anything likely to be unearthed in a journalistic expose or a congressional committee hearing. "Our civilization is builded on competition," Lloyd continues, "and competition evolves itself crime—to so acute an infatuation has the lunacy of self-interest carried our dominant opinion. We are hurried far beyond the point of listening to the new conscience which, pioneering in moral exploration, declares that conduct we think right because called 'trade' is really lying, stealing, murder. 'The definite result,' Ruskin preaches, 'of all our modern haste to be rich is assuredly and constantly the murder of a certain number of persons by our hands every year.' "[5]

This sort of writing strikes the modern ear as Victorian, overwrought, and quaint. But the language of Lloyd and Ruskin is far better tailored to the genuine moral plight of the contemporary economic citizen than the grotesque fictions trundled out under such deliberately self-distancing jargon as "consumer sovereignty" or "the rational market hypothesis." Indeed, where the older rhetoric of economic confrontation was visceral and personal, the governing rhetoric of latter-day financial crises is studiously ambient and clinical. To take just one example, these crises are no longer spoken of, as they were in Lloyd's day, as "panics"—a word that admirably summons the vivid, all-too-human feeling that accompanies the realization that an investment, a securities deal, or, indeed, an entire speculative sector has become a worthless stack of paper. Instead, the ever-more-frequent maladies of the investment world are now depicted as mysterious, causeless epidemics—"infecting" foreign markets, accruing "toxic" debt, moving "risk" around in ways that ultimately only made markets that much more risk prone.

As the Santelli episode makes clear, what's surpassingly odd about our present vocabulary for economic affairs is that it tends to sound most specific precisely at its points of greatest analytical vagueness. Any casual reader of the business press knows that the threat of "class warfare" is omnipresent and to be smote ever vigilantly. But those who would actually prosecute this species of war are maddeningly diffuse and anonymous. They certainly can't be labor militants, with just 7 percent of the private-sector workforce now belonging to unions. Nor can they be the sort of socialist intellectuals who'd formed the backbone of the heady New Left uprisings in places like Paris and Prague. Our intellectual class has grown far too jaded and media addled for any dalliance with ideas of mass social rebellion. Socialism itself is dead as an ideological force. It's only spoken of now as a mysteriously viral trait held in common among our elite liberal governing class— sort of like an embarrassing sexually transmitted disease picked up at an Ivy League reunion. Socialism no longer serves as a universal rallying cry to the disenfranchised; it is, rather, an irksomely gnomic floating signifier, used here to describe the alleged redistributionist schemes of an Obama economic team dominated by investment bankers, and there to decry a health-care reform plan that is nearly a letter-perfect replica of the plan offered up by congressional Republicans in 1993.

The analytic fog only thickens when you consider the odd way that terms of economic conflict have migrated into cultural debate. It's now standard form, in any discussion of any mass-culture genre— reality TV, pop music, video gaming, and what have you—to plot all points of contention on the undeviating axis of "populism" versus "elitism." In this debased scheme of things, to endorse any product of the mass-entertainment complex, no matter how cynically executed or smarmily marketed, is to advertise one's populist sensibilities. And to suggest that perhaps the *Saw* movie franchise has gotten a bit out of hand, taste-wise, or that Dan Brown can't write his way out of an open phone booth, is to be exposed as a monocle-and-cummerbund-sporting elitist of the first order. Confusion in these matters is now so deep that to criticize a work that viciously lampoons lower-class Americans, like the never-funny Sacha Baron Cohen vehicle *Borat*, is somehow to place oneself out of the comforting range of respectable "populist" opinion.

In this tangled, dumbed-down terminology, it's impossible to recall that the economic populists of the nineteenth century promoted rural literacy as a key plank in their platform. There was an immediate, practical rationale for this reform: to safeguard farmers from entering into (yes) predatory contracts with landlords and railroad interests that they could barely read or comprehend. But more broadly, the historical populists, far from scorning book-learning as a highfalutin "elitist" affection, were keen to advance their constituents' education in political economy. That's why the national newspaper of the People's Party—which its founder and editor Thomas L. Nugent significantly called the *Economist*—featured a running column on the founding principles of democratic government, beginning with Polybius' classical dissection of the separation of powers on down to David Ricardo and the labor theory of value. To the latter-day sensibility—which roughly equates "populism" with the canons of reality TV and the semiliterate blathering of Sarah Palin—the Nugent program must seem like a distant, indecipherable transmission from another planet.

And so, in a sense, it is. To clearly counterpoise the positions of "the people" and "the money interests" in the political sphere—and in the process, to promote the widest possible diffusion of economic literacy—is a project bound up with the discipline once known as "political economy." The spheres of economic production and political discourse were understood as a unity throughout most of the nineteenth century because the idea of promoting formal democracy in the absence of economic self-determinism struck most social critics of the age as a cruel and dangerous pursuit.

The legacy of slavery, if nothing else, should have underlined that point. Indeed, the populists proved an intolerable force for the white supremacist regime of the Deep South precisely because they began to assert a cross-racial solidarity of interests among white and black tenant farmers over and against the power of the former planter class. In the racist synthesis of the postbellum South, the lords of the new economic order undid the dangerous ideas of populist political economy by creating a virulent new system of legal segregation. Tragically, they did so by recruiting many former populist political leaders, such as Georgia's Tom Watson and Alabama's "Pitchfork" Ben Tillman, as the bigoted face of the New South's system of racial and economic exclusion. C. Vann Woodward masterfully recounted this ugly history in *The Strange Career of Jim Crow*.[6]

But the disassembling of political economy had a broader, less provincial motive force behind it as well. Beginning in the early twentieth century, economics and political science were each professionalized—carved up into separate academic disciplines, credentialed with new postgraduate programs and professional associations, and fully vested with the flowing ermine raiment of social-scientific jargon. Specialists in each field set about performing work that became steadily less public-minded while ensuring that no one in either new specialization ventured too far onto the turf of the rival discipline.

Indeed, the closest the two disciplines have lately come to cross-pollinating is in the unsightly, quasi-delusional discipline known as "rational choice" theory—the heroic effort of empirically minded political scientists to reduce all public political deliberation to binary, econometric, and radically private calculation. Rational choice is in fact a grotesque parody of political economy and a discipline drained of any coherent intellectual content for the sake of positing a fanciful universe where political choices are plotted on a simple cost-benefit axis and carried out by undeviatingly rational market actors.

All it takes is a cursory glance at the behavior of the financial markets circa 2008—and at the countless perverse doctrines of the Tea Party right—to note that the rational choice school is very much a dead letter when it comes to describing how political and economic thinking occurs in consensual reality.

Part of what makes it so difficult to connect our talk about economic life with how we actually experience it has been the long-standing American taboo about discussing social class. We can never own up fully to the powerful and specific ways that class determines individual life outcomes, since that notion defies the foundational American myth of upward social mobility. So our understanding of class has long been mired, as Benjamin DeMott has noted, in the muddy force field of "the imperial middle." In our public discourse, the middle class occupies the same everywhere-and-nowhere quality that the Virgin Mary does for many Catholic worshipers around the globe: a beneficent, reassuring presence that possesses little practical cultic authority, but who's mainly kept on hand as a household god to ward off misfortune and bad spirits. We have middle-class targeted tax cuts, middle-class car models,[7] a middle-class case for a new New Deal,[8] and a middle-class argument for restoring the gold standard.[9] We've seen a steady stream of self-appointed cable tribunes, such as Bill O'Reilly and Lou Dobbs, who position themselves heroically to redeem the middle class's somehow beleaguered footing in public life—even though no leader or policy hand of any serious ambition could survive for a moment in today's climate by besmirching the American bourgeoisie. We have legislation named ceremoniously in the middle class's honor, with the honorific being more prayerful than policy oriented. The Middle Class Opportunity Act and the Middle Class Investor Relief Act are the two signature initiatives to emerge from the 2008 meltdown.

Don't get me wrong; our middle class embodies many hardy virtues, and we certainly don't need to set about vilifying them in the vein of the bohemian French literati or the American New Left. But

the outsize space we've cleared for the middle class in our economic rhetoric makes it that much harder to see how the middle orders
themselves are actually faring—as well as the significant rearrange-
ment of life outcomes both above and below the imperial middle.
Among other things, this makes it hard to speak intelligibly about
times like now, when the self-identified American middle class is
plainly losing its economic footing.

Consider the futile task of reliably defining the middle class in
these United States. More than half of respondents in most surveys on
the subject identify themselves as "middle class," but they also cover
an objective range of socioeconomic circumstances so vast as to render that designation almost empirically meaningless. In the last major
Pew Research Center poll on the subject from late 2008, 40 percent of
respondents from households earning less than $20,000 a year called
themselves middle-class—but so did a third of respondents whose
households took in more than $150,000 a year.[10] The designation, in-
terestingly, held remarkably consistent across racial and ethnic lines,
with Anglos, blacks, and Hispanics all calling themselves middle class
at a rate of 50 percent or more. (Mathematically, of course, a figure
making up more than half of a larger number can't logically be aggregated in the middle of a numeric field—but Americans wouldn't be
having these difficulties with class self-designation if they were better
at arithmetic.)

What might be called the aspirational feature of middle-class
identification is the ready conflation of middleness in America with
upward mobility. No one, after all, places him- or herself in the middle with the expectation of slipping beneath the mean. Yet that is the
story of American wealth and income over the past decade—a steady
erosion of real earning power only made superficially tolerable by a
massive explosion of consumer debt. As the 2008 Pew study notes,
the paper-enabled prosperity of the last two decades largely skipped
the middle orders and rewarded the nation's upper classes at a wildly disproportionate rate. "The upper-income tier (households with

annual incomes above 150 percent of the median) has outperformed the middle tier (household with annual incomes between 75 percent and 150 percent of the median)—not just in terms of income gains, but also in wealth accumulation. From 1983 to 2004, the median net worth of upper-income families more than doubled, while the median net worth of middle-income families grew by just 29 percent."[11] That's roughly a fourfold disparity in net worth achieved over a period of broad general growth.

In the developing world, countries that tolerate that sort of chronic inequality over a long enough interval are known variously as kleptocracies, banana republics, and oligarchies. But here, once again, words fail us for the simple reason that our social mythology of ever-upward mobility will not permit us to call the most basic material conditions of our lives by their true names. We have no publicly acknowledged working class, or inequality crisis, or any basic grasp of what might constitute economic justice for the same reason we have no political economy: We are committed in advance to the dogmatic belief that we are all affluent entrepreneurs waiting to happen.

One rarely acknowledged consequence of this self-inflicted blind spot is that we grow estranged not merely from the core economic decisions that leaders of industry and government routinely hand down; we also lose any sense of how we ourselves directly participate in central economic outcomes. When the 2010 Gulf oil spill disabled an entire regional economy and poisoned wetlands, beaches, and marine ecosystems for generations to come, we were reduced to fulminating about the rank incompetence of oil executives in "fixing" the catastrophe—parroting callow cable-pundit demands that our president "get mad" or "get tough," testosterone apparently being the most efficient oil solvent on offer.

These impotent wishes seemed to hinge on the belief that the toy-soldier-style surrogates of the corporate and political world possessed some concealed super powers that could suddenly deactivate an unprecedented massive flow of oil, or magically stop up a busted well a mile beneath the surface of the ocean. Meanwhile, efforts to boy-cott BP stations sidestepped the entire complex supply chain of the oil industry, where franchised BP station owners are no more likely to be selling the company's oil than bars exclusively market the beer brand that furnished the neon signs in their front windows. Indeed, the irony of BP consumer boycotts is that they most directly harmed small gas station proprietors who were every bit as aggrieved at the British oil giant as the average environmentally minded consumer tends to be.

All these gestures, in other words, bespeak a public world where we not merely have long lost the capacity for effectively identifying the actual scourges of the public's interests—putting a true face to the ene-my—but also have abandoned any coherent understanding of our own participation in profoundly damaging economic arrangements. Incit-ing political leaders to anger, or symbolically scorning the BP logo in the consumer marketplace, does nothing to mitigate the insatiable de-mand for oil that makes calamities like the Gulf spill a dead certainty.

Likewise, complaints about the deficient efforts of BP and the Obama White House to contain the spill's damage neatly insulate us from processing the abundant evidence that simple greed was the ef-ficient cause lurking behind every proximate decision taken in the run-up to the rig explosion that triggered the spill. BP declined to carry out safety measures to secure the drill wall's casing because the company was behind in its optimal drilling schedule and losing $500,000 a day on the Deepwater Horizon project at the time of the April 20 explosion. Subcontractors charged with conducting follow-up safety tests on the facility were sent abruptly packing with the evi-dent mandate not to obstruct the fastest possible exploitation of the underwater oil and to secure its rapid delivery at a moment when oil prices were rising.

The only way to ensure that BP-style catastrophes don't simply be-come the sort of chronic dystopian eyesore one finds in a Don DeLillo novel or a Ridley Scott movie is to clearly apprehend the way we all conspire, wittingly or otherwise, in creating an epically unsustainable way of life. In the end, these are not really technical or policy questions, but rather questions about how best to live and what sort of livelihoods do and do not contribute to the common good. Here again the forgotten language of Henry Demarest Lloyd commends itself as a new way of thinking and acting:

Our tyrants are our ideals incarnating themselves in men born to command. What these men are we have made them. All governments are representative governments; none of them more so than the government of industry. We go hopelessly astray if we seek the solution of our problems in the belief that our business rulers are worse men in kind than ourselves. . . . Every idea finds its especially susceptible souls. These men are our most susceptible souls to the idea of individual self-interest. They have believed implicitly what we have taught, and have been the most faithful in trying to make the talent given them grow into ten talents. They rise superior to all our half-hearted social corrections: publicity, private competition, all devices of market-opposition, private litigation, public investigation, legislation and criminal prosecution—all. Their power is greater to-day than it was yesterday, and will be greater tomorrow. The public does not withhold its favor, but deals with them, protects them, refuses to treat their crimes as it treats those of the poor, and admits them to the highest places. The predominant mood is the more or less concealed regret of the citizens that they have not been able to conceive and execute the same lucky stroke or some other as profitable. The conclusion is irresistible that men so given the lead are the representatives of the real 'spirit of the age' and that the protestants against them are not representative of our time—are at best but intimators of times which may be.[12]

NOTES

Introduction

1. C. Wright Mills, *The Power Elite* (New York: Oxford University Press, 1956), 332.

1: The US Constitution

1. Quoted in Charles Beard, *An Economic Interpretation of the Constitution of the United States* (New York: Free Press, 1965), 6.
2. Jackson Turner Main, *The Antifederalists: Critics of the Constitution, 1781–1788* (New York: Quadrangle Books, 1964), 3.
3. Ibid., 61.
4. Quoted in Beard, *Economic Interpretation*, 179–80.
5. Quoted in ibid., 158.
6. Main, *Antifederalists*, 132.
7. Quoted in ibid., 131.
8. Quoted in ibid., 133–4
9. Ibid., 134
10. Beard, *Economic Interpretation*, 151.
11. Ibid., 324.

2: The New York Times

1. http://www.observer.com/2008/media/special-investment-fund-increase-business-coverage-i-times-i.
2. http://www.bostonphoenix.com/boston/news_features/other_stories/multi_3/documents/04731992.asp.

3. http://www.nytimes.com/2005/05/15/national/class/OVERVIEW-FI-NAL.html.

4. http://www.nytimes.com/2005/05/24/national/class/EDUCATION-FINAL.html.

5. http://www.nytimes.com/2005/05/24/national/class/EDUCATION-FINAL.html.

6. http://www.workinglife.org/blogs/view_post.php?content_ id=7694.

7. http://www.nytimes.com/2010/01/17/world/americas/17class.html.

8. Robert Warshow, *The Immediate Experience* (Cambridge, MA: Harvard University Press, 2001), 76.

3: Meritocracy

1. Michael Young, *The Rise of the Meritocracy* (London: Penguin Books, 1958), 133.

2. Ibid., 115.

3. Ibid., 14–15.

4. http://www.guardian.co.uk/politics/2001/jun/29/comment.

5. http://www.nytimes.com/1992/11/29/opinion/the-smart-club-comes-to-the-white-house.html?scp=717&sq=Smart%20House&st=nyt&pagewanted=1.

5: David Brooks

1. David Brooks, *Bobos in Paradise: The New Upper Class and How They Got There* (New York: Simon & Schuster, 2000), 137.

2. Ibid., 102.

3. Ibid., 271.

4. http://www.phillymag.com/articles/booboos_in_paradise/.

6: The Free Market

1. Michael Perelman, *The Invention of Capitalism: Classical Political Economy and the Secret History of Primitive Accumulation* (Durham, NC: Duke University Press, 2000), 176.

2. http://www.truth-out.org/070709E.

3. Alfred D. Chandler, *The Visible Hand: The Managerial Revolution in American Business* (Cambridge, MA: Belknap/Harvard University Press), 492–3.

7: The Stock Market

1. Steven Brill, "What's a Bailed-Out Banker Really Worth? *New York Times Magazine,* January 10, 2010. http://www.nytimes.com/2010/01/03/magazine/03Compensation-t.html?pagewanted=.
2. Doug Henwood, *Wall Street* (New York: Verso, 1997), 171.

8: "Class Warfare"

1. http://articles.latimes.com/2009/feb/28/nation/na-obama-budget28.
2. http://www.nytimes.com/2006/11/26/business/yourmoney/26every.html.
3. http://www.netcharles.com/orwell/ctc/docs/cancrtcs.htm.
4. A.J. Liebling, *The Press* (New York: Pantheon, 1981), 123–124.

9: The Democratic Party

1. http://www.heritage.org/Press/Commentary/ed110607a.cfm.
2. http://www.usatoday.com/news/washington/2009-10-13-House-wealth-gap-Democrats-richest-districts_N.htm.
3. http://dissidentvoice.org/Sept05/Street0929.htm.
4. http://prorev.com/2007/09/reagan-bush-clinton-bush-years.html.
5. Daniel Gross, *Bull Run: Wall Street, the Democrats and the New Politics of Personal Finance* (New York: Public Affairs, 2000), 16.

10: The Prosperity Gospel

1. Joel Osteen, *Become a Better You: 7 Keys to Improving Your Life Every Day* (New York: Free Press, 2007), 95.
2. Ibid. 346.
3. Ibid., 348.
4. http://www.cnn.com/2009/LIVING/wayoflife/12/25/RichJesus/index.html.

11: Wired Magazine

1. http://www.nytimes.com/2003/07/27/books/the-coolest-magazine-on-the-planet.html?pagewanted=1.
2. Quoted in Chris Anderson, *Free: The Future of a Radical Price* (New York: Hyperion books, 2009), 3.
3. Ibid., 3 and passim.
4. http://online.wsj.com/article/SB123335678420235003.html.

5. http://www.vqronline.org/blog/2009/06/23/chris-anderson-free/.
6. http://www.edrants.com/chris-anderson-plagiarist/.
7. http://www.plagiarismtoday.com/2009/06/24/the-chris-anderson-vaplagiarism-controversy/.
8. http://www.leighbureau.com/speaker.asp?id=373.

12: The Creative Class

1. Paul H. Ray and Sherry Anderson, *The Cultural Creatives: How 50 Million People are Changing the World* (New York: Harmony Books, 2000), 5.
2. Richard Florida, *The Rise of the Creative Class: And How It's Transforming Work, Leisure and Everyday Life* (New York: Basic Books, 2002), 37.
3. Ibid., 115.
4. Ibid., 115.
5. Ibid., 80.
6. Ibid., 13.

13: Malcolm Gladwell

1. Steven Pinker, "Malcolm Gladwell, Eclectic Detective," *New York Times Book Review* (November 15, 2009), 1.
2. Ibid.
3. http://www.sheldensays.com/Res-three.htm.
4. http://www.slate.com/id/2246732/pagenum/2.
5. http://www.gladwell.com/2005/2005_09_12_a_warren.html.
6. Ibid.
7. Ibid.
8. Ibid.
9. http://www.dailykos.com/story/2009/11/30/809224/-Rick-Warren-refuses-to-condemn-Ugandas-gay-execution-law.

14: Reality Television

1. http://www.guardian.co.uk/business/2010/apr/18/undercover-boss-television-comment.
2. http://www.huffingtonpost.com/kimberly-freeman-brown/undercover-boss-as-underc_b_544065.html.
3. http://www.aceshowbiz.com/news/view/00026581.html.
4. http://watching-tv.ew.com/2009/08/24/ryan-jenkins-dead-murderer-a-bigger-tv-star/.

5. http://www.theatlantic.com/magazine/archive/2007/05/the-case-for-reality-tv/5791/.

15: Damien Hirst

1. Chin–tao Wu, *Privatising Culture: Corporate Art Intervention Since the 1980s* (New York: Verso, 2002), 157.
2. http://www.telegraph.co.uk/culture/art/7560280/Damien-Hirst-Money-deserves-respect.html.
3. Ibid.

16: Ayn Rand

1. http://www.aynrand.org/site/News2?page=NewsArticle&id=22869&news_iv_ctrl=1221.
2. Ayn Rand, *Atlas Shrugged* (New York: Signet Books, 1957), 42.
3. Ibid., 731–2.

17: The Memoir

1. Walter Benn Michaels, "Going Boom," *Book Forum*, Feb/March 2009, 44.
2. Margaret Jones, Love and Consequences: A Memoir of Hope and Survival (New York: Riverhead Books, 2008), 29.
3. Ibid., 60.
4. Ibid., 234.
5. http://www.nytimes.com/2008/02/26/books/26kaku.html?_r=1&pagewanted=1&ref=garden.

18: The Supreme Court

1. http://www.scribd.com/doc/25537902/Citizens-Opinion.
2. Ibid.
3. http://supreme.justia.com/us/118/394/case.html.
4. http://unequalprotection.com/articles/2002/12/railroad-barons-are-back-and-time-theyll-finish-job.
5. http://www.jimrobison.org/node/68.
6. http://www.ratical.com/corporations/ToPRaP.html.
7. http://www.newyorker.com/reporting/2009/05/25/090525fa_fact_toobin?currentPage=all.
8. http://www.newyorker.com/reporting/2009/05/25/090525fa_fact_toobin?currentPage=all.

9. http://www.newyorker.com/reporting/2009/05/25/090525fa_fact_toobin?currentPage=all.

19: Higher Learning

1. http://docs.google.com/viewer?a=v&q=cache:f5-WxhueOAYJ:www.pewtrusts.org/uploadedFiles/wwwpewtrustsorg/Reports/Economic_Mobility/PEW_EM_Haskins%25207.pdf+university+education+upward+mobility&hl=en&gl=us&pid=bl&srcid=ADGEEShrtij9_jin-2_rWfaQYKVfz5DT2plWWJvgQhumz8X0iNPjiVOM3Us59-pRY_FKorzq8M8ZXbgjvQUscspxbaNR9IK4U16LaoUrLUI3zeOD-MHWIsCuT_cA5wKA3lGxrkRwd4TKON&sig=AHIEtbRJ4Mp8is_UHMvkJLXY6YcvLvlYYg.
2. Ibid.
3. http://money.cnn.com/2008/08/20/pf/college/college_price.moneymag/.
4. Ibid.
5. http://www.newamerica.net/blog/higher-ed-watch/2009/sallie-maes-full-court-press-11132.
6. http://usinfo.org/docs/democracy/16.htm.
7. http://www.theamericanscholar.org/the-decline-of-the-english-department/.
8. Ibid.
9. Jennifer Washburn, *University Inc.: The corporate Corruption of Higher Education* (New York: Basic Books, 2006), x.
10. http://www.propublica.org/feature/at-u-of-phoenix-allegations-of-enrollment-abuses-persist-1103.
11. http://www.propublica.org/feature/university-of-phoenix-settles-suit-over-recruitment-practices.
12. http://www.reuters.com/article/idUSSGE62S0HX20100329.
13. http://www.propublica.org/article/at-u-of-phoenix-allegations-of-enrollment-abuses-persist-1103.

20: The Troubled Asset Relief Program

1. http://dailybail.com/home/bank-bailout-news-tarp-oversight-chaperone-elizabeth-warren.html.
2. http://www.cnn.com/2010/POLITICS/04/20/obama.goldman.donations/index.html.
3. http://nymag.com/daily/intel/2010/02/tarp_overseer_it_is_hard_

to_se.html?utm_source=feedburner&utm_medium=feed&utm_c
ampaign=Feed%3A+nymag%2Fintel+%28Daily+Intelligencer+-
+New+York+Magazine%29.

4. http://www.nytimes.com/2010/05/24/business/24reform.html.
5. http://www.publicintegrity.org/articles/entry/2096/.

21: The Lobbying World

1. http://www.publicintegrity.org/articles/entry/1953/.
2. http://www.politico.com/news/stories/0510/37594.html.
3. http://articles.chicagotribune.com/2009-12-20/news/0912190289_1_
   health-care-lobbyists-insiders.
4. Thomas Frank, *The Wrecking Crew: How Conservatives Ruined Government, Enriched Themselves, and Beggared the Nation* (New York: Henry Holt, 2008), 5.
5. http://www.thenation.com/article/democracy-sale; http://motherjones.com/politics/2004/11/ralph-reeds-other-cheek.
6. http://www.cnn.com/2005/POLITICS/05/09/real.delay/.

22: Libertarianism

1. http://tpmlivewire.talkingpointsmemo.com/2010/05/rand-paul-defends-criticism-of-civil-rights-act-to-rachel-maddow.php.
2. http://www.econlib.org/library/NPDBooks/Moss/mslLvM6.html.
3. Ibid.
4. Lisabeth Cohen, *A Consumer's Republic: The Politics of Mass Consumption in America* (New York: Knopf, 2003); Bethany Moreton, *To Serve God and Wal-Mart: The Making of Christian Free Enterprise* (Cambridge, MA: Harvard University Press, 2009).
5. http://swopec.hhs.se/ratioi/abs/ratioi0131.htm.
6. http://www.msnbc.msn.com/id/37273085/ns/politics-decision_2010/.
7. http://www.unbossed.com/index.php?itemid=2819.

23: The iPad

1. http://mashable.com/2010/05/26/apple-most-valuable-tech-company/.
2. http://www.reuters.com/article/idUS47469936120100528.
3. http://www.thewrap.com/ind-column/sales-not-exactly-brisk-gqs-ipad-edition-17483.
4. http://www.prnewswire.com/news-releases/air-display-turns-ipad-into-extra-pc-monitor-for-70-more-screen-space-95022234.html.

5. http://www.businessweek.com/news/2010-05-27/apple-ipad-draws-lines-in-sydney-tokyo-as-global-sales-start.html.

6. http://news.cnet.com/8301-17852_3-20004899-71.html.

7. http://www.businessweek.com/news/2010-05-28/apple-ipad-out-shines-mona-lisa-as-global-sales-start-update2-.html.

8. http://www.dailymail.co.uk/news/worldnews/article-1282481/iPad-factory-suicides-China.html.

9. http://www.guardian.co.uk/commentisfree/2010/may/30/nick-cohen-apple-factory-china.

10. http://www.telegraph.co.uk/finance/china-business/7763699/Protest-at-Chinese-iPad-maker-Foxconn-after-11th-suicide-attempt-this-year.html.

11. http://www.dailymail.co.uk/news/worldnews/article-1282481/iPad-factory-suicides-China.html.

12. http://www.folklore.org/StoryView.py?project=Macintosh&story=90_Hours_A_Week_And_Loving_It.txt.

24: Steve Forbes

1. http://money.cnn.com/magazines/fortune/fortune_archive/1996/02/05/207332/index.htm.

2. http://money.cnn.com/magazines/fortune/fortune_archive/1996/02/05/207332/index.htm.

3. http://www.antifascistencyclopedia.com/allposts/pioneer-fund-the-steve-forbes-connection; http://news.google.com/newspapers?nid=336&dat=19960129&id=tscRAAAAIBAJ&sjid=D-0DAAAAIBAJ&pg=4994,7606832.

4. http://sensuouscurmudgeon.wordpress.com/2009/02/06/forbes-magazine-promotes-creationism/.

5. Steve Forbes and Elizabeth Ames, *How Capitalism Will Save Us: Why Free People and Free Markets Are the Best Answer in Today's Economy* (New York: Crown Business, 2009), 6.

6. Haynes Johnson, *Sleepwalking Through History: America in the Reagan Years* (New York: W.W. Norton, 1991), 436.

7. Ibid., 437.

8. http://economistsview.blogspot.com/2005/03/optimetrics-part-1-does-presidential.html.

9. Forbes and Ames, *How Capitalism Will Save Us*, 5.

25: Alan Greenspan

1. Bill Bonner and Addison Wiggin, *Empire of Debt: The Rise and Fall of an Epic Financial Crisis* (New York: Wiley, 2006), 255.
2. http://www.usatoday.com/money/economy/fed/2004-02-23-greenspan-debt_x.htm.
3. http://trueslant.com/allisonkilkenny/2009/10/04/alan-greenspan-is-the-definiton-of-epic-fail/.
4. Bonner and Wiggin, *Empire of Debt*, 257.
5. http://www.foreignpolicy.com/articles/2005/01/05/think_again_alan_greenspan?page=0, 2.
6. Quoted in Bonner and Wiggin, *Empire of Debt*, 259.
7. http://www.federalreserve.gov/boarddocs/speeches/2003/20030304/
8. http://globaleconomicanalysis.blogspot.com/2008/12/case-shiller-cpi-vs-cpi-u-november-2008.html.
9. http://www.bloomberg.com/apps/news?pid=newsarchive&sid=a_IH5AnCyOm4.
10. Ibid.
11. http://www.washingtonpost.com/wp-dyn/content/article/2009/ 09/26/ AR2009092602706.html.
12. http://www.washingtonpost.com/wp-dyn/content/article/2009/ 09/26/ AR2009092602706.html.
13. http://www.usnews.com/articles/opinion/2008/09/24/from-enron-to-the-financial-crisis-with-alan-greenspan-in-between.html.
14. Ibid.
15. Roger Lowenstein, *When Genius Failed: The Rise and Fall of Long-Term Capital Management* (New York: Random House, 2001), 231.
16. Ibid., 231.

26: The Sporting Life

1. http://sports.espn.go.com/mlb/columns/story?columnist=quinn_tj&id=3270983.
2. http://news.bbc.co.uk/sport2/hi/other_sports/olympics_2012/3939219.stm.
3. http://www.tribuneindia.com/2000/20000930/sports.htm#2.
4. http://communities.canada.com/theprovince/blogs/edwilles/archive/2009/10/09/andrew-jennings-a-true-olympic-hero.aspx.
5. http://www.ajr.org/article.asp?id=505.
6. http://socialistworker.org/2008/08/08/whos-grabbing-olympic-gold.

7. http://news.bbc.co.uk/sport2/hi/other_sports/olympics_2012/3939501. stm http://www.novinite.com/view_news.php?id=49608.
8. http://www.washingtonpost.com/wp-srv/digest/daily/jan99/ioc23.htm.

27: Frank Gehry

1. http://findarticles.com/p/articles/mi_m0268/is_10_39/ai_80485033/ pg_4/?tag=content;col1.
2. http://entertainment.timesonline.co.uk/tol/arts_and_entertainment/ visual_arts/architecture_and_design/article4304855.ece.
3. Mike Davis, *City of Quartz: Excavating the Future in Los Angeles* (New York: Vintage Books, 1992), 236.
4. Ibid., 240.
5. Ibid.
6. http://www.hrw.org/en/reports/2009/05/18/island-happiness-0.
7. http://www.mediabistro.com/fishbowlny/frank-gehrys-100m-west -side-iac-building-oddly-tame_b4662.
8. http://www.nytimes.com/2011/02/10/arts/design/10beekman.html? _r=1.

28: Social Media

1. Evgeny Morozov, *The Net Delusion: the Dark Side of Internet Freedom* (New York: PublicAffairs, 2011), 213.
2. Ibid., 15.
3. Ibid., 12–13.
4. Ibid., 21.
5. Clay Shirky, *Cognitive Surplus: Creativity and Generosity in a Connected Age* (New York: Penguin Press, 2011), 49.
6. Ibid., 109.
7. Ibid., 57–58.
8. Ibid., 82.

29: Tax Cuts

1. http://money.cnn.com/2010/09/08/news/economy/reagan_years_taxes/ index.htm.
2. http://www.nytimes.com/2010/06/09/business/09estate.html?_r=1.
3. http://moneywatch.bnet.com/investing/blog/against-grain/tax-deal -making-work-pay-credit-out-payroll-tax-cut-in/835/.
4. http://www.nytimes.com/2010/12/13/us/politics/13tax.html.

5. http://www.bloomberg.com/news/2010-12-23/tax-cutters-set-up
   -tomorrow-s-fiscal-crisis-commentary-by-simon-johnson.html.

6. http://www.cbp.org/pdfs/2008/0804_pp_taxes.pdf.

7. http://articles.sfgate.com/2011-01-16/opinion/27032088_1_tobacco-tax
   -revenues-tax-swap-tax-increases.

Conclusion: The Language Problem

1. http://econlog.econlib.org/archives/2010/04/what_i_think_ab_1.html.

2. http://www.npr.org/templates/story/story.php?storyId= 127762995.

3. http://article.nationalreview.com/435966/the-transformative-power-
   of-rick-santellis-rant/michael-barone.

4. http://www.let.ru

5. g.nl/usa/D/1876-1900/reform/lloyd.htm.

6. Ibid.

7. C. Vann Woodward, *The Strange Career of Jim Crow* (New York: Oxford
   University Press), 1955.

8. http://findarticles.com/p/articles/mi_m3012/is_7_180/ai_ 63974706/.

9. http://www.valleyadvocate.com/article.cfm?aid=11899.

10. http://mises.org/daily/2983.

11. http://pewsocialtrends.org/pubs/706/middle-class-poll.

12. http://pewsocialtrends.org/pubs/706/middle-class-poll.

13. Henry Demarest Lloyd, *Wealth Against Commonwealth* (New York:
    Prentice-Hall, 1963), 169–170.

Also from Haymarket Books

Breaking the Sound Barrier
Amy Goodman, Edited by Denis Moynihan • Amy Goodman, award-winning host of the daily internationally broadcast radio and television program *Democracy Now!*, breaks through the corporate media's lies, sound bites, and silence in this wide-ranging new collection of articles. • ISBN 9781931859998

Essays
Wallace Shawn • In these beautiful essays acclaimed playwright and actor Wallace Shawn takes readers on a revelatory journey through high art, war, politics, culture, and privilege. • ISBN 9781608460021

Field Notes on Democracy: Listening to Grasshoppers
Arundhati Roy • Combining fierce conviction, deft political analysis, and beautiful writing, this essential new book from Arundhati Roy examines the dark side of democracy in contemporary India. Roy looks closely at how religious majoritarianism, cultural nationalism, and neo-fascism simmer just under the surface of a country that projects itself as the world's largest democracy. • ISBN 9781608460243

Hopes and Prospects
Noam Chomsky • Noam Chomsky surveys the dangers and prospects of our early twenty-first century. Exploring challenges such as the growing gap between North and South, American exceptionalism (including under President Barack Obama), the U.S.-Israeli assault on Gaza, and the recent financial bailouts, he also sees hope for the future and a way to move forward—in the democratic wave in Latin America and in global solidarity movements. • ISBN 9781931859967

In Praise of Barbarians
Mike Davis • No writer in the United States today brings together analysis and history as comprehensively and elegantly as Mike Davis. The author of *City of Quartz* and *Planet of Slums* attacks the current fashion for empires and white men's burdens in this blistering collection of radical essays. • ISBN 9781931859424

Live Working or Die Fighting: How the Working Class Went Global
Paul Mason • This is a story of urban slums, self-help cooperatives, choirs and brass bands, free love, and self-education by candlelight. *Live Working or Die Fighting* celebrates a common history of defiance, idealism, and self-sacrifice shared by the global working class. • ISBN 9781608460700

About Haymarket Books

Haymarket Books is a nonprofit, progressive book distributor and publisher, a project of the Center for Economic Research and Social Change. We believe that activists need to take ideas, history, and politics into the many struggles for social justice today. Learning the lessons of past victories, as well as defeats, can arm a new generation of fighters for a better world. As Karl Marx said, "The philosophers have merely interpreted the world; the point, however, is to change it."

We take inspiration and courage from our namesakes, the Haymarket Martyrs, who gave their lives fighting for a better world. Their 1886 struggle for the eight-hour day, which gave us May Day, the international workers' holiday, reminds workers around the world that ordinary people can organize and struggle for their own liberation. These struggles continue today across the globe—struggles against oppression, exploitation, hunger, and poverty.

It was August Spies, one of the Martyrs targeted for being an immigrant and an anarchist, who predicted the battles being fought to this day. "If you think that by hanging us you can stamp out the labor movement," Spies told the judge, "then hang us. Here you will tread upon a spark, but here, and there, and behind you, and in front of you, and everywhere, the flames will blaze up. It is a subterranean fire. You cannot put it out. The ground is on fire upon which you stand."

We could not succeed in our publishing efforts without the generous financial support of our readers. Many people contribute to our project through the Haymarket Sustainers program, where donors receive free books in return for their monetary support. If you would like to be a part of this program, please contact us at info@haymarketbooks.org.

Shop online at www.haymarketbooks.org or call 773-583-7884.

ABOUT THE AUTHOR

Chris Lehmann is employed, ever precariously, as an editor for Yahoo!
News, *Bookforum*, and the *Baffler*. He is also the author of *Revolt of the
Masscult* (Prickly Paradigm Press, 2003), and has written for *Harper's*, the
Atlantic Monthly, *Raritan*, the *Nation*, *Slate.com*, and the *Columbia Jour-
nalism Review*. He lives in Washington, DC.